THE DIMENSIONS OF EVIL AND OF TRANSCENDENCE:

A Sociological Perspective

Natalia R. Moehle
Southwest Texas State University

 University Press
of America™

Library of Congress Catalog Card Number: 78-59124

The author wishes to express appreciation to
The Viking Press (New York) for permission to quote
selections from Eichmann in Jerusalem: A Report on the
Banality of Evil, by Hannah Arendt, copyright 1963, 1964
by Hannah Arendt; to Random House, Inc., (New York) for
permission to quote selections from The Best Short
Stories of Fyodor Dostoyevsky by Fyodor Dostoyevsky,
translated by David Magarshack; to W. W. Norton and
Company Inc. (New York) for permission to quote selections from Civilization and Its Discontents by Sigmund
Freud, translated and edited by James Strachey, copyright 1961 by James Strachey; to Harcourt Brace
Jovanovich, Inc. (New York) for permission to quote
selections from Ideology and Utopia: An Introduction
to the Sociology of Knowledge by Karl Mannheim,
translated and edited by Louis Wirth and Edward
Shils; to W. W. Norton and Company Inc. (New York) for
permission to quote selections from Man's Search for
Himself by Rollo May, copyright 1953 by W. W. Norton
and Company Inc.; to Dr. Rollo May and W. W. Norton
and Company Inc. (New York) for permission to quote
selections from Power and Innocence: A Search for the
Sources of Violence by Rollo May, copyright 1972 by
Rollo May; to the University of Chicago Press (Chicago)
for permission to quote selections from Mind, Self, and
Society from the Standpoint of a Social Behaviorist:
George H. Mead by George H. Mead, edited and with an
Introduction by Charles W. Morris, copyright 1934 by
The University of Chicago, copyright 1962 by Charles W.
Morris; to Alfred A. Knopf, Inc. (New York) for per-
mission to quote selections from Freud: Political and
Social Thought by Paul Roazen, copyright 1968 by Paul
Roazen; and to Jossey-Bass, Inc., Publishers (San
Francisco) for permission to quote selections from
Sanctions For Evil: Sources of Social Destructiveness
by Nevitt Sanford, Craig Comstock, and Associates,
copyright 1971 by Jossey-Bass, Inc., Publishers.

CONTENTS

To
My Parents
Diana Wallace
and
My Favorite Gremlin

ACKNOWLEDGEMENTS

Since Sociology is my chosen field of study, it is not surprising that I have come to adopt the sociological perspective as my personal world-view. The fundamental tenet of this perspective, which my teachers have conveyed, sometimes directly and often deviously, is that people are the products of society. In terms of ethical consciousness, this means that an individual's conception of evil and transcendence is a function of interaction with significant others. Consequently, I wish to express my gratitude to the many significant others who have contributed so much to my own understanding and concern with ethical issues. In addition to those listed in the dedication, I would like to thank Cynthia Castillo, William Pharo, Howard A. King, Mildred Hatch, Rollo Newsom, Clarence Schultz, Arthur Horn, Louis A. Zurcher, and Gideon Sjoberg.

Another crucial aspect of the sociological world-view is that social interaction is the mechanism which develops and maintains the individual's sense of self and of reality. In this respect, I am deeply indebted to the faculty members, graduate students and office staff of the Department of Sociology at the University of Texas at Austin whose constant emotional support sustained my sanity during the writing of this manuscript. Similarly, I am most grateful to my colleagues and students in the Department of Sociology and Anthropology at Southwest Texas State University for their advice and support during the process of revision. Special thanks go to Ms. Pamela Meyer and Ms. Denise Munn whose understanding and humor have sustained me during the traumas of heartache and headache, desolation and despair, rejection and revision. Truly, this project could not have been conceived or completed without the inspiration, challenging criticism and tolerance of my significant others.

——N.R.M.

April 1978

PART ONE: INTRODUCTION

CHAPTER 1: The Role of Science in the Study of Ethical Issues

Introduction

For what is virtue? Answer me that, Alexey. It's one thing to me and another thing to a Chinaman—it's a relative thing. Or isn't it? Is it not relative? A shrewd question! You won't laugh if I tell you it kept me awake for two nights. I only wonder now how people can go on living and not think about it. Vanity! (Dostoevsky, 1958:696).

The ideas about good and evil embodied in manners and morals depend upon society; but good and evil in themselves do not depend upon it; on the contrary, social institutions depend upon the ultimate nature of good and evil... And it is utterly impossible to substitute society for the good. Durkheim tried to put society in the place of God, but this is the most monstrous form of idolatry. Society itself stands in need of moral evaluation and presupposes the distinction between good and evil (Berdyaev, 1945:20-21).

Sociology is not moral philosophy, but it is surely intimately related to it, since it must attempt to assess, scientifically and rationally, the social consequences of a particular value commitment (Means, 1969:35).

In recent decades, however, mankind has imperceptibly, suddenly, become one, united in a way which offers both hope and danger, for shock and infection in one part are almost instantaneously transmitted to others, which often have no immunity (Solzhenitsyn, 1973:13).

When society demands total commitment it is in the very act of destroying itself; to refuse to make the commitment then is a way of saving society from itself (Goodheart, 1963: 8).

Ethics must begin by opposing the final socialization of man which destroys the freedom of spirit and conscience. The socialization of morality means a tyranny of society and of public opinion over the spiritual life of man and his moral evaluations (Berdyaev, 1945:58).

The problem of evil and the possibility for transcendence of evil, because of its ostensibly esoteric and empirically inaccessible nature, has traditionally comprised a subject of philosophical speculation rather than scientific investigation. Although the ontological ground or ultimate nature of such phenomena—as the Russian philosopher Nicolas Berdyaev (1945) aptly observed—is unquestionably impervious to scientific method, the catastrophic events of this century signify that the scientist's cultivated detachment and neutrality with respect to ethical questions—specifically, for example, the potentially harmful consequences of research, and the possibility for an empirical examination of the exoteric and immediate dimensions of evil and transcendence—can no longer be justified. The experience of two devastating world wars, of numerous smaller-scale conflicts, the invention of concentration camps, gas chambers and atom bombs, the continuing development of increasingly sophisticated weaponry, and the prospect of a final nuclear holocaust all testify to the fact that scientific ingenuity is amenable to the perpetration of the greatest evil as well as the production of the greatest good.

Furthermore, as the novelist Solzhenitsyn (1973) warns, the ever-accelerating advance of technology is rapidly establishing a fundamental interdependence among the world's societies such that the dislocations and difficulties of any one society immediately affect every other, and the misunderstandings and conflicts of ethnocentric interests and values between societies could easily culminate in genocide. The exigencies of the modern world, thus, preclude the customary practice of science as though it were beyond good and evil, particularly in terms of

4

the dogma of ethical neutrality which effectively negates the critical consciousness in which scientific
endeavor is originally grounded, and therefore necessitate a radical revision in the philosophy and practice of science.

This revision should include, in the first
place, the realization that science itself constitutes
a variable in the human condition—that it is not detached from social reality, but that its activities
and products have ramifications in social life, and
that the resultant transformations, in turn, affect
the practice of science. This being the case, in the
interest of preserving science and the human species,
it behooves the scientist to recognize that the human'
consequences of research guided by the traditional
principle of accumulating knowledge for the sake of
knowledge are not always nor necessarily beneficial,
and that science should instead be guided by a commitment to the production of good and the prevention
of evil. This is not to say that science—in contrast to philosophy or ethics—should be concerned
with the discovery of ultimate values, which is, ad-
mittedly, beyond the scope of its competence, but
rather that every aspect of scientific endeavor must
be grounded in commitment to an ideal which envisions
the welfare of human beings. In general terms such an
ideal could be conceived as the improvement of the
quality of life for which the pragmatic techniques of
science are eminently suited.

In accordance with this ideal, the first revision applies to the methodology of science, and requires the extension and incorporation of the critical
consciousness from which scientific activity originally derives to every stage of the research process.
In other words, it is the duty of each scientist—
utilizing either his/her own faculties of critical reflection and judgment, and/or the advice of social
scientist consultants—to meticulously analyze the
influence of personal values in the choice of research topics, the underlying motives and interests
of funding agencies, the values, needs, and the consequences of research for target populations, in short,
the possible and probable consequences of each research project.

If, moreover, scientific activities are to
ameliorate the quality of life in actuality, this
modification of methodology must be supplemented by a

5

revision in the content or subject of research projects. In essence, the volatile and precarious conditions of the world today, and in the foreseeable future—i.e., the expanding interdependence of societies and the prospect of total destruction—signify that science, as humanity's most innovative and successful problem-solving tool, must be reoriented toward dealing directly with the value-laden issues of evil and transcendence. This would entail, specifically, the utilization of scientific method in the identification and resolution of the conflicts and dilemmas that disrupt individual, interpersonal and societal life, and which decrease the possibilities of world peace. Research projects organized according to this perspective would focus, in the first place, on the empirical determination of the conditions which, on the one hand, detract from the quality of life, and those which, on the other hand, enrich the quality of life on the individual, interpersonal and societal levels, and secondly, on the innovation of techniques designed to minimize the former and maximize the latter. In this fashion, the experimental, pragmatic, and intrinsically nonmetaphysical techniques of scientific endeavor, directed by an explicit commitment to the welfare of human beings, and grounded in the aforementioned revised conception of objectivity as a critical awareness of implicit personal and professional values, could be productively applied to the study and solution of the esoteric problem of evil and transcendence in its exoteric and perceptible manifestations.

The reformulation of scientific means and ends along these lines could, conceivably, result not only in realizing the ideal—ameliorating the quality of life—but furthermore and perhaps more importantly, in ensuring the continued existence of the human species. That is, the empirical determination of the types of conditions—universally characteristic of all societies and cultures—which are either beneficial or detrimental to the welfare of human beings, may well evoke a consciousness of common humanity among the multitudinous peoples of the world which would mitigate the divisive conflicts of ethnocentric interests, encourage voluntary cooperation in stabilizing the interdependence of societies, and expedite the establishment of world peace. In sum, given the unstable and perilous state of the world today, it is incumbent upon the scientist to revise the archaic conception of objectivity, to discard the counterproductive dogma of ethical neutrality, to become committed to an ideal that envisions the preservation of the human species, to direct research in accordance with that ideal, and thus to willingly and wittingly engage in an intrinsically ethical endeavor. Again, this is not to deny that the discovery or prescription of ultimate values is outside the province of science, but it is to say that, given an ideal originating in the exigencies of contemporary life, it is within the province of science to investigate and ascertain the conditions which preclude or facilitate realization of that ideal.

Speaking pragmatically, this generalized ideal of improving the quality of life must be delineated more precisely if it is to function in fact as the guiding principle for a science which confronts rather than evades the issue of evil and transcendence. Specification of the ideal, as previosuly noted in regard to its original derivation, must also draw upon sources outside science itself. In this respect, it can be proposed—drawing from the evidence of past history—that improving the quality of life essentially requires protection and preservation of human dignity and moral judgment. The concept of human dignity is based on and refers to the unique constellation of distinctively human attributes, such as, for example, self-consciousness, reason, imagination, and moral judgment. It is this constellation of qualities characteristic only of human beings that comprises the special worth or dignity of the human species. As the history of the first half of the twentieth century dramatically demonstrates, it was precisely the deliberate suppression of these distinctive attributes that produced the drastic deterioration in the quality of life under totalitarian regimes such as Nazism and Stalinism. Indeed, the ultimate goal of totalitarianism, in its past and present forms, is to effect a transformation in human nature such that these attributes are totally and irrevocably eradicated, in which the individual becomes completely a product and instrument of society, and the creative human being is reduced to a mindless, infallibly obedient automaton. The intrinsic evil of such a transformation is most vividly illustrated in its deleterious effect on the attribute of moral judgment. One of the essential means by which totalitarian regimes endeavor to transform human nature involves the construction of an alternate social reality in which the concepts of morality and immorality, legal actions and illegal actions are fundamentally reversed. As the case of

Nazi Germany illustrates, when the state itself becomes
a criminal institution, then actions which, in normal
times, would have been classified as immoral and illegal become instead moral and legal. Thus, for example, in the Nazi regime, the administration of genocide became the moral and legal obligation of law-
abiding citizens, whereas failure to participate constituted an immoral and even criminal action. Such
conditions dramatically expose the essence and vulnerability of human moral judgment, for individuals
are forced to choose between the moral code represented by societal norms and the ethical principles
deriving from their own personal experience. In essence, totalitarian regimes create situations which
nullify human judgment, in which it becomes virtually
impossible to distinguish right from wrong. As
Hannah Arendt commented with regard to the Nazi war
criminals:

> ... What has come to light is...a quite ex-
> traordinary confusion over elementary ques-
> tions of morality—as if an instinct in such
> matters were truly the last thing to be
> taken for granted in our time (Arendt,
> 1973:295).

In other words, the totalitarian "<u>social
construction of reality</u>" (Berger and Luckmann, 1967:3)
renders individual moral judgment equivocal, inoper-
able, and superfluous, and it is this nullification of
a fundamental and indispensable human quality that
makes possible, and indeed inevitable, the perpetration of unforgivable and unforgettable atrocities.
Thus, if subversion of the ontological foundations of
human dignity facilitates and engenders such irredeemable evils as genocide, then, without doubt, the protection of human dignity and judgment against violation should constitute an ethical imperative, informing and directing the practice of science. The proposed ideal, moreover, consists of two immediately
discernible interrelated dimensions. On the one hand,
if the quality of life deteriorates as a result of
violations of human dignity—i.e., subversion or annihilation of the distinctive human attributes such as
moral judgment—then, the prevention of such violations comprises one aspect of the ideal. On the other
hand, if the quality of life improves as a result of
preserving human dignity—i.e., continued development
of the distinctive human qualities—then the other re-

8

related aspect of the ideal entails cultivation and refinement of these immanently transcendental qualities.

It could be argued, however, that it is both unreasonable and futile to formulate an ethical ideal on the basis of qualities which are apparently so highly vulnerable to the influence of evil. In response to this, and taking again the problematic issue of moral judgment, the atrocities committed by totalitarian regimes were and are implemented by people subjected to intensive socialization processes imposed either by society as a whole or by particular institutions, which determine to an as yet unknown extent their mode of consciousness and being. The critical question, then, is whether or to what extent moral judgment (and, analogously, the other distinctive qualities) is merely a learned faculty acquired through socialization and hence dependent upon the definitions of society, or whether it is an innate faculty existing prior to socialization and transcending the limitations of a particular society's definitions.

While certain of the social sciences, and sociology in particular, have produced much evidence to the effect that the individual is essentially a microcosmic replica of society as a whole, and thus automatically and unavoidably infused with the idiosyncratic values of that society (which supports the first alternative), the very fact of the practice of science provides evidence supporting the second alternative. That is, science is founded upon the critical and reflective faculties of the human intellect, and the intellect, like human judgment, remains an enigma—for it has not yet been determined to what extent the intellect is a function of social learning, innate ability, or both. And yet from the intellect arises the apotheosis of science, which fact testifies to the creativity of the human faculties, whatever their origins. Thus, it can be concluded that it is both reasonable and worthwhile to construct an ethical ideal in terms of the unique human faculties, because, on the one hand, these exist as a creative potentiality, and because, on the other hand, the subversion of these faculties results in irremediable evil.

In sum, it is proposed that if science is to respond constructively to the crise de conscience of the modern world, it must incorporate and fulfill a

9

commitment to the welfare of human beings. Such a
commitment would require several fundamental revisions
in the practice of science. In the first place, research activities should be directed toward the prevention of evil and the production of good. Secondly,
research projects oriented toward the prevention of
evil should focus on empirical identification of conditions which detract from the quality of life on the
individual, interpersonal and societal levels, whereas
research directed toward the production of good should
focus on determining the conditions which enrich the
quality of life on the individual, interpersonal, and
societal levels. Thirdly, a generalized construct
which envisions the well-being of humanity is the improvement of the quality of life. Fourth, an ethical
ideal formulated on the basis of this construct is
the protection and preservation of human dignity and
moral judgment. Finally, this ideal contains two interrelated dimensions: (1) preventing violations of
human dignity and moral judgment which can be implemented through empirically determining the conditions
of life (on the individual, interpersonal, and societal levels) that foster such violations, and thus
detract from the quality of life, (2) expediting the
development and exercise of the transcendent human
faculties such as moral judgment which can be implemented through identifying the conditions of life
that sustain these faculties, and thus enrich the
quality of life. Thus the efforts and ingenuity of
science must simultaneously be directed against evil
manifested as "the final socialization of man"
(Berdyaev, 1945:58) and directed toward the continuing
maturation of those faculties constituting the special
worth or dignity of human beings.

What can thus be said of science in general
should be applied with even greater emphasis to social
science which is concerned sui generis with social
life. Since its divorce from social philosophy, social science has conceived a slavish attachment to
the traditional goals of natural science, i.e., objectivity and ethical neutrality. Within those disciplines where the scientist is intrinsically involved with the objects of his investigation, these
goals become ever more questionable. However, social
science has not been completely negligent in regard to
these issues, even though no one solution has been
unanimously approved. Thus far, the most promising
recommendation comes from the sociology of knowledge,
a number of whose adherents advocate the cultivation

10

of ethical consciousness and critical reflection as specified above with regard to science. The discovery and explication of the social scientist's personal assumptions about the world, the assumptions about the world implicit in his/her discipline, the recognition of personal motive and the interests of others implicated in the research process is recommended as an approach to objectivity more appropriate to the nature of the discipline.

Given that the principal manifestation of evil in the modern world has been identified as the "final socialization of man" (Berdyaev, 1945:58)—as in the totalitarian subordination of individual life to collective life, it follows that the field of sociology—which examines the nature of social life, and, moreover, the interrelation of individual and society—is especially well-equipped to investigate this form of evil, and to contribute to realization of the proposed ethical ideal. Hence, it is necessary to specify the nature of sociology's role with respect to the "eternal problems" (Dostoevsky, 1958:272) of evil and transcendence, of moral valuation. As the Russian philosopher Nicolas Berdyaev (1945) has gone to considerable lengths to demonstrate, sociology is not philosophical ethics, and thus is not qualified to discover or elucidate the nature of ultimate reality. Sociology is defined as the empirical study of human social behavior. As such, sociology analyzes the modes and processes of interpersonal interaction, the structures and dynamics of social groups, social systems at all levels from the small group to society, and the influence of social groups on individual behavior. In Berdyaev's philosophical terms, sociology deals with secondary facts—the nature of social reality—which are merely the projection of the primary facts of spiritual reality. Moreover, Berdyaev accuses sociology of equating the moral with the social which is ..."the most monstrous form of idolatry" (Berdyaev, 1945:21). Indeed, the last accusation is well-founded, for Durkheim, to whom Berdyaev was referring, contended that:

> The moral rule cannot emanate from the individual since no act is moral which has as its exclusive end the conservation and self-development of the individual. The moral fact can only represent a value higher than the self. This higher moral fact is God, which is only society conceived

11

symbolically. Thus religion and the moral life have the same origin. (Martindale, 1960:89).

It is certainly no exaggeration to say that within sociology today this equation of the moral and the social continues to prevail. For instance, in most contemporary sociological schools, social reality (as opposed to human nature) is identified as the realm of causality from which derive all aspects of human behavior including morality, and similarly, deviance, crime, mental illness and all manner of "social problems" are conceived of as aberrations from the social order. It seems that sociology's predominant focus on the nature and process of collective life, on the group influences on individual behavior, has led to an unscientific neglect of the complementary reverse process of individual influence on the collective, culminating in an unconscious one-sided view of causality. Thus, the sociologistic determinism which Berdyaev noted in 1945 remains today one of the most unreflected domain assumptions of the discipline which vitiates its claim to ethical neutrality.

With regard to the first Berdyaev's contentions, contemporary sociology traces its origins to the speculations of social philosophy, but in the process of its historical development has become grounded in the empirical orientation of natural science, and thus has been transformed into a social science. As such sociology no longer delves into the transcendental phenomena of ultimate realities, but investigates the empirically accessible phenomena of social reality. Such phenomena are identified as the patterns and processes of collective life which are understood as deriving from the social construction of reality. That is, sociology only attempts to deal with phenomena having a specifically social origin, and in this sense it is irrelevant whether such phenomena are primary or secondary facts. It matters only that "If men define situations as real, they are real in their consequences" (Thomas, as cited in Theodorson, 1970:370). In terms of the social construction of reality and the derivative definitions according to which people live, that aspect of social organization known as the normative order, which consists of moral notions and conceptions about good and evil, is a proper and an essential subject matter for sociology. The unique perspective of sociology—in contrast to philosophical ethics—explores the origin and development of such

12

ideas, the role of these ideas in structuring and directing human behavior, and especially, as Richard Means indicates, "the social consequences of a particular value commitment" (Means, 1969:35).

It is precisely this area of the normative order that provides the opportunity for sociology to exercise its commitment to the ethical ideals of human dignity and moral judgment. The nature of sociology's contribution was also outlined by Berdyaev in his fascinating analysis of The Destiny of Man:

> The moral judgment is made not by a free personality in the presence of God, but by the family, the nation, the party, the denomination, etc. ... Our conscience is confused and polluted ... because we belong to various social units, which find falsity more useful than truth for purposes of self preservation (Berdyaev, 1945:161).

In view of these societal influences on the nature of human judgment—which become constituents of human consciousness primarily through the unconscious learning process of socialization—the ethical task of sociology is to expose these influences, and bring them to the level of critical reflection. Consistent with the perspective of the sociology of knowledge, this means that: the social structural origins of various moral notions should be traced and identified; the process by which such notions are internalized into the individual consciousness should be delineated; the extent to which these unexamined propositions control human behavior should be clarified; the nature of the consequences of these notions in structuring inter-personal relations, in influencing self-esteem, and in precluding reflections upon society should be explicated; and finally, the character of the fundamental interests of the social structures which prescribe such notions should be revealed. The task is, then, to disclose these socially produced extra-cognitive constituents and determinants of human judgment, and to bring them to the level of consciousness in order to facilitate critical reflection and moral judgment. Sociology's ethical obligation entails unmasking the covert social determinants of human judgment in order to liberate this faculty from the confines of the social construction of reality.

13

In addition to exposing the covert societal factors which restrict the exercise of moral judgment, the task of examining and exposing to public awareness the conditions of life on the individual, interpersonal, and societal levels which violate human dignity by extinguishing mankind's distinctive faculties, and conversely, the conditions of life which preserve human dignity by sustaining these faculties, also falls within the province of sociology. In this respect, it is necessary to delineate the nature of evil and transcendence in terms of the social conditions or factors conducive to the minimal and maximal development of individual potentials, which inhibit or induce harmonious interpersonal relations, and which detract from or contribute to the creative interdependence of individual and society.

The combination of these two strategies—the unmasking of societal factors in human judgment, and the detection and disclosure of conditions beneficial and detrimental to the constellation of faculties on which human dignity is based will serve, on the one hand, to expedite the free exercise and development of human judgment, and on the other, to provide empirically grounded and accurate data for human judgment and decision-making. In this manner, sociology can fulfill its obligation to the ethical ideal generated by the crisis of the modern world.

The Structure of the Book

This study, then, is founded on a sociological perspective, and is designed to examine, in an exploratory fashion, the theories of selected writers in the fields of literature, psychoanalysis, social psychology, and social philosophy, who have dealt with the issue cf evil and transcendence, in an effort to discern existing knowledge relating to the nature of evil and the capacity of human judgment to recognize and transcend evil. The novelists and scholars whose theories were considered germane to this issue include: D. H. Lawrence, Anton Chekhov, and Alexander Solzhenitsyn - in the field of literature; Sigmund Freud and Erich Fromm - in the field of psychoanalysis; Rollo May and George Herbert Mead - in the field of social psychology; Herbert Marcuse and Hannah Arendt, in the field of social philosophy. Finally, an original sociological theory of evil and transcendence within the context of bureaucracy, which draws from several of the previous theories, was written specifically for this study.

14

The central assumption guiding this analysis is that the principle of causality may be ascribed either to human nature, interpersonal interaction, or social reality, and that, consequently, a scholar's approach to the problem of evil and transcendence of evil will depend on which of these phenomena is identified as causal. For example: (1) if human nature—here defined as the innate biological characteristics of human beings—is identified as the locus of causality, then the existence of evil in social reality is an external function of human nature. Hence, if evil is to be eliminated, human nature must be transformed. Secondly, if human judgment exists as an innate quality of human nature, thus having a referent external to social reality, then it transcends the definitions of social reality, and is capable of evaluating those definitions. (2) If interpersonal interaction—here defined as the forms and processes of symbolic communication—is identified as the locus of causality, then the existence of evil in human nature and social reality is a function of interaction processes. Hence, if evil is to be eliminated, the processes of human interaction must be revised. Secondly, if human judgment and the social construction of reality both originate in the process of interaction, then the valuations of judgment and the definitions of reality will be continuous—human judgment will not be transcendent. (3) If social reality—here defined as the world-view or "...conception of what actually exists, that is established and maintained by the consensus of the group" (Theodorson, 1970:393)—is identified as the locus of causality, then the existence of evil in human nature and the social order will be a function of social reality. Thus, if evil is to be eliminated, social reality must be reconstructed. Secondly, if human judgment is a derivative of the social construction of reality, it will be constrained by social definitions, and hence will not be capable of functioning in a transcendent manner.

As these examples indicate, it will be of vital importance to specify the underlying assumptions about causality implicit in each writer's perspective. Consequently, in each case, the following interrelated aspects of evil and transcendence will be delineated: (1) definitions of evil and transcendence; (2) the realm of reality (either human nature, interpersonal interaction, or social reality) identified as causal; (3) the sources of evil and transcendence identified within the causal realm of

15

reality, and classified as: (a) one or more components of one system of reality, (b) components from two or more systems of reality, (c) interaction of two or more systems of reality, (d) action of one system of reality upon another system of reality; (4) the forms (causes and effects) in which evil and transcendence are generated; and (6) the detrimental and beneficial consequences for the individual and society of the existence of evil and transcendence.

The two-fold strategy of unmasking societal influences on human judgment, and the provision of accurate data for moral evaluation here advocated, may be construed as an attempt to eradicate evil in the world by means of a transformation in human consciousness. In this respect, sociology would be following a venerable tradition in the history of literature. For centuries literature has transcended the doctrine of "art for the sake of art," and has responded to the challenges of changing times and historical crises. Sociologists, and other scientists as well, could not do better than to emulate the moral courage of novelists who understand art as a form of social criticism, i.e.:

> Literature that is not the breadth of contemporary society, that dares not transmit the pains and fears of that society, that does not warn in time against threatening moral and social dangers—such literature does not deserve the name of literature... (Solzhenitsyn, 1972:ix),

and who portray in their writings the vision of a better future:

> These are writers who attempt to reconstruct the world they reject...to enunciate a radical vision of possibilities within the world even while shattering the very foundations of self and society as we know them (Hochman, 1963:259).

The example of such critical novelists can provide unique and invaluable guidance for contemporary social scientists in fulfilling their ethical commitments. Thus, although the major portion of this study analyzes the theories of selected scholars of social science, chapters 2, 3, 4, and 5 examine the writings of three critical novelists for

16

perceptions relevant to the problem of evil and transcendence. These three authors have been chosen not
only for the astuteness of their observations, but
also for the general similarity of their world-views
to the selected disciplines of psychoanalysis, social
psychology, and social philosophy. D. H. Lawrence
was chosen as representative of the psychoanalytic
orientation; Anton Chekhov was chosen as representative of the social psychological orientation; and
Alexander Solzhenitsyn was chosen as representative of
the social philosophy orientation. Turning to the
scholars of social science, Part Three examines the
works of Sigmund Freud (Chapter 6) and Erich Fromm
(Chapter 7), representing the field of Psychoanalysis.
Part Four examines the theories of Rollo May (Chapter
9) and George Herbert Mead (Chapter 10), representing
the field of Social Psychology. Part Five examines
the works of Herbert Marcuse (Chapter 12) and Hannah
Arendt (Chapter 13), representing the field of Social
Philosophy. In Part Six, Chapter 15 presents a sociological theory of evil and transcendence within the
context of bureaucracy, and Chapter 16 briefly summarizes the key issues and major conclusions of this
study.

PART TWO: THE PERSPECTIVE OF LITERATURE

CHAPTER 2: D. H. Lawrence

Introduction

Let us hesitate no longer to announce that the
sensual passions and mysteries are equally
sacred with the spiritual mysteries and passions. The only thing unbearable is the degradation, the prostitution of the living mysteries in us.... The creative spontaneous
soul sends forth its promptings of desire and
aspiration in us. These promptings are our
true fate, which is our business to fulfill.
A fate dictated from outside, from theory or
from circumstance, is a false fate.... Nothing that comes from the deep, passional soul
is bad, or can be bad (Lawrence, 1969:n.p.).

In the above quote, taken from Lawrence's
foreward to that most controversial novel, Women in
Love, Lawrence expressed his deep faith in the innate
goodness of human nature, and the integrity of the
impulses arising from the human's essential being,
which impulses he believed revealed the direction of
human destiny, and the natural course of individual
development. Owing to this belief in the integrity of
the impulses from the "spontaneous soul," Lawrence vio-
lently protested against the repression of such impulses by any external source. Thus, he opposed the
final socialization of human nature which threatens
the violation of essential being, which renders impossible the fulfillment of the destiny dictated from
within, and which subordinates human nature to the perverse dictates of a corrupt society.

In the industrialized world of the early twentieth century, Lawrence perceived a tragic antithesis
between the requirements of civilization and the fundamental impulses of human nature--an antithesis which
was expressed in the unnatural tension between self and
society, in a perverse separation of reason and passion,

21

of spirit and flesh, and in the overcultivation of reason and the repression of passion. Yet unlike Freud,
he did not consider this antithesis as endemic to the
human condition, for in his view, the contemporary situation was merely a corruption of the natural harmony
between self and society, between human nature and civilization—for civilization was a natural outgrowth and
expression of human creativity. While his great novels
contained an implicit criticism of current conditions,
they also revealed a utopian vision of the reintegration of human nature and civilized society—a thorough-
going transformation of the corrupted world ensuing
from individual transcendence. In this utopian vision
of a revitalized world, Lawrence perceived reason and
passion to be essential and natural polarities of the
human soul—that reason, arising from the impulses of
aspiration in the spontaneous soul bound humans to civilization as the condition and expression of creative
fulfillment, and, that passion, arising from the impulses of desire in the spontaneous soul bound humans to
their fellow beings in the fulfillment of relationship.
It is only through this combination of intellectual
creativity and erotic experience that all the latent
potentials of human nature are realized in a harmonious
relation of self and society.

Definitions of Evil and of Transcendence

Given this perception of the natural harmony
of self and society in accordance with the promptings
of essential being, evil for Lawrence, consists of the
estrangement of human beings from their spontaneous inner selves, the coterminous alienation of people from
society, and the corruption of civilization which is no
longer a natural outgrowth of the spontaneous self. In
his novels, especially evident in Women in Love, evil
is symbolized in the disparity between the lush, green,
teeming world of nature, and the ugly brutality and
barbarity of industrialization superimposed on nature,
and similarly, in the distance between the greater life
of the body, and the falsity of the social self. Transcendence, in this perspective, consists of the individual's coming to consciousness of the estrangement from
his/her inner self, of the return to communion with the
promptings from the inner self, and of the self-
conscious rejection of the alienated mode of being.
Transcendence is defined as a capacity and a function
of individuals, whose self-transformation in turn
transforms the forms of social life also.

Locus of Causality

Lawrence's belief in the goodness and creativity of the spontaneous self, in the nature of transcendence as an individual capacity, and in the falsity of the social forms of a corrupted society indicate that he identifies human nature as the dimension of causality, social reality as the dimension of effect. One critic pointed directly to this identification:

> "The System," Lawrence had written elsewhere, "...is only the outcome of the human psyche, the human desires."... The fallen world is the objective expression of man's inner fallen state, the outward manifestation of his inward spiritual malaise (Lawrence, as cited in Hochman, 1970:118).

Lawrence symbolizes this conception in the portrayal of his characters' relation to the social environment. For example, in Women in Love, the degrading mechanization of the industrial world—specifically, the mining industry at Beldover—is depicted as an externalization of Gerald Crich's corrupted psyche—a psyche alienated from pure sexuality, and dominated by the abstract intellect and impotent will. Similarly, Rupert Birkin's dreams of a transformed renatured world, and his efforts to attain that vision—as illustrated in his relation to Ursula Brangwen—is portrayed as the outward expression of his inner psychological rejection and transcendence of the perverted social self. The existence of evil and the capacity for transcendence both originate in the diverse potentials of human nature, and are manifested externally in social reality. The forms of social reality may act to sustain the tendencies originating in human nature, but, this function of maintenance is itself derivative.

Sources of Evil and of Transcendence

This derivative nature and function of social reality, furthermore, indicates that the source of evil and transcendence resides in the action of one dimension of reality on another, that is, the action of human nature on social reality. In regard to the phenomena that he defined as evil, Lawrence's basic premise is that at some point in human history, human nature became alienated from the flesh, from passion and sexuality. This psychological estrangement was exteriorized in individual social relations, and, consequently

23

became incorporated into the social construction of reality. This incorporation of evil into the forms of social reality, in turn, resulted in the maintenance of evil through the transformation of the modes of consciousness and being that social reality imposed upon individuals. Thus, evil originates in an initial corruption of human nature, is incorporated into social reality, and is sustained through corrupted social roles which mask and distort spontaneous being. In a similar fashion, the capacity for transcendence of evil derives from the natural impulses of the spontaneous self. When individuals are able to re-establish contact with the promptings of desire and aspiration, when they attempt to realize these impulses in creative activity and erotic relation, these activities effect a readjustment of social relations, and finally, a transformation of the forms of social reality. In both cases, the condition of human nature determines the condition of social reality.

Manifestations of Evil and Transcendence

In his polemics against the evil estrangement of human nature and civilization from the spontaneous self, Lawrence depicts the manifestation of evil in several ways. He saw evil evinced primarily in the constricting mode of consciousness and experience fostered by society: "Within the drama men assume masks, not in accord with their natures, but in keeping with arbitrary roles defined in the social scenario" (Hochman, 1970:6). It is the mode of consciousness concomitant with the social roles that maintains the alienation from the real self, sustains the division of reason and passion, promotes the overcultivaton of reason and the repression of passion, perverts sexuality, stimulates a will to power rather than realization of potentials, and culminates in a catastrophic tension between self and society. Lawrence's criticisms center on the alter-ego of the social self, which in repressing and distorting the spontaneous soul, creates a deathly mechanization of human life detrimental to both the individual and society. He proclaimed in regard to industrial England:

> It was producing a new race of mankind, over-conscious in the money and social and political side, on the spontaneous intuitive side dead— but dead! Half corpses, all of them...(Lawrence, 1962:9).

24

On the other hand, Lawrence perceived evidence of transcendence in the "return to the natural life of the body and the senses" (Lawrence, 1962:6). That is, transcendence is manifested in individual intuitive recognition of the falseness and corruption of prevailing social forms—especially in the trappings of conventional morality—the self-conscious rejection of those social forms, and the development of a radically new mode of consciousness and being which directly expresses the natural morality of the passions, the impulses of the spontaneous self. In the individuals thus liberated from confining social roles, reason is directed toward participation in the creation of civilization, passion becomes a means of emotive fulfillment, the will to realize one's potentials displaces the will to power, and self and society are restored to a harmonious relation.

Processes of Evil and of Transcendence

As stated above, the premise of human nature as the dimension of causality, signifies that if evil is evident in the social order it must have been generated by a prior corruption of human nature. In this regard, the fact that civilization has turned against human nature reflects the previuos fact that human nature turned against itself. As a matter of historical development, Lawrence traces this inversion of human nature to the Elizabethan era when the nature and consequences of syphilis were discovered. It was this horrifying discovery that generated the psychological alienation from sexuality, which in turn, perverted interpersonal relations, was eventually assimilated into social reality, and finally, was maintained throughout social life as an estrangement within consciousness.

The alternate process of transcendence involves primarily the experience of sexual love, and secondarily creative and purposive activity in civilized life. As one critic has summarized this unusual conception of liberation through eroticism:

> Sexuality becomes the path to transcendence and the quest for fulfillment through sexual love becomes a way of salvation that culminates in a transfiguration of the parties to it (Hochman, 1970:23).

Lawrence contended that in the authentic erotic experience, the individual momentarily escapes the confines of the social self, experiences a lapse into the unknown beyond civilized consciousness, confronts and is reunited with the spontaneous self, and returns from this journey into the unknown with a re-awakened sense of the real self that transcends the restricted social self, and generates a transformation of life-style consistent with the impulses of the spontaneous self. Thus, the trauma and transfiguration of eroti-cism culminate in a recognition and rejection of the death-in-life forms imposed by social reality. In add-ition, in his later novels, Lawrence realized that sex-uality itself could be corrupted by civilized society, and he revised his concept of transcendence to include a moral and spiritual re-awakening through creative activity:

> ...man's fulfillment depends on participation in the daylight life of society as well as on the nighttime experience of <u>eros</u>. Man must return from the blood-darkness of sexuality, where he is submerged in nature, to the day-light world of history, there to participate in the purposive activities of men (Hochman, 1970:72).

Thus, the processes of the manifestation of evil and of transcendence both originate from impul-sions in human nature—evil in social life is the con-sequence of a corruption of human nature, and the tran-scendence of evil in social life results from a conver-sion of human nature.

Consequences of Evil and of Transcendence

Throughout his novels, Lawrence portrayed an idyllic vision of the fulfillment of individuality in relationship which he posed as an alternative to the final socialization of human beings, and the violation of individuality which he viewed as the ultimate conse-quence of the evil estrangement of self and society from the natural order of spontaneous being. Lawrence intuited that the total domination of self by society would prove fatal for society as well as for the indi-vidual—since the dynamic and healthy development of civilization derived from and depended upon the dynamic and imaginative creativity springing from the spontan-eous being of human nature. It is clear, however, that Lawrence's affirmation of the value of the promptings from the spontaneous soul did not signify giving free rein to the impulses. Rather, Lawrence idealized a

26

productive tension of impulse and resistance within the spontaneous being—as opposed to the unnatural and destructive tension between self and society. It is the creative resolution of this inner tension which generates both the natural development of individual life, and the historical progress of civilization.

Thus, the consequence of the triumph of evil in terms of the radical estrangement of self and society from the one and only source of natural motivity in the world was envisioned as an absolute dehumanization of individual life—the transformation of human beings into social automatons, and the degeneration of civilized society into "a diabolical world of death and destruction..." (Hochman, 1970:96). And, in contrast, the consequence of the victorious transcendence of evil—i.e., the reintegration of self and society with spontaneous being effected by vital individuals—was envisioned in terms of the re-establishment of natural harmony between self and society, and the transfiguration of civilization into a dynamic setting conducive to the fulfillment of individuality in creativity and relationship. In conclusion, Lawrence did not condone a nihilistic rejection of an evil society, since he believed that the possibility always existed for the transformation of society by means of the capacity for transcendence in human nature.

CHAPTER 3: Anton Chekhov

Introduction

Andrei: "Oh, where is it, where has it all
gone, my past, when I was young, gay, clever,
when I dreamed and thought with grace, when
my present and future were lighted up with
hope? Why is it that when we have barely be-
gun to live, we grow dull, gray, uninterest-
ing, useless, unhappy..." (Chekhov, 1964:305).

In her biographical and critical study, Princess Nina Toumanova has aptly described Anton Pavlovich
Chekhov as "the voice of twilight Russia," a "true son
of his generation" (Toumanova, 1937:6). There was indeed a striking contrast between Chekhov's world-view
and art, and that of the great writers of the Golden
Age of Russian literature—Pushkin, Lermontov, Turgenev,
Tolstoy, and especially, Dostoevsky. These writers established the tradition in Russian literature of literature as a form of social criticism, as an instrument
of social change, as the expression of an ethical commitment above and beyond the ideal of "art for art's
sake." Their novels both reflected contemporary life,
and were directed toward a transformation in social
consciousness. The heroes of their short stories and
novels symbolized the "men of action" of mid-19th century Russia, and reflected their ideals, revealed their
weaknesses, and glorified their accomplishments. In
the 1840's, the vociferous and vituperative polemics of
the Westernizers and the Slavophils; in the 1860's, the
revolutionary activity of the rasnochintsy as exempli-
fied by the literary critic Belinsky and the radical
leaders Chernyshevsky, Dobrolubov, and Pisarev; in the
1870's, the "return to the people" of the populist movement—provided the drama of real-life from which these
writers drew their inspiration. But, by the time of
the late nineteenth century, the forces of literary and
revolutionary circles seemed to have disintegrated, dis-
pelled perhaps by the ever-increasing and powerful reaction of Tzarist autocracy. The atmosphere of fin de
siecle Russia was pervaded by a sense of depression,

29

gloom, and passive despair. The intelligentsia of <u>fin</u> <u>de siecle</u> Russia retained the dissatisfaction character-istic of their forbears, but exhibited also an uncharac-teristic impotence in the face of impending disaster. Such was Chekhov's intellectual heritage. It is not surprising, then, that his art, grounded in a meticulous observation and analysis of contemporary conditions, conveys a mood of lassitude, alienation, disillusion, meaninglessness, and impotence.

Definitions of Evil and of Transcendence

As the introductory quotes illustrate, the heroes of Chekhov's stories and plays are not the "men of action" of the Golden Age who sought to transform a wicked world. They are instead passive victims who are annihilated by a wicked world. Perpetually confused and unhappy, the unwilling but helpless victims of circum-stance, these people give in imperceptibly to the vicis-situdes of social life, and gradually, irrevocably, are deprived of hope, and emptied of their humanity. Chek-hov's primary insight is that evil is not a function of human nature, but rather, is a function of the forms of interaction of the social world. These modes of inter-action are alien to fundamental human needs, and yet, the alien modes persist, indeed predominate, and human needs are stifled, distorted, and destroyed. Thus, he defines as evil the prevalence of falsity in social life, the dehumanizing falsity of alien forms of inter-action. This evil falsity he perceives as originating in social reality, is manifested in the perversion of interpersonal interaction, and culminates in the dehu-manization of human nature. This understanding of evil as falsehood is evident in one of his letters:

> ...You once said that my stories lack an ele-ment of protest, and don't show my sympathies and antipathies...but in my story don't I pro-test from beginning to end against falsehood? (Chekhov, as cited in Hingley, 1966:95).

Within Chekhov's vision of the thorough-going degenera-tion of the world, the possibility of transcendence is extremely remote. However, in conjunction with his de-finition of evil as falsehood, he tentatively defines transcendence as the recognition and rejection of false-hood, which would perhaps someday be made possible by an evolving social consciousness. As he expresses this:

> I believe in individual people; I look for salvation to individual personalities, scat-tered here and there throughout Russia,

whether they are intellectuals or peasants.
It is in them that strength lies, though they
are few in number. The individual personalities of which I speak play an unobtrusive
role in society; they do not dominate, but
their work leaves its mark. Whatever else
may be going on, science keeps moving forward
and social consciousness is growing (Chekhov,
as cited in Hingley, 1966:177).

Locus of Causality

Through his observations of <u>fin de siecle</u>
Russia, Chekhov must have been impressed by the evident
futility of romantic humanitarian ideals, the complete
absence of heroic social reformers, the abdication of
the intelligentsia from its leading political role, the
decline of all the furious intellectuals into pathetic
apathy, and the subordination of the whole society to a
degenerate social life typified by deceit, falsity and
triviality. As the dramatic action of his plays suggests, such observations must have signified to Chekhov
the relative weakness of human nature in contrast to the
apparent strength of social reality. Hence, he perceived social reality as the locus of causality from
which derives evil in the world.

This evil is manifested in the dimension of
interpersonal interaction in the form of social conventions alienated from the natural spontaneity of human nature, and which inform social life with falsity,
deceit, and interpersonal estrangement. The disconnec-
ted dialogue of his plays demonstrates the pernicious
influence that social reality exerts on interaction,
transforming it from a vehicle of genuine communication
and relationship into a deceitful ritual of falsity devoid of human spontaneity.

In view of this identification of social reality as the realm of causality from which evil derives,
Chekhov, rather inconsistently, defines human nature as
the realm of causality from which transcendence derives.
He places his hope for transcendence in the activities
of enlightened individuals, whose dedicated pursuit of
truth would eventually stimulate the evolution of social
consciousness and a rejection of alienated forms of
interaction. Thus, he assumes a dichotomous conception
of causality in which social reality is the locus of
evil and human nature is the locus of transcendence.

31

Sources of Evil and of Transcendence

As suggested previously, with respect to the phenomena of evil, Chekhov identifies social reality as the dimension of causality and social interaction as the dimension of effect in which the corrupted conventions of interaction serve as the medium for the externalization and maintenance of evil. The source of evil —of falsehood—is thus the action of one system upon another, the action of an evil social construction of reality upon interaction, through which interaction is corrupted, and becomes an instrument of evil. With regard to the phenomena of transcendence, Chekhov identifies human nature as the dimension of causality and social reality as the dimension of effect. Thus, the source of transcendence is the action of one system upon another—the action of human nature upon social reality in the effort to transform that reality. In this manner, Chekhov remained true to the heritage of the radical intelligentsia of earlier decades:

> The strength and salvation of a country lies in its intelligentsia—in that section of it which thinks honestly and is capable of work (Chekhov, as cited in Hingley, 1966:169).

Manifestations of Evil and of Transcendence

Chekhov's critics have been most concerned with analyzing the nature of his dialogues, for it is the dialogue which reveals the extent to which interaction has been corrupted, and relationship vitiated. Princess Toumanova and Prince D.S. Mirsky, respectively, have provided most insightful analyses of the dialogue, and of Chekhov's intuition:

> The dramatic dialogue disappears, to give place to a peculiar form of speech built along two parallel lines that never meet. One is constantly aware of an undertone of sorrow and pain expressed in detached, inconsistent, often incoherent words. Long pauses and reticence create an odd feeling that important things, indeed the most important ones have never been said and never will be said (Toumanova, 1937:7),

32

and;

> The dialogue form is also admirably suited to
> the expression of one of Chekhov's favorite
> ideas: the mutual unintelligibility and
> strangeness of human beings, who cannot and
> do not want to understand each other. Each
> character speaks only of what interests him
> or her, and pays no attention to what other
> people in the room are saying. Thus the dia-
> logue becomes a patchwork of disconnected re-
> marks (Mirsky, 1958:381).

Indeed, the first thing that strikes a reader
of a Chekhovian play is, as these critics note, the fact
that all the characters continually "talk past each other." The things they say to each other, more often
than not, are totally unrelated. There seems to be no
common ground of interest or sympathy, and the parallel
lines of speech never connect. The reader intuits that
the most important things simply cannot be expressed.
In the instances when one character reaches out to another, and attempts to relate an event of utmost importance to him or her, the other character either responds
with indifference, or reveals an utter inability to
understand and respond at all. For example, in The
Three Sisters, Masha attempts to confide in her sister
Olga about her unhappy marriage, and her increasing love
for another married man—yet when she does, Olga reacts
indifferently—"...I'm not listening. Whatever silly
things you may say, it doesn't matter, I shan't hear
them" (Chekhov, 1964:291). Similarly, in A Dull Story,
when the Professor's ward, Katya, begs him hysterically
to advise her, and help her reconstruct her ruined life,
the Professor is simply at a total loss. He has no
idea at all what to tell Katya, despite the fact that
he is suffering from a similar misery, and despite the
fact that he genuinely cares about Katya. He is unable
to respond. And further, in The Cherry Orchard, Chekhov
demonstrates that what needs to be said, cannot be said—
the most important things in life have become virtually
incommunicable. In The Cherry Orchard this tragedy is
so unbearable it becomes almost comical—that is, when
Lopachkin decides to propose to Varya—whose life is
wrecked by the loss of the Cherry Orchard—they talk
instead about a pair of lost galoshes!

The conventional forms of interaction render
impossible geniune communication, understanding, and
relationship. Even when people attempt to understand
each other—as the Professor and Katya—they can't, and

33

the growing realization of their mutual unintelligibility eventually results in utter self-absorption, indifference to others, reluctance to try to communicate, and finally, a blank incapacity to respond at all. In one of Chekhov's masterpieces, the short story The Name-Day Party, each of these tragic defects of interaction are illustrated dramatically, and are revealed as the inevitable consequence of decadent social conventions, unrelated to human needs—or as Richard Mathewson aptly summarizes this tragedy:

> The social roles of guest and host at the interminable party constrict movement, stifle feeling and spread a gloss of falsehood over everyone's behavior. Facial expressions are masks, gesture and utterance respond to the cultural norm, not to human need. Chekhov invokes this inhuman world at regular intervals through the story be citing a frozen smile, an affected remark, a self-serving diatribe, or a partisan political attitude. This aspect of the world is held together by hatred and lies under the surface of party manners (Chekhov, 1965:381).

Chekhov demonstrates the prevalence of falsehood primarily be noting facial expressions that are inconsistent with the character's feelings, and the tendency to mask true feelings in flippant, frivolous conversations. Thus, the heroine, Olga, moves through the party continually smiling and chatting politely with guests, when in reality she is furious with her husband for his flirtations, is physically miserable due to the corset she wears to conceal her pregnancy, despises her guests for their deceitfulness, frivolity, and because they stay so long.

> No one realized how agonizing all these trifles were to the hostess, and indeed, it would have been hard to tell, as Olga Mikhaelovna went on smiling amiably and talking nonsense (Chekhov, 1965:327).

In similar fashion, Olga's husband, Pyotr Dmitrich, smiles and chats nonchalantly about the matter of his upcoming trial, which in fact, arouses his anxiety and fear. The unintelligibility of each to another, and the isolation that evolves from this predominant falsity is illustrated in the self-absorption, indifference, and reluctance to communicate that characterizes the relations of Pyotr and Olga, husband and

wife. Thus, for instance, at one point, Pyotr escapes
from the party into his study, and sits brooding over
his misfortune. Olga finds him there, and his misery
touches her—she attempts to comfort him, but instead,
when Pyotr sees her, he withdraws into himself:

> Meeting his wife's eyes, Pyotr Dmitrich's
> face instantly assumed the expression it had
> worn at dinner and in the garden—indifferent
> and slightly ironical; he yawned and stood up
> (Chekhov, 1965:313-314).

They pass each other without touching—when Olga reaches out, Pyotr retreats and withdraws. It is not surprising at the end of the story that a shared tragedy
does not bring them together, but further estranges
them. Their child is still-born, and Pyotr, overcome
with grief and remorse—realizes his love for his wife
—but the tragedy drains Olga of all feelings, she is
unable to respond to Pytr beyond a dull indifference.
Each passes the other unnoticed.

The tragic falsehood of social conventions
that irrevocably stultifies the original spontaneity of
human nature provides the basic theme for another of
Chekhov's masterful short stories, The Dull Story. In
the case of the central character, a brilliant and
highly esteemed professor of science, it is his fame
and the social and psychological repercussions of his
reputation that have turned his life into a dull, meaningless routine, and has severed his relation to real
life. The professor becomes increasingly aware of the
emptiness in his life and notes it especially in the
monotony of dinner:

> In the old days I would either enjoy my dinner
> or be indifferent to it; now it induces in me
> nothing but boredom and irritation. Ever
> since I became an "Excellency" and was made a
> dean of faculty, my family has, for some rea-
> son, found it necessary to make a complete
> change in our menu and dining habits. Instead
> of the simple dishes I was in the habit of eat-
> ing when I was a student and in practice, I am
> now fed soup puree with some sort of stalac-
> tites floating in it.... Gone is the gaiety
> of the old days, the spontaneous talk, the
> jokes and laughter, all the mutual affection
> and joy that used to animate my wife and
> children when we came together at the table
> (Chekhov, 1965:187).

The professor realizes that his fame is the cause of his unhappiness, of the drifting apart of his family, of his general boredom with life, and of his inability to understand and love the people he once loved. This realization, however, comes too late, as he is about to die, and he realizes also that there is nothing he can do to change anything. Each individual in Chekhov's world becomes encapsulated within his/her individuality, unable to break through the external social, and the internalized barriers that separate him or her from others.

Although transcendence of societal evil forms only a tentative hope in Chekhov's world-view, he expresses this hope in his writings in a call to enlightened individuals to put their talents to work for the good of society. Recognizing the inefficacy of most programs of social reform, and realizing also that it would probably take some great historical convolution to produce a radical change in social life, he nonetheless calls for an almost existential revolt, and struggle against the fraudulent decadence of Russian society. He advocates patient and dedicated individual effort directed toward educating the social consciousness of the people. In the words of Trofimov in The Cherry Orchard Chekhov says:

> Mankind goes forward, perfecting its powers.
> Everything that is now unattainable will some
> day be comprehensible and within our grasp,
> only we must work, and help with all our might
> those who are seeking the truth. So far,
> among us here in Russia, only a very few work
> (Chekhov, 1964:346).

Processes of Evil and of Transcendence

The process by which the evil falsehood of social reality takes hold of human life, mutilates, and demolishes it, Chekhov perceives as a gradual, almost imperceptible displacement of the authentic spontaneous individual self by the superficial, insincere social self. He depicts this displacement in terms of a progressive drifting apart of people who had once been close, a dissolution of the bonds that linked people to their ideals, vocations, and interests, and a gradual recognition of the futility and meaninglessness of life. Thus, in A Dull Story, the Professor gazes at his wife in bewilderment, wondering whatever happened to the beautiful and vital woman he had once loved. He looks at his wife and daughter, and realizes that they

36

have nothing in common with him, that they have been
strangers to him for years. He remembers that he had
been delighted to take Katya in as his ward, and then
regrets that he never had the time to spare from his
busy schedule, to come to know her, to guide her, and
love her. He finally discovers that his profession had
taken him from his family, that it had received all his
devotion, and that even this profession was now only a
burden to him. He had sacrificed everything for his
belief in science, and now all his accomplishments were
meaningless, for when he died there would be no one to
mourn him, no one to miss him. He had never had the
time for others, and now, no one would have time for
him. Similarly, in The Three Sisters, the sisters despair because their heritage of aristocratic life has no
place in modern society—they are displaced, alienated,
trapped in a senseless and terminal existence. Life
has somehow passed them by, and their brother Andrei
mourns the fact that he never even noticed it slipping
away. Irina cries:

> Where? Where has it all gone? Where is it?
> Oh, my God, my God!...it's all muddled in my
> head...I'm forgetting everything, every day
> I forget, and life is slipping by, never to
> return, never... (Chekhov, 1964:289).

The process of transcendence, as stated previously, Chekhov envisions in terms of the creative cultural activity of enlightened individuals who stimulate
the social consciousness of the people by their example.
In Chekhov's vision, the role of the intelligentsia—
whether they were aristocrats or peasants—was to re-
discover the nature of human beings' basic and genuine
needs, of their real selves, and the fundamental self-
actualizing function of interpersonal interaction. It
was the intelligentsia who were capable of recognizing
the dehumanizing effect of the false social conventions
that society had imposed on human nature. On the basis
of such realizations, Chekhov believed the intelligentsia could construct a vision of a new society in which
the conventions of interaction were consonant with genuine human needs, and where interpersonal communication
would serve as the medium of developing individuals'
real selves. Having this vision before them as the
ideal toward which society should progress, the intelligentsia would endeavor to stimulate such progress
by restructuring their own lives and interaction in
consonance with the ideal. In doing so, their function was to present to the masses a model of a new and

better stage of social life. This model, then, would arouse the interest of the masses, generate their recognition of the existing degenerate phase of social life, and stimulate a desire for and willingness to work toward a regeneration of both collective and individual life. Thus, the initial impetus and the driving force behind social change and transcendence of societal evil arises from the intelligentsia.

Consequences of Evil and of Transcendence

Tragedy is the only word that summarizes the disastrous consequences of the perversion of interaction Chekhov dramatized. Interaction is transformed into an instrument of suffering, and worse, of meaningless suffering. In The Name-Day Party, Olga Mikaelovna is reduced to a state of inner emptiness. The Professor of A Dull Story slowly descends from a sense of unreality to disillusion, to disgust, and finally to indifference The Three Sisters bewail the futility of existence, and surrender to the anguish of isolation. All regret the passing of their lives from hopeless solitude into quiet oblivion, yet they are completely unable to change their destiny.

Through his melancholy characters Chekhov shows that there is no faint hope for the alleviation of this societally-induced misery in the near future. There is only the remote possibility of a better life in the distant future for the descendants of their descendants—and that possibility depends on the ceaseless effort of the present unfortunates. Their efforts, their agony will perhaps, someday, evoke a change for a better life—but the play ends with Olga's cry—"If we only knew, if we only knew!" (Chekhov, 1964:312).

CHAPTER 4: Alexsander Solzhenitsyn

Introduction

It was a universal law: everyone who <u>acts</u>
breeds both good and evil. With some <u>it's</u>
more good, with others more evil
(Solzhenitsyn, 1972:88).

"...the wolfhound is right and the cannibal
is wrong!" (Solzhenitsyn, 1973b:466).

"A human being," Kondrashev continued, "possesses from his birth a certain essence, the
nucleus, as it were, of this human being.
His "I." And it is still uncertain which
forms which: whether life forms the man or
man, with his strong spirit, forms his life!
...because he has something to measure himself against... Because he has in him an
image of perfection which in rare moments
suddenly emerges before his spiritual gaze"
(Solzhenitsyn, 1973b:297).

What is the most precious thing in the world?
Not to participate in injustices. They are
stronger than you. They have existed in the
past and they will exist in the future. But
let them not come about through <u>you</u>
(Solzhenitsyn, 1973b:397).

The dehumanization of Soviet life in the Stalin era extended to the realm of literature, and was
reflected in the decline of socialist realism. Today,
however, there is a movement in literature oriented
toward a return to the challenging artistic consciousness of the 1920's. The standard-bearer of this movement is Alexsander Isaevich Solzhenitsyn whose courageous revelations of Stalinist atrocities has shocked
the entire world, has made him an anathema in the eyes
of the Soviet political elite, and has resulted in
exile from his native land. Solzhenitsyn epitomizes

the artist whose consciousness and creativity are dedicated to an ethical ideal, indeed, an ethical imperative. He maintains that the artistic perception entails a unique perspective on society, and comprises a moral obligation to function as social critic, to serve as an instrument of social change by evoking a radical transformation in the reader's consciousness. This belief in the revolutionary possibilities of art was expressed in a rare interview:

> Because he observes the world with an artist's eye and because of his intuition, many social developments reveal themselves to a writer earlier than to others, and from an unconventional aspect. This is what comprises his talent. And from his talent springs his duty. He must inform society of what he has seen, especially about everything that is unhealthy and cause for anxiety...Russian literature has always addressed itself to those who suffer. Sometimes the opinion is offered in our country that one should write about what is coming tomorrow touching up where necessary. But this is falsification —and justifies lies (Solzhenitsyn, as cited in Burg and Feifer, 1974:239).

Solzhenitsyn's conception of art as a commentary on life, of the continuity of art and life, and of the revolutionary potential of art to transform life, reflects not only the critical consciousness of the Silver Age of socialist realism, but moreover, the radical consciousness of the Golden Age of Russian literature, especially as represented in Dostoevsky and Tolstoy. Solzhenitsyn's art, like that of Tolstoy and Dostoevsky, arises from a transcendent perspective, grounded in critical reflection, and an unwavering sense of duty. Again, like Tolstoy and Dostoevsky, he presupposes the existence of moral absolutes, of an innate conscience consonant with those absolutes, and of an ethical imperative that people exercise human judgment in regard to their own actions, their relations with others, and the values and activities of their society.

Solzhenitsyn conceives of justness as a moral absolute, and of conscience as an innate faculty. He contends that morality is not at all a relative matter. There are moral absolutes, and furthermore, it is the human being's very nature to be cognizant of those absolutes—such is the implication of

the distinction between the "wolfhound" and the
"cannibal." The inner image of perfection to which
Kondrashev refers provides the inherent guide to moral
behavior, which, as the last quote indicates, consists
of acting with justness in relation to others, and in
opposing injustice. In this respect, Solzhenitsyn de-
parts sharply from Tolstoy's doctrine of non-resistance
to evil. Moral behavior, for Solzhenitsyn, is a matter
of action—of the active effort to realize justness in
relation to others, and to resist to the end, without
compromise, the manifestations of injustice. Awareness, reflection, commitment, and action—these are
fundamental constructs of Solzhenitsyn's ethics. Possessing an innate conscience grounded in the moral absolute of justness, and being by nature a conscious animal—i.e., conscious of conscience, the human being is
implicitly morally committed to critical reflection,
and action grounded in moral valuations. The failure
to reflect and to act thus constitutes deliberate evil.
Being conscious, human beings are responsible, accountable for evil—and their transcendence of evil—in accord with the moral absolutes—is never relative, but
always and inevitably, absolute.

Definitions of Evil and of Transcendence

Writing of the system of arrest, deportation,
exile, imprisonment, and slaughter that characterized
the Stalin era, Solzhenitsyn exposes, and protests
against the indignities to which a human being can be
subjected. The prisons, the labor camps, the concentration camps were all founded on the violation of human dignity and integrity. Survival in these camps
often depended upon the surrender of the last vestiges
of humanity.

> Here every real compromise must lead to a
> loss of human dignity. A refusal to compro-
> mise in all human and social essentials thus
> forms a prerequisite for anyone wishing to
> remain really human in the camps (Lukacs,
> 1970:58).

The horrifying choice these people faced was
either to refuse to compromise, and thus to retain human dignity and die, or to compromise, to give up their
dignity, and live. In such conditions, the price of
life was too great—as one of Solzhenitsyn's most tragic characters, Oleg Kostoglotov, relates:

How much can one pay for life, and how much
is too much? It's like what they teach you
in school these days. "A man's most precious
possession is his life. It is only given to
him once." This means we should cling to
life at any cost. But the camps have helped
many of us to establish that the betrayal or
destruction of good and helpless people is
too high a price, that our lives aren't worth
it (Solzhenitsyn, 1972:295).

It is the injustice of such conditions which
destroy human dignity and integrity that Solzhenitsyn
defines as evil, as unbearably evil. He protests
against the fundamental injustice of conditions of
humiliation, deprivation, degradation, and dehumanizing fear that drive people to irredeemable moral compromises or to death.

By exposing such atrocities Solzhenitsyn
strives to evoke a transfiguration of the reader's
consciousness. For contemporary Soviet citizens,
he seeks to invoke a kind of collective catharsis—
a traumatic recognition of past evils which will generate a conscious resistance, and opposition to evil in
the present and future. The people of today, he believes, must be forced to remember the evil injustice
of Stalinism in order to prevent a recurrence of such
a horror in the future. The critic Lukacs comments
that Solzhenitsyn's novels succeed in this endeavor by
confronting the reader with the questions:

> ...what demands has this era made on man?
> Who has proved himself as a human being? Who
> has salvaged his human dignity and integrity?
> Who has held his own—and how? Who has re-
> tained his essential humanity? Where was
> this humanity twisted, broken, destroyed?
> (Lukacs, 1970:13-14).

And Solzhenitsyn's biographers, Burg and Feifer, summarize the favorable reaction to One Day in the Life of
Ivan Denisovich as:

> ...that with one stroke, One Day had wrought
> a fundamental change in Soviet literature,
> and this, in turn, would spark an equally ra-
> dical change in Soviet life (Burg and Feifer,
> 1974:173).

42

This cathartic and transformative orientation of Solzhenitsyn's novels signifies that he understands transcendence as the awakening of moral consciousness, the establishment of contact with the inner conscience which necessarily results in individual recognition of evil, and motivates individual resistance to evil, the evil of injustice. Transcendence is the ethical imperative for survival as a human—as a moral being:

> ...grave moral compromises were acceptable for the sake of sheer survival—but for survival as a human being with a moral core, a prisoner had to fix a line beyond which he would not step (Burg and Feifer, 1974:73).

Locus of Causality

The focus of Solzhenitsyn's novels on the nature of diverse forms of societal evil—that is, the injustice inflicted on human beings by an evil social order—signifies, on the one hand, that social reality is the dimension of causality. However, on the other hand, his emphasis on the primacy of individual conscience, and the transcendence of societal evil in accord with the promptings of conscience, signifies that human nature is the dimension of causality. In the first place, in The First Circle, he dramatically portrays the entrapment of individuals within the Stalinist system—even the officers in charge of the prison camps are revealed to be human beings with ambivalent feelings about the system—and yet their ambivalence is impotent for they see no way to escape the system or to change it. Everyone, from the top ranks of official circles to the prisoners themselves, is a victim of the system, and always at Stalin's mercy. Similarly, in Cancer Ward, the patient Shulubin rages against the inability of a whole people to rebel against, and to prevent complete subordination to the evil system:

> In no more than ten years a whole people lost its social drive and courageous impulse.... What happened to us? How could we have given in? (Solzhenitsyn, 1972:439).

However, in the second place, the wickedness that pervades the social order, is also shown to emanate from Stalin himself, and from others like him. And, further, it is only through the unremitting efforts of individuals who recognize and resist evil that Solzhenitsyn sees the hope for eradiction of societal evil. Both the hero of Cancer Ward—Oleg Kostoglotov—

and the hero of The First Circle—Gleb Nerzhin—conclude from their experiences in the prison camps that a person must fight the evils of society, no matter how futile that fight may appear to be. Both realize that only individuals possess the necessary inner guide, the understanding and the courage that are needed to transcend and transform societal evil. Solzhenitsyn apparently assumes a dichotomous conception of causality—both social reality and human nature are dimensions of causality. These dimensions are interpenetrating, interdependent, and mutually determinative, but in the final analysis, human nature is primary, and social reality is secondary. Although human beings receive their mode of consciousness and being from social reality, it is this consciousness and being that constructs social reality in the first place—as the critic Lukacs phrases it:

> ...every proving of oneself, and every failure to prove oneself point to the future normal mode of human relations; they are—implicitly—preludes to a real future life among men (Lukacs, 1970:22).

Sources of Evil and of Transcendence

Solzhenitsyn illustrates his concept of interdependent realms of causality—stressing the primacy of human nature—through examples of confrontation. The characters of his novels are inevitably personally confronted with manifestations of societal evil, and the dramatic action of the novels revolves around the choices they make in regard to such confrontations. For example, the inmates of The First Circle are imprisoned within a special section of the prison system— the "sharashka." To the sharashka are brought all manner of intellectuals, professionals, and people of special skills, whose talents are put to use in service of the State Security System. The prisoners are all involved in tasks essential to the improvement of the security system. The central character, Gleb Nerzhin, is one whose talents are especially valuable to the NKVD. During his internment in the sharashka, Nerzhin comes to the realization that his work is expediting the effectiveness and success of the NKVD—that he is facilitating the imprisonment of more innocent and helpless people. Nerzhin eventually revolts, and refuses to further collaborate with "the enemy," even though he knows this means he will be deported from the relative luxury of the sharashka to one of the worst prison camps. He discovers the limit of his ability to

44

compromise, even though his survival depends on that ability. Thus, human nature is confronted with evil in social reality, and responds with transcendence of evil.

The interdependence of human nature and social reality as dimensions of causality is evident in the fact, that, on the one hand, human nature (individuals) transforms social reality (the social order) by means of the active resistance to and transcendence of societal evil, and on the other hand, social reality transforms human nature by providing situations of confrontation which awaken the innate moral conscience, necessitate individual human judgment, and result in either conscious transcendence or conscious capitulation to societal evil. The interaction of these two causal systems manifested in the individual experience of confrontation of evil is the means by which the innate ambivalent tendencies of human nature for evil and for transcendence are realized. The existence and the predominance of evil in the social order derives from a capitulation to evil in the confrontation situation— the failure of individuals to adhere to the dictates of conscience, the failure to choose for transcendence. Each individual failure to prove oneself, to make the moral choice, contributes to the existence of evil in the social order, the generation of a social construction of reality which is evil. And the elimination of evil in the social order depends upon the exercise of human judgment according to conscience in confrontation situations.

Thus, human nature is the locus of causality from which originates the possibilities of evil and transcendence, and the interaction of causal systems of human nature and social reality is the source of the manifestation of evil and transcendence in the world. Solzhenitsyn would agree with Berdyaev that humans are both spiritual and social beings belonging to two worlds, and would concur also with Berdyaev's intuition of the primacy of the spiritual aspect of human nature. Moral consciousness is not a function of social reality, but implicitly transcends social reality.

The spiritual aspect of human nature is antecedent to the social aspect. By virtue of conscience— the inherent and absolute knowledge of good and evil— human beings transcend the collective, and are by nature ethically obligated to exercise judgment in regard to collective life, the social construction of reality. The wolfhound is right because it has no awareness of

45

good and evil; the cannibal is wrong because he or she is conscious of good and evil. The wolfhound is not responsible for its action; human beings are.

Manifestations of Evil and of Transcendence

Owing to his stubborn faith in the spiritual aspect of human nature Solzhenitsyn places the highest value on the preservation of human dignity, integrity, and freedom as prerequisites for the realization of all the human being's latent inner potentials. Consequently, he vigorously protests any conditions which detract from or violate dignity and integrity. The concept of injustice symbolizes for him the nature of such conditions, and thus he equates evil with injustice. In terms of collective life, evil as injustice is epitomized in the final socialization of people which utterly destroys their freedom of spirit, and reduces them to the status of social automatons or as Dostoevsky phrased it, an "organ-stop" or "piano-key" (Dostoevsky, no date:136). The individual is greater than the collective and the collective life; he or she cannot become a mere function of the collective without irreparable damage to his or her dignity, integrity, and freedom. In this respect, Solzhenitsyn denounces as manifestations of evil-injustice both the total absorption of the individual into the ant-heap of society, and the dehumanization promoted by science which reorients "people from ultimate values to exclusive preoccupation with things" (Burg and Feifer, 1974:152). He sees the danger of science, as Dostoevsky did:

> It is, of course, quite true that if one day they really discover some formula for all our desires and whims, that is to say, if they discover what they all depend on...that is, a real mathematical formula, man may perhaps at once stop feeling any desire.... For who would want to desire according to a mathematical formula? And that is not all. He will at once be transformed from a man into an organ stop, or something of the sort. For what is man without desires, without free will, and without the power of choice but a stop in an organ pipe? (Dostoevsky, no date:131-132).

For Solzhenitsyn as for Dostoevsky, the purpose of human life is realized in the individual exercise of judgment in situations of choice between good and evil, made possible by the possession of reason, conscience, and free will:

46

Not by birth, not by the work of one's hands,
not by the wings of education is one elected
into the people. But by one's inner self.
Everyone forges his inner self year after
year. One must try to temper, to cut, to po-
lish one's soul so as to become a human being. And thereby become a tiny particle of
one's own people (Solzhenitsyn, 1973b:452).

Similarly:

...for it seems to me that the whole meaning
of human life can be summed up in the one
statement that man only exists for the purpose of proving to himself every minute that
he is a man and not an organ-stop!
(Dostoevsky, no date:136).

The human being's nature as a spiritual being
thus determines that the final socialization of people
into society, and the tendency of science toward dehumanization constitute manifestations of evil on the societal level. Similarly, on the individual level, this
spiritual nature signifies that the failure of the individual, confronted with evil in the form of injustice, to resist that injustice, and failure to act with
justness in relations to others, also comprises evil.
Solzhenitsyn assumes that individuals cannot remain unaware of the promptings of conscience, and therefore
the failure to act with justness, and to resist injustice is the result of deliberate negligence for which
the individual is morally responsible and accountable.
In his novels, he gives as specific examples of such
negligence moral compromises which "enhance one's
own well-being. . . in violation of one conscience"
(Burg and Feifer, 1974:100), the "pre-occupation
with things" rather than "ultimate values" (Burg
and Feifer, 1974:152); isolation from the spiritual
unity of humanity; and the degrading "...herd instinct,
the fear of remaining alone, outside the community"
(Solzhenitsyn, 1972:435) that reduces people to the
status of groveling slaves of society. All of these
conditions Solzhenitsyn identifies as instances of individual negation of humanity, as violations of the
dignity, integrity, and freedom of human beings.

Transcendence of evil, in contrast, is evident in individual adherence to the promptings of conscience—i.e., the manifestation of justness in relations to others, and the active opposition to injustice, and on the societal level, is evident in the

reorganization of society itself in accordance with the
ethical principles arising from conscience. In his novels, Solzhenitsyn depicts as evidence of transcendence
the refusal to make moral compromises; the concern for
ultimate values rather than preoccupation with things;
the exercise of individual judgment; the value of skepticism as "a way of freeing the dogmatic mind..."
(Solzhenitsyn, 1973b:41); the feeling of oneness with
humanity; the exercise of compassion, "selfless gener-
osity," toward others (Burg and Feifer, 1974:200); the
realization of individual responsibility for others;
the resistance of injustice (Solzhenitsyn, 1973b:397);
and the dedication to truth and goodness realized
through active affection for others (Solzhenitsyn,
1974:17). In sum, the organization and direction of
individual life in consonance with the dictates of conscience constitutes transcendence. Individual activities such as these constitute prerequisites for the
protection and preservation of human dignity and integrity. In Solzhenitsyn's view, the transcendence of
evil must also be incorporated into the social construction of reality. He sees the possibility for the
preservation of essential values through the reorganization of society itself according to the dictates of
the human being's inner moral consciousness. The concept of ethical socialism summarizes, for Solzhenitsyn,
such a reconstruction of society founded on a dedication to human dignity.

Processes of Evil and of Transcendence

As previously indicated, it is in the process
of personal experience in confrontations with evil that
the individual faces the necessity of moral decision,
the choices between good and evil. Solzhenitsyn assumes that the psychic trauma of such dramatic confrontations necessarily awakens the moral consciousness.
Although the intuitive knowledge of good and evil may
have previously lain dormant and unrecognized, the
personal confrontation with evil brings this knowledge
to the conscious level. Therefore, the individual confrontation with evil renders imperative the choice between evil and transcendence of evil, and the consequences of each decision either contribute to the existence of evil in society or toward the elimination of
evil, and the transformation of society.

The impact on the individual of such confrontations stems from the fact that certain areas of the
world are rendered problematic. The individual is
faced with the uncertainty or unreliability of his or

her own previously unrecognized assumptions about reality. He or she is forced to question and to reflect on the "given"—those beliefs and judgments that have always been taken for granted. Confrontation engenders problematic doubt, critical reflection, and moral choice. In his novels, Solzhenitsyn depicts as instances of such critical experience, radical changes in everyday life, especially as evident in the tranposition to a new setting—i.e., hospitalization in a "Cancer Ward," or interment in a labor camp. The novelty of conditions in an unfamiliar environment, and the concurrent exposure to transformed and unpredictable social relations cannot be perceived by the individual involved as natural or self-evident. The result is that a new analysis of existence is triggered in the individual—he or she begins to question, and to reflect upon the givens of his or her world. As Lukacs observes, the novelty of the situation is the paramount factor in evoking such a reaction:

> Here it depends above all on whether this
> socially necessary reality...is simply accep-
> ted as "normal" existence, as a "natural"
> continuation of their previous lives, or whe-
> ther such a contac of a character's own
> life with a sphere of social reality will
> cause him to regard his existence and its
> meaning for himself and for his fellow man
> with new eyes, and to make himself and others
> aware of it (Lukacs, 1970:44).

Removed from the security of the "normal" surroundings and the habitualized routine of everyday life, the new inmate or patient perhaps initially experiences a sense of unreality, and refuses to adapt to the new existence. But in order to survive in the new situation, the individual must eventually recognize the necessity of reviewing, reflecting upon, and revising his or her previous world-view and its concomitant intellectual and moral guidelines for conduct.

> For the individual always bases his decisions
> on a certain social situation; his decisions
> depend principally on the idea he has of so-
> ciety, of his position in it and of his atti-
> tude towards it, as well as on the command-
> ments that because of this position he re-
> gards as binding...(Lukacs, 1970:57).

And moreover, the repercussions of individual decisions in such crisis situations, have significant consequences not only for the course of individual destiny, but also for the progress or the decline of society.

Consequences of Evil and of Transcendence

The pivot of Solzhenitsyn's ethics has been shown to be the primacy of conscience which necessarily requires the exercise of human judgment with regard to individual conduct, relations with others, and the values and activities of society. The individual's failure to exercise this judgment contributes to the existence of evil in the social order, and in Solzhenitsyn's vision, culminates in the ultimate evil of the final socialization that destroys the freedom of the spirit, the essential dignity and integrity of human beings. Solzhenitsyn perceives and denounces the pernicious tendency toward final socialization in the ethical neutrality of science, in totalitarian political systems, and in all forms of government not grounded in the principle of human dignity.

The alternative to the predominance and the eventual victory of evil implicit in such institutions is given in the prospect of ethical socialism—the reconstruction of society in consonance with the guidelines of the "inner ethic." Through ethical socialism, Solzhenitsyn envisions the possibility of incorporating the transcendence of evil in the principle of justness into social reality, and thus establishing societal safeguards of human dignity and integrity. In ethical socialism, justness would be established in society as the reflection and the equivalent of individual conscience. The life of society, as the life of the individual, would be directed by moral consciousness and human affection—the two attributes that distinguish humans from all other animals. As Shulbin expresses this ideal to Oleg in Cancer Ward:

> We have to show the world a society in which all relationships, fundamental principles and laws flow directly from ethics, and from them alone.... As for scientific research, it should only be conducted where it doesn't damage morality, in the first instance, where it doesn't damage the researchers themselves (Solzhenitsyn, 1972:442).

CHAPTER 5: Concluding Remarks on the Perspective of Literature

Each of the writers considered in this section define evil in terms of conditions that detract from or are detrimental to the special qualities of human beings which distinguish them from the rest of nature. Specifically, Lawrence protests the suppression of impulses from the inner moral and spontaneous self; Chekhov protests the repression of authentic human needs by the falsehood of social conventions; and Solzhenitsyn repudiates the injustices that devastate freedom of the spirit and conscience. This implicit belief in the special qualities of human nature informs also their definitions of transcendence of evil as a function of individual consciousness and arising from the inherent knowledge of good and evil.

The three authors differ, however, in determining the locus of causality—Lawrence emphasizes the primacy of human nature, Chekhov stresses social reality, and Solzhenitsyn recognizes the priority of human nature. The sources of evil and transcedence are identified, accordingly, in terms of the action of human nature on social reality (Lawrence), the action of social reality on interpersonal interaction (Chekhov), and an interaction of human nature and social reality (Solzhenitsyn).

With regard to the manifestations of evil and transcendence, whether evil is perceived in terms of confining social roles, or decadent social conventions, or in a tendency to ignore the promptings of conscience, all of these forms of evil have in common a perception of an estrangement between the human being's social and spiritual aspects—between the superficial and the real selves. Similarly, transcendence is perceived in terms of the individual's coming to consciousness of innate morality, and the consequent rejection of evil—i.e., the rejection of a terminal mode of consciousness (Lawrence), of the falsehood of social conventions (Chekhov), and of injustices of the social order (Solzhenitsyn).

51

The processes by which evil and transcendence
are realized, in all three cases, involve an interaction of individual consciousness and the social construction of reality. According to Lawrence, evil is
manifested as the corruption of human nature is incorporated into and maintained by social reality, and
transcendence is manifested as the experience of eroti-
cism and creative activity transform social reality.
According to Chekhov, evil is manifested as authentic
human needs are displaced by false social requirements,
and transcendence is manifested as the creative cultural activity of the intelligentsia transforms society. According to Solzhenitsyn, both evil and transcendence are manifested as a consequence of individual
confrontations with evil. Finally, each author envisions the consequences of evil and trancendence in
terms of the alternative possibilities for the dehumanization of human beings that will follow the final socialization, or the fulfillment of individual and societal potentials that will ensue from a creative and
harmonious interaction of self and society.

Most significant for the purposes of this essay is the fact that two of these writers (Lawrence and
Solzhenitsyn) concur in the perception of the primacy
of human nature —in contrast to social reality—as the
locus of causality. In this respect, Solzhenitsyn is
most optimistic regarding the capacity of human nature
to transcend, and to transform social reality, Lawrence
is moderately optimistic, and Chekhov is the most pessimistic. None of these authors underestimate the significance of social reality as a factor influencing human consciousness and judgment, but this influence is
conceived as a secondary factor. Human consciousness
and moral judgment depend also and derive primarily
from a source external and prior to social reality,
i.e., human nature. Secondly, as Lawrence and
Solzhenitsyn both emphasize, the conditions which
awaken the latent moral consciousness are ubiquitous
and endemic to the human condition: erotic experiences, creative participation in social life, and confrontation situations which call into question basic assumptions about the world are "givens" of human experience
which can be taken for granted.

These two conceptions—the primacy of human
nature and the natural inevitability of conditions that
awaken consciousness of conscience—signify that the
function and exercise of human judgment is a quality
which can be taken for granted. Individuals are

52

responsible for, and can be held accountable for the evils of society, and an evil society can and must be transformed by the individual recognition and transcendence of evil.

Furthermore, the metaphysics of these authors' world-views support Berdyaev's identification of the final socialization of human beings as the ultimate evil which must be opposed and resisted by all ethical individuals, and ethically oriented institutions. To this end, a responsible sociology and all the sciences must undertake:

> ...activity which contributes not to dehumanization, but, through deeper understanding of the world and mankind, to conscience... (Burg and Feifer, 1974:152).

PART THREE: THE PERSPECTIVE OF PSYCHOANALYSIS

CHAPTER 6: Sigmund Freud

Introduction

The notion of a human nature in conflict with
itself, disrupted by the opposition of social
and asocial inclinations, the view that the
social self develops from an asocial nucleus
but that the social trends are also dynamic
and emotional in nature, and finally the conception that reason's control can be extended
by a detailed knowledge of the repressed asocial tendencies—all this was not known before Freud (Roazen, 1968:250).

For Freud, neither the assumed causality of
events nor the possibilities of retrodiction
or prediction denies the psychological ideal
of the responsible human being. Any textbook
on psychoanalytic technique could demonstrate
the extent to which, far from absolving pa-
tients of responsibility for their acts,
psychoanalysis entails an ever-widening
sphere of accountability to oneself. "The
patient must learn to renounce guidance and
to settle his conflicts by himself." Freud
did not offer psychoanalytic doctrine as an
alibi: according to Fenichel, analysts "demonstrate, whenever it is possible, that the
patient in reality brings about things which
he seems to experience passively." Although
"every human being's responsibility is
limited, because no human act is performed
under the full control of the conscious ego,"
Freud's central therapeutic intention was to
extend the realm of that control, to make men
more genuine masters of themselves (Roazen,
1968:299).

This contention holds that what we call our
civilization is largely responsible for our
misery, and that we should be much happier if

<u>we gave it up and returned to primitive con-</u>
<u>ditions</u> (Freud, 1962:33).

A certain degree of direct sexual satisfaction appears to be absolutely necessary for
by far the greater number of natures, and the
frustration of this variable individual need
is avenged by manifestations which, on account of their injurious effect on functional
activity and of their subjectively painful
character, we must regard as illness (Freud
1972:26).

The implicit theoretical assumptions and explicit therapeutic strategies and goals of psychoanalysis are founded upon an ethical substructure which
closely approximates the central premises of this study. The shared premises of this ethical substructure
revolve around the fundamental conception of science as
a variable in the human condition. From this conception of science derives the notion of its consequent
responsibility, on the one hand, to expose and eliminate conditions of life detrimental to human dignity and
freedom, and on the other hand, to discover and reinforce conditions favorable to the exercise of responsible human judgment. This ethical substructure is evident in the most elementary definitions of psychoanalysis:

A theory of the structure and development of
personality, and a method of psychotherapy
for the treatment of neurosis, originated by
Sigmund Freud. Psychoanalysis is particularly concerned with problems of repression
and inner conflict, and is designed to bring
unconscious desires into consciousness. The
analysis of dreams and the techniques of free
association are used in freeing the patient
from the "tyranny of the unconscious"
(Theodorson, 1970:320).

It was Sigmund Freud's meticulous and brilliant analysis of neurotic behavior patterns which led
him to the discovery of the debilitating effects exerted by the irrational processes contained in the unconscious. From his observations of neurotic distur-
bance, Freud deduced that the contents of the unconscious were comprised of impulses and desires deemed
unacceptable by the prevailing moral standards of society. The social unacceptability of these impulses

58

required their exclusion from behavior and awareness, and Freud hypothesized the existence of the mechanism of repression by which these impulses were relegated to the realm of the unconscious. Thus removed from consciousness but not eliminated, the forbidden impulses are manifested in distortions of consciousness and behavior that undermine the normal and healthy functioning of the personality. To correct this pernicious process and to return the personality to mental health, Freud devised the techniques of free association and dream analysis through which he attempted to liberate the rational processes of consciousness from the surrepticious control of irrational forces in the unconscious. Thus Freud, through basically pessimistic and critical of both human nature and society, by attempting to bring the repressed contents of the unconscious to the level of consciousness and reflection, sought to reduce the degrading bondage of personality to the moral dictums of society, and to expand the range of human freedom, responsibility, and rational judgment.

Definitions of Evil and Transcendence

As the foregoing definition of psychoanalysis indicates, Freud's psychoanalytic method of psychotherapy also entails a theory of the structure and development of the personality. Basically, Freud conceived of the personality as a coherent system composed of three interdependent and interacting sub-systems—the id, the ego, and the superego (Hall, 1954:22-35). He identified the id as the source of the instincts, that is, of the human being's innate biological drives, and thus as the psychological representative of human evolutionary and biological heritage. The instincts are of a conservative nature in that the satisfaction of an instinct always involves a regression from a state of excitation or tension to a state of relaxation or the release of tension. In terms of instinctual satisfaction, then, tension is equivalent to pain, and the release of tension to pleasure. The satisfaction of instinctual needs is the sole function of the id, and this function is governed by the pleasure principle, the aim of which is the avoidance of pain and the experience of pleasure, in other words, the reduction of tension within the organism.

The id's function of obtaining instinctual satisfaction under the guidance of the pleasure principle consists of the discharge of tension by means of image formation (wish formation) and impulsive motor activity. While this process of image formation does

provide the organism with a visual representation of
the object of the instinct, it does not produce the
tangible object necessary for the satisfactory release
of tension. This process, Freud hypothesized, constitutes a function of the ego. The ego fulfills this
function through the utilization of thought and reason
in developing a plan of action to discover or produce
the actual object in the external world that will satisfy the instinct. This activity necessarily entails
a postponement of the discharge of tension until the
desired object is present. Thus, the operation of the
pleasure principle must be temporarily suspended until
the ego's transactions with the external world of reality is completed. Freud called the ego's suspension of
the pleasure principle in view of the exigencies of external reality the operation of the reality principle.
The definitive characteristic of the ego, then, is its
rational, cognitive, problem-solving activity by which
it effects transactions with the external environment
that satisfy more efficiently than the processes of the
id the instinctual needs of the organism.

Whereas the id represents that aspect of personality deriving from biological and hereditary factors, and the ego represents the product of the organism's interaction with the external world, the third
component, the superego, represents that aspect of personality which results from the influence of culture,
transmitted through the socialization process. The
superego provides the moral code of the personality,
and develops from the child's identification with his
or her parents, and the internalization of their moral
concepts and the authority with which they enforce
those concepts. As such, the superego is a vehicle of
tradition and cultural continuity. The internalization
of parental moral values provides the superego with definitive conceptions of virtue and vice, and the internalization of parental authority imbues the superego
with the power to enforce the value-system. According
to Freud, the prohibitions of the superego are directed
against those instinctual needs and consequent actions
which would disrupt or endanger the stability of society—the instincts of sex and aggression. By rewarding
the person for thoughts and actions beneficial to society with feelings of pride, and by punishing the person for thoughts and actions detrimental to society
with feelings of shame and guilt, the superego enforces
the law-abiding conduct of the individual and ensures
the stability of society.

According to Freud, this triadic constellation of complementary functions in the personality system serves the overall purpose of effecting realistic transactions with the external environment which satisfactorily fulfills the human being's basic biologically grounded needs given in the instincts. The satisfaction of these innate needs, he conceived, as the primary and indispensable condition of mental health. And thus, he defined as the highest good of human life the maintenance of mental health by the coordinated and harmonious functioning of the three sub-systems of personality. Conversely, he conceived of evil in terms of the disruption of these interrelated processes, the subversion of mental health, and the decline of the personality system into mental illness. That is, he perceived as evil whatever predispositions in human nature or conditions of social reality detracted from the maintenance of mental health by interfering with, inhibiting, or precluding the satisfactory fulfillment of the innate biological needs of human nature. As is evident in Freud's innovation of psychoanalytic technique to counteract and correct the processes of mental illness, he defined the transcendence of evil in terms of the restoration of mental health. That is, he identified as transcendent whatever predispositions in human nature or conditions of social reality oppose, overcome, and eliminate factors inimical to mental health.

Locus of Causality

Freud's conception of the personality as an integrated system constituted by the combined influences of biological and cultural factors indicates that he perceived two realms of causality, i.e., human nature, as the origin of biological influences and social reality, as the origin of cultural influences. The biological predispositions inherent in human nature, and represented in the instincts contained in the id, and the cultural conditioning to which the instincts are subject—manifested in the regulative activities of the superego, are both instrumental in the determination of personality. Although Freud's biological terminology may mislead the superficial reader to infer a one-sided biological determinism, Freud was, in fact, very specific in emphasizing the significant influence of cultural factors. For example, in his essay "Thoughts for the Times on War and Death," he states:

61

that the inmost essence of human nature consists of elemental instincts, which are common to all men and aim at the satisfaction of
certain primal needs.... These primitive instincts undergo a lengthy process of development before they are allowed to become active
in the adult being. They are inhibited, directed towards other aims and departments, become commingled, alter their objects, and are
to some extent turned back upon their posses-
sor.... The influences of civilization cause
an ever-increasing transmutation of egoistic
trends into altruistic and social ones, and
this by an admixture of erotic elements
(Freud, 1965:213-215).

The biological foundation of human nature
provides the basic material from which the personality
is fashioned within the context of life in society, and
hence determines the range of development possible for
human personality. The cultural conditioning, on the
other hand, imposed upon this biological foundation by
life in society, determines the direction of development of innate potentials not only by eliciting that
which is innate, but by redirecting, altering, or even
preventing the manifestation of those potentials.
Human nature, as a realm of causality, determines
the original nature and the range of possible development of personality, while, social reality as a realm
of causality, determines which of the innate drives and
potentials will become active, and the form in which
they will be manifested in the personality. The char-
ges of biological determinism, and of a possible foundation for eugenics in Freud's theories are refuted not
only by his emphasis on the cultural factors but also
by his fundamental assumption of a human nature common
to all people. The racial theories of de Gobineau, Cham-
berlain, and others, are founded, in contrast, upon the
assumption of innate biological inequality among races,
and the determination of human nature by biological and
hereditary factors alone. Nothing could be further removed from Freud's dynamic conception of interdependent
causal realms.

Sources of Evil and of Transcendence

Freud's dichotomous conception of causality
signifies further that the sources of evil and of transcendence of evil must derive from both the realms of
human nature and social reality. The biological

62

foundation of human nature provides several components
of the personality system which detract from mental
health, and may be identified as sources of evil. In
the first place, although the satisfaction of the instincts through the immediate discharge of tension regulated by the pleasure principle is the sole function
of the id, the processes of releasing tension through
image formation and impulsive motor activity with no
reference to the exigencies of the external environment
do not always result in satisfaction of the instincts.
That is, when an actual object is required to fulfill
an instinctual need, the processes of the id are inadequate, and produce instead an increase of painful tensions, and thus endanger the harmonious functioning of
the organism. Secondly, although the processes of the
ego, under the governance of the reality principle,
provide more efficiently for the satisfaction of the
instincts that does the id, by taking into account the
available objects in the environment, the necessary
postponement of gratification also results in a diminuition of the capacity for the enjoyment of pleasure.
This is not to say that the pursuit of pleasure through
the discharge of tension is abandoned in the 6peration
of the reality principle, but it does signify that the
organism must be able to tolerate painful tensions temporarily. Ideally, there must be an equilibrium between the immediate discharge of tension and the temporary postponement of this release, and consequently,
an imbalance between the operations of the pleasure
principle and the reality principle increases painful
tensions within the organism, and undermines its stability and mental health. Thirdly, the regulatory activity of the superego in repressing those instincts,
which if unrestricted, would disrupt the social order,
on the one hand promotes a pragmatic integration of
individual and society, but on the other hand, produces
instinctual frustration painful to the organism.
Further, the debilitating effects of this frustration
are exacerbated by the punishment for wrong-thinking
and wrong-doing inflicted on the ego by the superego in
the form of anxiety, shame, and guilt.

          As these examples illustrate, the stability
and health of the human organism depend on the distribution of energy throughout the personality system.
That is, if most of the organism's psychic energy is
controlled by the superego, which thus dominates the
personality, the organism will suffer the painful frustration ensuing from instinctual renunciation. If most
of the energy is controlled by the id, which thus

dominates the personality, the organism will suffer the painful increase of tension ensuing from the inefficient processes of the id. Obviously, the most functional and desirable arrangement from the standpoint of the organism is the control of most of the psychic energy by the ego, which is most effective in fulfilling instinctual needs, and preserving the stability and health of the organism. Although Freud usually maintained that the instincts in themselves were neither good nor evil, and that the satisfaction of the instincts was necessary to mental health, he qualified this position with regard to the instinct of aggression. He states in Civilization and Its Discontents:

> The existence of this inclination to aggression...is the factor which disturbs our relations with our neighbor and which forces civilization into such a high expenditure [of energy]. In consequence of this primary mutual hostility of human beings, civilized society is perpetually threatened with disintegration.... Civilization has to use its utmost efforts in order to set limits to man's aggressive instincts and to hold the manifestations of them in check by psychial reaction-formations (Freud, 1962:59).

Indeed, he quite clearly realized the danger the instinct to aggression posed for both the individual and society, and hence, in this one case he supported the repression enforced by society, and justified by necessity. Finally, although the antisocial tendencies as a whole, are usually, in the process of socialization, either repressed or transformed into social tendencies, the fact remains that earlier mental states, in which hostile impulses are less restrained and more dominant, continue to exist alongside later mental states in which these impulses have been subdued. This condition indicates that there is always the possibility of regression to the earlier and more primitive states of mind and behavior which endangers both the health of the individual, and the stability of the social order.

With regard to the sources of evil in social reality, the principal condition which Freud perceived as inimical to mental health consists of the repressive influence exerted by society on human nature. In other words, it is the renunciation of instinct required by sexual morality, and enforced by the regulatory activity of the superego, that results in frustration, feelings of anxiety, guilt, and neurotic disturbances. In his analysis of civilization, Freud contended that the development of community life necessitates restrictions of individual freedom and possibilities of instinctual satisfaction in the interest of just and stable social relations. The required renunciation is embodied in the prevailing moral norms of a society. The standards and restrictions of these norms are imposed and enforced on children as new members of the society by their parents. With the formation of the superego by means of the child's identification with his or her parents, the moral norms are internalized as part of his or her own personality. From that point on, instinctual renunciation is maintained from within the personality as the superego blocks the operations of the id and the ego in the interest of instinctual satisfaction. The superego's opposition to these activities of the id and ego is reinforced as the aggressive instinct is turned inward and directed against the wicked ego in the forms of feelings of anxiety, shame, and guilt. In consequence, each instance of instinctual renunciation not only produces the agonies of frustration, but also, because the superego does not distinguish between wishes and actions, exacerbates the introversion of aggressiveness, and hence increases the painful burden of guilt. It was this culturally induced and internally sustained repression of the sexual instinct that Freud surmised to be the crucial factor in the etiology of the neuroses.

As a specific instance of civilized society's restrictions on sexuality, Freud noted that whereas the natural course of the sexual instinct was expressed in the exclusive and fully sensual love relationship between two people, the exigencies of communal life require and promote non-exclusive forms of love that bind together numerous individuals. In Civilization and Its Discontents he presented the dilemma thusly:

> We are saying much the same thing when we derive the antithesis between civilization and sexuality from the circumstance that sexual love is a relationship between two individuals in which a third can only be superfluous or disturbing, whereas civilization depends on relationships between a considerable number of individuals.... It favors every path by which strong identifications can be established between the members of the

community, and it summons up aim-inhibited libido on the largest scale so as to strengthen the communal bond by relations of friendship. In order for these aims to be fulfilled, a restriction upon sexual life is unavoidable (Freud, 1962:55-56).

He conceived of civilization as a process fulfilling the purpose of Eros to bind the whole of humanity into one great unity, the success of which depended upon the increase of non-exclusive aim-inhibited forms of love and the restriction of exclusive sensual relationships. It is precisely such prohibitions in regard to sexuality which generate the pernicious development of the neuroses.

Finally, the inimical influence of social reality upon human nature is evident also in a process exactly opposite the repression of sexuality. That is, in his essays on war, Freud voiced a protest against the disastrous consequences of chaotic societal events such as war which removed the cultural restraints on the aggressive and anti-social instincts. The removal of such restraints provokes a regression to earlier states of mind in which the hostile and aggressive instincts exist in more primitive form, as yet untouched by the subduing influences of culture. It is the regression to such states—precipitated by certain social conditions—that allows for the astounding display of "...deeds of cruelty, fraud, treachery and barbarity so incompatible with their civilization that one would have held them to be impossible" (Freud, 1965:212). Thus, Freud exhibited a certain ambivalence with reference to the cultural control of the instincts. On the one hand, he exposed the neurosis as a consequence of enforced renunciation of the sexual instinct, and accordingly protested the restrictions on sexuality. Yet, on the other hand, he exposed the implicit danger of the aggressive instinct, and thus protested the removal of cultural restrictions on aggressiveness. He considered the restriction of sexuality unjustifiable even from the standpoint of the progress of civilization, and conversely, he considered the repression of aggressiveness justifiable in terms of both individual and societal well-being.

In terms of the classification scheme for the sources of evil given in the Introduction, the sources of evil in human nature are each identified as components of the personality system, while the sources of evil in social reality each entail the action of social reality (culture) upon human nature (personality).

It is a curious fact, perhaps indicative of Freud's sometimes pessimistic world-view, that although the avowed aim of psychoanalysis is the transcendence of evil in the sense of restoring mental health, there are in his theories very few intimations as to the sources of transcendence either within human nature or social reality. With regard to components of human nature, only the ego can be identified as a source of processes in service of transcendence of evil. In the first place—as explained above—the processes of the ego—under the governance of the reality principle— carry out transactions with the external environment which achieve instinctual satisfaction more efficiently and adequately than the limited processes of the id. This attainment of gratification serves the purpose of reducing painful tension within the organism, and main- taining as low a level of tension as possible, thus contributing to the health and stability of the total personality system. Moreover, if most of the psychic energy of the organism is controlled by the ego rather than by the id or the super-ego, the rational transac- tions of the ego will prevent both the increase in ten- sions ensuing from the inefficiency of the id when it dominates the personality, and the agonies of instinc- tual frustration resulting from the domination of the personality by the super-ego. Thirdly, the ego functions to maintain mental health and indeed to pre- serve the very existence of the organism by transform- ing the primary death wish in the id into aggression against enemies in the external environment rather than allowing the organism to destroy itself.

Freud's dichotomous conception of causality— the intuition that both human nature and social reality are active in the determination of personality—pro- vides another source of transcendence in terms of the interaction of factors interior and exterior to the personality which engenders the transformation of anti- social impulses into social impulses. Specifically, this interaction involves the combined influence on the anti-social instincts—e.g., egoism—of the erotic in- stinct, that is, the need for love, and the moral val- ues of society which promote harmonious social rela- tions. The action of this combination of the biologi- cally given erotic need and the culturally given value

of social harmony upon the anti-social instincts transforms them into social ones, e.g., egoism into altruism.

> The influences of civilization cause an ever
> -increasing transmutation of egoistic trends
> into altruistic and social ones, and this by
> an admixture of erotic elements (Freud, 1965:
> 215).

This process serves the purpose of transcendence in
that it prevents the individual from coming into direct
conflict with other members of society through the expression of innate hostility and self-interest, and
thus preserves also the harmony of social relations.

Lastly, in one instance, Freud considered the
restrictive pressures exerted on the personality by
culture to be a positive process, and a source of transcendence of evil. That is, the perilous nature of the
aggressive instinct threatens both the destruction of
civilized society and the annihilation of the human
race. Although the positive value of civilized society
may be somewhat questionable, there was no doubt in
Freud's mind as to the ultimate evil of the latter prospect. Consequently, the redirection, restriction, and
repression of the inclination to aggression enforced by
societal sanctions and the processes of the super-ego
constitute transcendent processes in service of life
and mental health.

Manifestations of Evil and of Transcendence

Thus far, this examination of the Freudian
theory of psychoanalysis has shown, first that the
sources of evil in human nature are comprised of certain components in the personality system which thwart
the maintenance of mental health. Secondly, it has
shown that the sources of evil in social reality emanate from particular cultural pressures on the personality that either exacerbate the innate inadequacies of
the system or distort the normal functioning of its
efficient processes. Essentially, these components and
distortions give rise to the injurious non-satisfact-
ion, frustration, or repression of the elemental instincts, thus sabotaging the crucial condition of mental
health. The instincts of sex and aggression, primarily,
are the objects of this sabotage.

Upon closer scrutiny, it is apparent that the
principal consequence of both the punitive measures of
the superego and the external sanctions of sexual morality is the agonizing experience of anxiety. The

experience of anxiety is detrimental to the personality not only in the sense that it consists of tensions painful to the organism, but also in that it generates processes that interfere with the healthy and normal development of the personality. The response of the organism to the attack of anxiety is directed by the ego as the executive center of control in the organism. The ego's protective response may take either of two forms: rational and efficient methods of problem-solving, or the irrational and inefficient methods of defense mechanisms. Through the defense mechanisms, the ego attempts to reduce anxiety by denying, falsifying, or distorting reality. The result is that these irrational and unrealistic methods of denying the danger through repression, of externalizing the danger through projection, and of distortion the danger through reaction-formation— fail to eliminate the danger of anxiety effectively, and prevent the normal and necessary growth of the ego's rational control.

Similarly, the extended process of sexual development is also subject to disturbances that retard or distort the total personality. In particular, the frequent failure to overcome the Oedipus complex may lead to the disastrous consequences of fixation, perversion, or regression. In males, this failure is often manifested in the forms of a predominance of feminine traits, intense fear and hatred for the father, an excessively submissive attitude toward women, conflicting impulses, and drastic inhibitions in sexual life. In females, this failure may be manifested in a predominance of masculine traits, intense jealousy and hatred for the mother, Lesbianism, father-fixation, and inhibitions of sexual life.

The distortions of sexual development given above ensue primarily from parental lack of understanding, misconceptions, or improper handling of a child's sexual drives. However, further impetus to these and other distortions is also given by the excessive suppression of sexual life required by sexual morality. Above all, Freud expostulated against the demand for abstinence among the unmarried, and the prohibition of all sexual activity except in marriage. He contended that these rigid requirements— rather than freeing the energies of the libido for use in the pursuit of cultural activities—instead necessitate that all of a young man's energies be channeled into the struggle against sexuality at the very time when those energies are needed in his struggle to establish himself in society.

In the case of the young woman, Freud contended that these requirements, exacerbated by a critical
lack of education in sexual matters, result in a total
lack of emotional preparation for marriage. Hence,
when the young woman is finally permitted to experience
and express her sexuality within marriage, she is utterly incapable of doing so. The woman's frigidity
could then only induce disappointment and impotence in
her husband. Finally, these culturally-induced
sexual inadequacies of husband and wife culminate in
the dissipation of passion, and preclude the development of the "...mental affection between them which was
destined to succeed the originally tempestuous passion"
(Freud, 1972:32). Hence, the prohibitions of civilized
sexual morality undermine the very institution of marriage which they are intended to sustain. Furthermore,
the demand for abstinence essentially prohibits the
genital union of the sexes, and hence encourages an increase in the practice of perverse sexual activities
which, according to Freud are ethically reprehensible:

> ...for they degrade the love-relationship of
> two human beings from being a serious matter
> to an otiose diversion, attended neither by
> risk nor by spiritual participation (Freud,
> 1972:37).

Lastly, the anxieties and fears engendered by the prohibitions of sexual morality endanger the very existence of the human race, for people subject to them
become unwilling to produce children. Such observations
led Freud to denounce the malignant evil of sexual
morality:

> The inhibited sexual impulses are not expres-
> sed as such—and to that extent the inhibition
> is successful—but they are expressed in
> other ways which are quite as injurious to
> the person concerned, and make him quite as
> useless to society as satisfaction of those
> suppressed impulses in their original form
> would have done... (Freud, 1972:28).

As previously noted with regard to the
sources of transcendence, there are few indications in
the Freudian theory of psychoanalysis as to the specific causes and effects of transcendence. Since the
fundamental strategy of psychoanalysis, however, strives
to return the repressed contents of the unconscious
to the level of consciousness where the patient can
confront these inner conflicts, and, presumably, work

70

through these conflicts in a rational manner to devise
a functional solution, it seems logical to infer that
the human being's reasoning ability is the crucial factor of transcendence. The analyst attempts, as far as
is possible, to serve merely as a guide in helping the
patient discover and recognize his or her problem, to
become aware of and to understand the nature of the
conflicts involved, to trace the events that generated
the conflicts, and to rationally work through the conflicts to a solution most appropriate for his or her
personality. This strategy indicates that the capacity
for the transcendence of evil resides within the personality, and involves a combination of reason—that is
the awareness and understanding of the conflict—and
effort to overcome the conflict. The effect of this
process of combining the forces of reason and effort is
to deliver the person from the injurious control of irrational forces in the unconscious, to expand the range
of personal freedom, to increase the potential for rational self-determination, and to restore mental
health. Within human nature there is, apparently, the
ability to transcend and to overcome determination by
extra-cognitive factors, to establish the self as the
responsible agent of its own development. As Paul
Roazen states the matter:

> Psychoanalytic therapy is founded on the no-
> tion that a person's awareness of the motives
> behind a potential action can influence the
> action itself; neurotic symptoms can in
> theory be dissolved once their component mo-
> tives have been worked through (Roazen, 1968:
> 297)

There is a further conclusion regarding
transcendence which can be inferred from Freud's theories though it is not one of his postulations. If the
prevailing moral code of a society is indeed detrimental to mental health, and if the forces of reason and
effort are as effective as they appear to be in psychoanalysis, then it seems feasible to assume that
people can, by virtue of their reason, become aware of
the moral code's deleterious effect on their lives, and
with effort, free themselves from the moral determination by society. That is, through reason, people
could, not only recognize the deficiencies of the moral
code, but further, could evolve a new moral system better suited to their mode of life and beneficial to
their mental health. This process could be either a
matter of individual judgment and behavior, or a stra-

71

tegy for social change, and either case would constitute a transcendence of the evil "discontents" to which
civilization subjects personality.

Processes of Evil and of Transcendence

According to the Freudian theory of psychoanalysis, evil—defined as the frustration or non-sat-
isfaction of the instincts—emanates from both the components of the personality system, and from the repression exerted by culture on personality. In the normal
course of personality development, however, the evil
arising from components of the personality—e.g., from
th inefficient attempts of the id to satisfy the instincts, from the tension-producing conflict between
the pleasure principle and the reality principle, and
the tendency to self-destruction generated by the death
wish—is alleviated by being brought under the control
of the rational and realistic ego.

On the other hand, the satisfactory functioning of the ego in the interest of instinctual gratification is threatened and undermined by the restrictive
and repressive pressures imposed on the personality by
the culture. Since the existence and progress of
civilization depends upon the ever-increasing unifica-
tion of humanity, civilization must restrict and repress the expression of the sexual and aggressive instincts which are antithetical to the goal of unifica-
tion. Civilization cannot afford to tolerate exclusive
sexual relationships nor the innate mutual hostility of
human beings. The necessary restrictions on these instincts are, therefore, embodied in the moral code which
is inculcated into members of society through the process
of socialization, and the primary influence of the parents. The extensiveness of parental influence is ensured by the child's dependence on them for the satisfaction of his or her needs, including the need for
love. Through the system of being rewarded for good
conduct, and being punished for bad conduct, the child
is introduced to the ideals and prohibitions of the
moral code. One of the primary methods of the reward
and punishment system is to bestow love as a reward,
and to withdraw love as a punishment—which amounts to
the satisfaction or frustration of the basic need for
love. The child learns to conform to the moral standards his or her parents desire through fear of the
loss of love. Conformity to the moral code becomes an
attribute of the personality rather than a response to
parental expectations with the formation of the superego. Through the mechanism of identification, the

72

parents' ideals of virtuous behavior form the ego-ideal
and their conceptions of immoral behavior form the conscience of the superego. The power of the superego to
enforce these standards arises from the redirection of
the aggressive instinct from external enemies to the
ego, which, as the executive of the personality system,
is held responsible for immoral actions. Thus energized, the superego rewards the ego for good conduct with
feelings of pride, and punishes the ego for bad conduct
with feelings of anxiety, shame, and guilt. These experiences of pride and guilt, in effect, simulate the
parental bestowal and withdrawal of love, thus motiva-
ting the ego to conform to avoid the painful experience
of loss of love. The renunciation of the instincts of
sex and aggression is thus enforced through a manipulation of the need for love. This renunciation, however,
does not free the ego from the punitive aggression of
the superego. Since the superego does not distinguish
between a wish and an act, each instance of renunciation arouses its punitive retaliation, and increases
the ego's burden of guilt. The prohibitions and restrictions of civilized sexual morality inflict upon the
personality both the agonies of instinctual frustration
and the painful internal tensions of anxiety and guilt.
Thus the process of the manifestation of evil occurs
through a cultural subversion of the personality.

The process of the transcendence of evil involves, rather than the action of culture on personality, an interaction of components of the personality
system and cultural factors. This interaction of factors internal and external to the personality produces
a transformation of anti-social impulses into social
impulses. It is the combination of the fundamental
need for love and the cultural sanctions in support of
social stability and harmony that engenders this transmutation beneficial to both the individual and the
society.

Finally, it should be noted that the development of the faculty of reason and the extension of the
ego's control over the irrational tendencies of the id
constitutes a process of transcendence. The constellation of reason, awareness, and effort serves to
thwart and sometimes to overcome the pernicious influence of repressed irrational forces in the unconscious.

Consequences of Evil and of Transcendence

In the course of this inquiry into the nature of evil and transcendence as formulated in Freud's psychoanalytic theory, it has been established that evil and transcendence emanate from conflicting forces within and between the two causal realms. human nature, i.e, personality and social reality, i.e., culture.
That is to say, there are forces productive of evil within the personality—some of which are thwarted or overcome by forces of transcendence within the personality—some others are counteracted or overwhelmed by forces of transcendence arising from culture. Conversely, there are forces conducive to evil in the culture some of which are opposed and overcome by transcendent forces within the personality. For example, the evidence of psychoanalysis indicates that there are several opposing forces operating within the personality.
These forces are listed below. (1) The inadequate attempts of the id to provide instinctual gratification are supplemented by the efficient and realistic transactions of the ego with the external environment in the pursuit of instinctual satisfaction. (2) The tension-producing conflict between the operation of the pleasure principle and the reality principle is counteracted by the establishment of a functional equilibrium between these two operations. (3) The painful tensions ensuing from the ego's postponement of instinctual satisfaction until a suitable object is discovered is counterbalanced by th increase in the possibilities of satisfaction afforded by the ego in contrast to the id. There are, in addition, opposing forces which involve an interaction between personality and culture. Specifically, the interaction between the erotic instinct within the personality and the cultural values of societal harmony and stability effects the beneficial transmutation of anti-social to social impulses.
Finally, there are opposing forces operation within the culture. (1) The ever-increasing burden of guilt ensuing from the punitive measures of the cultural super-ego may be thwarted by a growing awareness and rational rejection of the claims of civilized sexual morality. (2) Similarly, the development of neuroses as a consequence of civilization's restrictions on sexuality may be undermined by the growing awareness of the cultural causes of neurosis. (3) The excessive suppression of sexuality may perhaps be alleviated by a rationally-directed transformation and liberalization of sexual mores. (4) The pernicious threat to individual and

social life posed by the aggressive instincts is reduced by the external sanctions of culture, and the internal restrictions of the superego.

What is, finally, the net effect of this complex system of interlocking conflicting forces? It
seems that Freud himself was somewhat uncertain concerning the end result, though he was, unhappily, more
convinced of the superior power of the forces of evil.
He voices this ambivalence in Civilization and Its Discontents thusly:

> A good part of the struggles of mankind centre
> round the single task of finding an expedient
> accommodation—one, that is, that will bring
> happiness—between this claim of the indivi-
> dual and the cultural claims of the group;
> and one of the problems that touches the fate
> of humanity is whether such an accommodation
> can be reached by means of some particular
> form of civilization or whether the conflict
> is irreconcilable (Freud, 1962:43).

Freud explicitly delineated the consequences for the
individual and society of the prospective triumph of
the forces of evil. That is, he perceived that the individual, perpetually subject to the repressive influence of civilization, suffers the intolerable agonies
of an ever-increasing sense of quilt, and a concomitant
diminuition of the possibilities for happiness. Thus,
he identifies "...the sense of quilt as the most important problem in the development of civilization..."
and demonstrates "...that the price we pay for our advance in civilization is a loss of happiness through
the heightening of the sense of quilt" (Freud, 1962:81)
And, conversely, he contends that the consequence for
society of the unmitigated repression of sexuality and
aggressiveness consists of an also ever-increasing
hostility against civilization, which if released,
would utterly annihilate civilized society.

Freud's pessimism regarding the possible triumph of forces transcending evil is again evident in
the fact that he did not outline the consequences of
transcendence for the individual and society. However,
these consequences can be inferred from the therapeutic
goals of psychoanalysis. The development of the ego as
the control center of the personality system and the
application of its rational processes in the interest
of instinctual satisfaction, the transmutation of the
anti-social into social impulses, and the beneficial

75

repression of the aggressive instinct are all processes
that serve to preserve the integrative and progressive
development of the personality, thus contributing to
the maintenance of mental health. Furthermore, the development and constant application of the rational cognitive faculties afford the
nition and critical evaluation of the determinative and
detrimental influence exerted on the personality by extra-cognitive factors. The exercise of rationality is
thus the indispensable condition that makes possible
the liberation of personal judgement from the invidious
influence of cultural values, and generates within the
individual the development of freedom, independence,
and self-determination. In regard to the consequences
of transcendence for society, this exercise of the
rational function signifies that the detrimental
effect of repressive mores can be undermined by
the transformation of the mores in a direction supportive of the practice of life and beneficial to mental health. Such a transvaluation would benefit both
the individual and society in that it would aid in preventing the decline into mental illness, and also promote a constructive and stabilizing integration of individual and society.

CHAPTER 7:   Erich Fromm

Introduction

...mental health cannot be defined in terms
of the "adjustment" of the individual to his
society, but, on the contrary...it must be
defined in terms of the adjustment of society
to the needs of man, of its role in furthering or hindering the development of mental
health. Whether or not the individual is
healthy, is primarily not an individual matter, but depends on the structure of his society (Fromm, 1955:71).

In trying to avoid the errors of biological
and metaphysical concepts we must not succumb
to an equally grave error, that of a sociological relativism in which man is nothing
but a puppet, directed by the strings of social circumstances. Man's inalienable rights
of freedom and happiness are founded in inherent human qualities: his striving to live,
to expand and to express the potentialities
that have developed in him in the process of
historical evolution (Fromm, 1965:121).

...the nature or essence of man is not a
specific substance, like good or evil, but a
contradiction which is rooted in the very
conditions of human existence. This conflict
in itself requires a solution, and basically
there are only the regressive or the progressive solution (Fromm, 1971a:152-153).

The ability to act according to one's conscience depends on the degree to which one
has become a citizen of the world (Fromm,
1971b:128)

The position of normative humanism presented by Erich Fromm in The Sane Society is quite in accord with the thesis of this monograph of the need for a scientific ethic devoted to the amelioration of the quality of human life. Deriving his inspiration from the provocative notion of collective neurosis developed by Freud in Civilization and Its Discontents, Fromm contends, in the first place, that society itself can be sane or insane depending on whether it is conducive to mental health or mental illness, and secondly, that it is the task of the social sciences—as sciences of human nature and society—to determine the sanity or insanity of society. He defines the sane society as that which contributes to mental health by correspond-ing to the needs of human beings. Fromm, therefore, like Freud, considers the satisfaction of human needs to be the requisite condition for mental health, though he differs from Freud in the identification of those needs.

The needs which, according to Fromm, must be satisfied in order to preserve mental health, are of an ontological rather than biological nature. This iden-tification arises from his fundamentally evolutionary perspective, and the corresponding teleological view of nature and human nature. According to the evolutionary perspective, the phenomena of nature are regulated by a process of immanent development characterized by the "...emergence of new forms from unique combinations of pre-existing elements of older forms... The new forms are qualitatively different from the older forms..." (Theodorson, 1970:137). In this context, human nature represents the emergence of a new form of life qualita-tively different from the rest of nature.

As a product of evolution and subject also to the process of immanent development, the essence of human nature is given as a contradiction between the qualities which humans share with the rest of nature, and the emergent qualities which separate them from the animal world—i.e., reason, freedom, and love. The solution required by this agonizing contradiction con-sists of the reestablishment of a union between human beings and nature, and the character of the specific-ally human—that is, ontological needs—is determined by this primal drive toward union. The satisfaction of these needs through which humans are re-united with nature can be achieved in either a regressive or a pro-gressive fashion—that is, by regression to a pre-human state in which the uniquely human qualities are relin-quished and the animal qualities predominate, or by progression to a fully human state in which these unique qualities are developed and predominate. The progressive tendency thus entails the realization of embryonic humanity through growth toward ever-increasing complexity, and accords with the teleological character of the evolutionary process, while the regressive tendency involves the degeneration of the human organism from a more complex to less complex state, and is antithetical to the intrinsic purpose of evolution. According to Fromm, the resolution of the contradiction in human nature and the reunion of human beings and nature attained through the satisfaction of the ontological needs in the progressive fashion—i.e., the development of the unique and emergent qualities—is conducive to mental health, whereas the resolution achieved in the regressive fashion—i.e., the failure to develop human qualities—is conducive to mental illness.

Definitions of Evil and of Transcendence

As a psychoanalyst concerned with the cure of mental illness and the preservation of mental health, Fromm necessarily defines mental illness as evil and mental health as good. Consequently, he identifies as evil the tendency to regression in human nature, and as good—or, in this case, as transcendent, the opposite tendency to progression in human nature.

> Evilness...is the attempt to regress to the prehuman state, and to eliminate that which is specifically human: reason, love, freedom ... Good consists of transforming our existence into an ever increasing approximation to our essence... (Fromm, 1971a:192-193).

With regard to the influence of society on human nature Fromm identifies as evil the "insane society" which elicits and sustains the regressive tendency of human nature, and as transcendent the "sane society" which elicits and sustains the progressive tendency of human nature. Thus, within the context of his evolutionary perspective evil is defined as those predisopsitions in human nature and conditions in social reality which inhibit or preclude the full realization of the individual's embryonic human qualities, and conversely, transcendence is conceived as those predispositions in human nature and conditions in social reality which facilitate or engender the realization of the individual's emergent humanity. It is the ethical task of the social

scientist to discern to what extent the conditions
of social reality are conducive to the evil decline of
human nature or to its transcendent development.

Locus of Causality

Fromm's evolutionary and teleological assum-
tions also have definite implications with regard to
the locus of causality. That is, if human nature is
comprised of certain unique potentials for which the
initial impetus to development is provided by the contradiction between these qualities and the animal attributes, and if the actual realization of these potentials is elicited or prohibited by conditions of social
reality, then both human nature and social reality must
function as dimensions of causality. It is the interaction of these equally dynamic causal realms—of the
immanent potentials inherent in human nature and the
evocative conditions of social reality—that determines
the actual manifestations of human nature. Fromm contends, as did Freud, that the range of the possible
manifestations of human nature is determined by the innate qualities of human nature—however these are variously defined—and that which of these possibilities
will be realized in actuality is determined by the existing conditions of social reality.

Thus, both Fromm and Freud appear to agree in
the perception of dichotomous dimensions of causality—
i.e., that human nature provides the predisposing conditions for the manifestation of human nature, and that
social reality provides the necessary precipitating
conditions. However, in contrast to Freud's emphasis
on the primacy of cultural causality, Fromm stresses
the equality of causal factors arising from both
realms. That is, in reaction to Freud, Fromm emphasizes the dynamism of human nature which opposes and
may transform inimical social conditions—for instance:

> We arrive therefore at the fact that, al-
> though character development is shaped by the
> basic conditions of life and although there
> is no biologically fixed human nature, human
> nature has a dynamism of its own that consti-
> tutes an active factor in the evolution of
> the social process (Fromm, 1965:121).

Specifically, it is the progressive tendency
to develop and realize the uniquely human attributes
that Fromm identifies as the dynamic factor in human
nature that reacts against hostile social conditions,

80

and which may transform those into conditions favoring human development. That is:

> Needs like the striving for happiness, har-
> mony, love and freedom are inherent in his
> nature. They are also dynamic factors in the
> historical process which, if frustrated, tend
> to arouse psychic reactions, ultimately
> creating the very conditions suited to the
> original strivings (Fromm, 1955:78).

Thus, in contrast to Freud's pessimistic conception of the primacy of cultural causality, Fromm optimistically emphasizes the interaction of the equally dynamic factors in human nature and social reality.

Sources of Evil and of Transcendence

In The Heart of Man: Its Genius for Good and Evil, Fromm explores most extensively the notion of the contradiction in human nature as the seminal source of the human being's antinomic tendencies to evil and to the transcendence of evil. As mentioned above, this contradiction is manifested as the dichotomy between the attributes humans share with other animals, and the animal-transcending qualities. As such, this contradiction may be categorized as the interaction—or more accurately, the conflict between these dissimilar components of the human organism. Specifically, the conflict arises between the human's limited instinctual equipment and the practical intelligence shared with other animals, on the one hand, and on the other, the emergent faculties of reason which distinguish humans from the rest of nature. Human destiny, as it were, is determined by the fact that the human's under-developed instinctual equipment and the intelligence which provides for securing immediate aims are not sufficient to ensure survival—this depends upon the further development of the higher mental faculties. These higher mental faculties, however, ensure also the awareness of estrangement from nature:

> Man transcends all other life because he is,
> for the first time, life aware of itself.
> Man is in nature, subject to its dictates and
> accidents, yet he transcends nature because
> he lacks the unawareness which makes the
> animal a part of nature—as one with it
> (Fromm, 1971a:147).

81

Reason, self-awareness, and imagination comprise the newly evolved faculties which disrupt the harmony with nature, estrange humans from other forms of life, render them cognizant of this dilemma, give rise to the unique ontological needs, and which must be expanded and utilized to preserve the sanity and the very existence of the human species. According to Fromm, this inescapable existential dilemma necessitates a solution: the impact of the terrible realization of this inner division, of uniqueness and isolation, compels humans to attempt to integrate the divided self, to overcome their isolation, to somehow effect a return to nature, to harmony, to unity.

The resolution of this inner contradiction, as noted previously, is accomplished through the satisfaction of the ontological needs for relatedness, transcendence, rootedness, a sense of identity, and a frame of orientation and devotion in either a regressive fashion—arising from the animal aspects of human nature, or a progressive fashion—arising from the animal-transcending aspects of human nature. If, on the one hand, the attempt to overcome the inner contradiction and to return to union with nature takes the form of the satisfaction of these ontological needs in accord with the regressive tendency immanent in the animal atrributes, humans relinquish the very qualities which ensure their sanity and survival, and suffer a decline into the evil of mental illness. On the other hand, if this attempt occurs in the form of the satisfaction of the ontological needs in accord with the progressive tendency immanent in the distinctively human qualities, then human life is enriched, stablizied, and integrated through the gradual development of the qualities necessary to mental health and continued existence. The elemental contradiction in human nature, the antithesis of the animal and animal-transcending components of the human is the inner source of the human being's intrinsic ambivalent tendencies to evil (i.e., mental illness) and to transcendence of evil (i.e., mental health).

The actual manifestations of human nature, however, as is evident in Fromm's dichotomous conception of causality, are functions not only of inner motivations, but also of the conditions of social reality. In brief, the real possibilities existent in the conditions of social life for the satisfaction of human ontological needs serve as the precipitating factors which induce manifestation of the regressive or progressive predispositions of human nature. That is, the exigencies of social life may prove favorable

82

to the manifestation of evil by providing for the satisfaction of human needs in an unhealthy regressive manner, and thus ⌐licit and sustain the intrinsic predisposition to re⌐ ess to a pre-human level. Conversely, the exigencies of social life may favor the manifestation of transcendence of evil by providing for the satisfaction of human needs in a healthy progressive manner, and thus elicit and sustain the alternative predisposition to progress to a fully human level. The existing conditions of social life thus interact with the inherent drives of human nature, and function as catalytic factors to precipitate the actual manifestations of human nature. The specific components of social life which Fromm identifies as significantly involved in this interactive process are the mode of production and the mode of social and political organization. Thus, the possibilities for evil and for the transcendence of evil arise also from the interaction of societal conditions—i.e., the mode of production, the social and political organization, and the given ambivalent tendencies of human nature.

Manifestations of Evil and of Transcendence

Consistent also with the dichotomous conception of causality presented in The Sane Society, Fromm maintains that the particular causes of evil and of transcendence—ensuing from sources in human nature and social reality—similarly involve an interaction of internal psychological tendencies and external societal conditions. He represents the effect of this determinative interaction in the construct of the "social character" which is defined as:

> ...the nucleus of the character structure which is shared by most members of the same culture in contradistinction to the individual character in which people belonging to the same culture differ from each other (Fromm, 1955:76).

Assuming the constancy of the intrinsic contradictory predispositions to evil and transcendence, the status of the social character is an indication of the relative strength of societal conditions conducive to evil and to transcendence. That is, the function of the social character is to channel human energies in a direction consistent with the requirements of the social system in order to secure the continued functioning of the society. In function, then, the social character is analogous to the Freudian superego. This

83

determination of human behavior in accord with the requirements of the social system reveals also the ways
in which human ontological needs can and must be grati-
fied within the limitations of a particular social system. The existing possibilities for the satisfaction
of these needs provided by the society and imposed upon
members of the society through socialization into the
social character, elicit either the regressive or progressive tendencies, in varying degrees, thus precipitating mental illness or mental health. Hence, the
predominance of regressive or progressive elements in
the social character reflects the relative insanity or
sanity of the society.

      The point of departure for Fromm's evaluation
of the sanity of modern Western society is an analysis
of the contemporary social character. The initial
thrust of the analysis is to ascertain whether contemporary social conditions engender evil by eliciting
the regressive tendency to satisfy human needs in an
unhealthy fashion, or engender transcendence by eliciting the progressive tendency to satisfy human needs in
a healthy fashion. The constellation of several drives
which compose the regressive tendency is identified as:
the drive to satisfy the need for relatedness through
narcissism; the drive to satisfy the need for transcendence through destructiveness; the drive to satisfy
the need for rootedness through incest; the drive to
satisfy the need for a sense of identity through "herd
conformity," and the drive to satisfy the need for a
"frame of orientation and devotion" through irrationality. Conversely, the constellation of drives comprising the progressive tendency is identified as: the
drive to satisfy the need for relatedness through love;
the drive to satisfy the need for transcendence through
creativeness; the drive to satisfy the need for rootedness through brotherliness; the drive to satisfy the
need for a sense of identity through individuality; and
the drive to satisfy the need for a frame of orientation and devotion through reason (Fromm, 1955:36-65)

      Each of these various drives, if evoked by
social conditions, functions as a cause of particular
forms of evil or transcendence. Specifically, the unhealthy and evil consequences of the drives constituting the regressive tendency are identified, respectively, as: destruction of personal integrity and increase in undue dependence on others (narcissism); the
infliction of suffering on self and others (destructiveness); unreflective identification with societal
values (incest); sense of self as passive and

84

determined creature (herd conformity); and a distorted, impractical, and dysfunctional world-view. In contrast the healthy and transcendent consequences of the drives comprising the progressive tendency are identified respectively as: growth of personal integrity and independence (love); discovery of meaning and purpose in life (creativity); reflective identification with universal human values (brotherliness); development of sense of self as active and volitional being (individuality); and an objective, pragmatic, realistic, and functional world view (reason) (Fromm, 1955:36-65).

The tendency to seek the satisfaction of human needs in the regressive direction thus forms a "syndrome of decay" (Fromm, 1971a:2) culminating in the deterioration of the distinctively human qualities of reason, freedom, and love, and the decline into mental illness. Conversely, the tendency to seek the satisfaction of human needs in the progressive direction forms a "syndrome of growth" (Fromm, 1971a:2) culminating in the full realization of the distinctly human qualities, and the preservation of mental health.

As previously indicated, the particular constituents of social reality which induce and sustain either of the innate antinomic predispositions of human nature are identified as the mode of production and the social and political organization of society. According to Fromm's stance at this point, these constituents of the social system determine the structure and process of interpersonal relations through which the social character is formed and internalized. His analysis of the capitalistic mode of production and social and political organization of modern western society identifies several specific social factors which generate a predominance of the regressive tendency in the social character. These factors are: the illusion of freedom promoted by the self-regulating mechanism of the modern market (Fromm, 1955:84); the principle of "the use of man by man" typical of class societies (Fromm, 1955:88); the capitalistic system of values which subordinates human beings to things (Fromm, 1955: 90); the "process of abstractification" which underlies all forms of relatedness (Fromm, 1955: 108); and the anonymity of social laws which regulate human life in capitalistic system
cial effects of these factors on the structure and processes of interpersonal relations are specified as, respectively: the loss of individual freedom (Fromm, 1955:84); the transformation of humans from being an end in themselves to being merely a means for another's

85

economic ends which negates the intrinsic value of the
individual person (Fromm. 1955:88); the subordination
to things alienates the individual from his or her
own volition and creativity (Fromm, 1955:90); the
"process of abstractification" undermines genuine relationship to self and others (Fromm, 1955:106), and the
regulation of life by anonymous social forces induces
the experience of personal powerlessness (Fromm, 1955:
125-126).

With regard to the ontological human needs
for relatedness, transcendence, rootedness, sense of
identity, and frame of orientation and devotion, the
consequence of these pernicious social factors is to
block the expression of the progressive tendency, and to
expedite the expression of the regressive tendency.
Specifically, with regard to (1) need for relatedness:
the satisfaction of this need through the simultaneous
intimacy and respectful independence of love is prevented by the abstractification of relationship, whereas
satisfaction through narcissism is promoted by the
practice of exploiting others as means to one's own
ends. With regard to (2) need for transcendence: satisfaction through creative activity is precluded by the
system of values which alienates humans from their own
creative powers, whereas satisfaction through destructiveness is promoted by the practice of exploitation.
With regard to (3) need for rootedness: satisfaction
through commitment to universal human values is prevented by the subversion of relationship through abstractification and the socially sanctioned practice of
exploitation, whereas unreflective identification with
societal values is induced by the loss of individual
freedom and the regulation of life by anonymous social
forces. With regard to (4) need for sense of identity:
satisfaction through the experience of personal volition, efficacy, and the growth of individuality is prevented by subordination to things, the exploitation by
others, and personal powerlessness in the face of social forces, whereas satisfaction through herd conformity is induced by the loss of personal freedom. With
regard to (5) need for frame of orientation and devotion: satisfaction through the utilization and development of reason is prevented by the subordination to
things which alienates human beings from their human
faculties, whereas satisfaction through the growth of
irrationality is promoted by the incomprehensible regulation of life by unseen and unknown social laws.
The predictable culmination of this interaction between
factors in human nature and social reality antithetical
to the healthy and continuous development of the human
organism is the ultimate evil of mental illness.

This exposition of the causes and effects of evil and transcendence arising from the interaction of psychlogical and sociological factors illustrates also the further point that in The Sane Society Fromm does not identify specific factors in social reality which may evoke the manifestation of the progressive tendency. The possibilities for the transcendence of evil are presented as arising only from the innate predisposition to transcendence, and the reaction of this dynamic striving for health against hostile factors in the social environment—which will be explained in the following section concerning the processes by which evil and transcendence are actualized.

Processes of Evil and Transcendence

In the course of this inquiry, it has become evident that Fromm conceptualizes the problems of evil and transcendence of evil as alternative responses to the existential dilemma posed by the implicit contradictions in human nature. Because of this contradiction human beings suffer a radical estrangement from all other forms of life, and their lives are characterized by an agonizing disequilibrium. The resolution of the contradiction is attained by means of the satisfaction of the uniquely human ontological needs for relatedness, transcendence, rootedness, a sense of identity, and a frame of orientation and devotion. There are within human nature two distinctive constellations of drives—one oriented toward resolution of the contradiction through the satisfaction of human needs in an unhealthy regressive fashion, and the other oriented toward resolution through the satisfaction of human needs in a healthy progressive fashion. The actual possibilities for the satisfaction of human needs are provided by existing conditions of social reality. These possibilities may allow for satisfaction in the regressive mode or the progressive mode, or both. If these possibilities generate satisfaction in the form of narcissism, destructiveness, incest, herd conformity and irrationality, then the tendency to regress to a pre-human level characterizes human existence. If these possibilities generate satisfaction in the form of love, creativeness, brotherliness, individuality, and reason, then the tendency to progress to a fully human level characterizes human existence. The satisfaction of human needs in the regressive mode results in neurosis, and the failure of social conditions to provide for need satisfaction even in the regressive mode results in insanity. The satisfaction of human needs in the progressive mode produces and sustains mental health.

There is, however, one other possibility for transcendence of evil—i.e., the transformation of pathological social conditions by the dynamic striving of the progressive tendency for mental health. Even when the social environment facilitates the manifestations of regression, the vital progressive drives may react against the inimical social environment by striving to transform detrimental conditions into beneficial conditions. According to Fromm, this transformation of social pathology is analogous to the course of the cure for individual pathology. In both cases, there first arises a conflict between the needs of human nature, and the possibilities for the satisfaction of these needs existent in the social order. Secondly, the suffering which ensues from the frustration or the satisfaction of basic needs in an unhealthy regressive manner, arouses the reaction of the progressive drives. The striving toward health immanent in these vital drives directs the energies of the progressive tendency against inimical social conditions in the attempt to transform them into conditions beneficial to mental health or to render them innocuous. The effectiveness of this organic reaction is enhanced, and must be supplemented by the individual's rational recognition of the societal causes of this conflict, and the utilization of reason, effort, and will to eradicate or transform detrimental societal conditions. Thus, it is possible for the combination of the vitality of the human organism's progressive predisposition and the dynamic power of the distinctively human qualities to disrupt, negate, and/or change the causal processes emanating from social reality. This emphasis on the potential primacy of causality arising from human nature, Fromm contends, coincides with the Freudian and Marxian conceptions of individual freedom in the social context:

> ...neither Marx nor Freud were determinists in the sense of believing in an irreversibility of causal determination. They both believed in the possibility that a course already initiated can be altered. They both saw this possibility of change rooted in man's capacity for becoming aware of the forces which move him behind his back, so to speak—and thus enabling him to regain his freedom (Fromm, 1971a:161).

Consequences of Evil and of Transcendence

In conclusion, what does the relative balance or imbalance of the forces of evil and transcendence of evil given in Fromm's theory of normative humanism signify for human destiny? Within human nature the evil arising from the regressive tendency to narcissism, destructiveness, incest, herd conformity, and irrationality is counter-balanced by the forces of transcendence emanating from the progressive tendency to love, creativeness, brotherliness, individuality, and reason. Within the context of social reality and in the particular structure of the capitalistic system, there are apparently no transcending social factors opposed to the evil deriving from the illusion of freedom, the practice of exploitation, the system of values that subordinates people to things, the process of abstractification, and the regulation of life by anonymous social forces. However, the evil arising from these societal circumstances may be counter-balanced, and even negated or transformed by the forces of transcendence in human nature—i.e., the organic striving toward health and the dynamic power of reason, effort and will. It seems, therefore, that while the quantitative sources of evil may be greater than the sources of transcendence, Fromm intimates that the quality of the strength of transcendent forces exceeds that of the forces of evil.

Fromm's critique of societal insanity identifies as the consequences of the forces of evil for the individual: devaluation of the significance of human life; alienation of the individual from his or her volitional being, and the consequent loss of productive and creative powers; deterioration of the capacity for genuine relatedness; the loss of a sense of meaning and purpose in life, and a crucial loss of the sense of identity as a unique individual, and also as a member of the human race. The consequences of evil for society consist essentially of the deterioration of the dynamic interaction and independence of creative individuals and society which ensures the continuance of the society by maintaining its necessary adaptability to change.

Conversely, the consequences for the individual of transcendence are delineated as: the significance of the individual life is retained as a central value; humans experience themselves as volitional beings, as self-determining and creative agents in the world; the experience of the genuine love relation increases the capacity to understand and relate to others in a brotherly fashion; the experience of personal volition, reason, and imagination enhances the meaningfulness of life; and the development of the distinctive human qualities of reason, freedom, and love engenders the realization of the unity of humanity. The consequences for society involve the maintenance of societal adaptability through the creative interaction of individuals and society, and the reorganization of social life in accord with the ideal of universal humanity. Human destiny, in collective life as well as individual life —like human nature, is emergent, always revolving around the crucial alternation between the regressive degeneration to a less than human state, and the progressive growth to fully developed humanity.

Taking a brief glance at The Chains of Illusion: My Encounter with Marx and Freud, it is interesting to compare this synthesis of Freudian and Marxian theory with the ideas Fromm presented in The Sane Society. The theory developed in The Chains of Illusion, again is based on an evolutionary perspective, assumes a teleological view of nature and human nature, and hence defines evil as whatever prevents the maximum realization of human potentials, and defines transcendence as whatever facilitates this realization. However, in contrast to the position of The Sane Society, it is here argued that in the interaction of causal factors in human nature and social reality, the factors of social reality predominate. That is, the primacy of social reality as a locus of causality is emphasized.

Fromm's basic ambivalence with regard to the issue of causality is especially evident in his identification of the sources of evil and transcendence. On the one hand, he stresses that evil arises from detrimental conditions of the social order which corrupt human nature, and on the other, he retains his previous emphasis on the transformative power of reason as a force of transcendence. The components of the social order which give rise to evil are identified as the implicit contradictions and irrationalities of the system which necessitate the repression of those human potentials which threaten to expose these irrationalities, and undermine the stability of the "insane society." That is, among the diverse immanent faculties of human nature there are some which, if developed, would lead to the discovery of societal contradictions, and hence threaten the continued existence of society in its present state—and there are other faculties, whose development would not undermine the society. The latter can be allowed to become manifest, whereas the former must be repressed, if society is to be preserved in its

90

present state. The determination of human nature in accord with these requirements of the social system demonstrates the action of one system—social reality, on another—human nature.

The societal determination of the manifestation of human nature is carried out by means of socialization into the social character, and, by the repression of forbidden faculties in the "social unconscious" effected by the "social filter" (Fromm, 1971b:121). That is, socialization into the desired social character provides the members of society with impulses, concepts and behavior patters, supportive of the society. The non-threatening faculties are elicited, developed, and directed through the processes of social interaction. Simultaneously, the formation within the social filter of taboos and restrictions on thought and behavior installs within the personality a regulatory mechanism which functions to repress—into the social unconscious —any thoughts or impulses which could lead to the discovery of societal contradictions. The contradictions of society thus preclude the maximum realization of human potentials by allowing only a few faculties to reach the level of awareness, and by relegating a great many to the reservoir of the social unconscious. This structuring of the person according to societal requirements—by preventing the perception of societal evils—arouses an unconditional commitment to the society and its values, and promotes a slavish conformity of the masses. Furthermore, this total encompassing of the person by society evokes in him or her a fear of isolation and ostracism so terrifying that her or her voluntarily participates in the repression of perceptions of societal evil. Thus, the individual is driven to believe what he or she is taught to believe, and conforms despite first-hand evidence of societal corruption.

On the other hand, Fromm contends that the innate and transcendent faculty of reason is also developed through the processes of social interaction. It must be assumed, then, that the development of reason is somehow essential to the maintenance of an irrational society, even though it is implicitly capable of transcending and transforming the irrationalities of the society. The transcendent power of reason is given in the fact that—whereas the contents of consciousness that is, the concepts which are used in the reflective precess, are determined by society—and while the reflective process itself is stimulated by social processes, the content and direction of reflection is not

91

determined by society, but is rather of an emergent and
creative nature. In the reflective process, the interaction of the reasoning and imaginative faculties uti-
lizes determined concepts but combines them in novel
and unique ways to produce perceptions, thoughts, and
values above and beyond those permitted by society.
Whereas the given contents of consciousness are peculiar to the person's society and bind him or her to
that society, the reflective process is a universal human quality, which binds the person to the whole of humanity. It is possible, therefore, for individuals to
discover universal human values on their own. Through
reflection—the combination of reason and imagination,
individuals are able to overstep and transcend society's restrictions, to conceive of universal ideals
beyond those of their society, and by which they can
evaluate their own society.

In the context of this theory, Fromm identifies
the specific causes of evil arising from social reality
as the social character, the social filter, and the social unconscious—the instruments of repression and restriction inculcated in human nature. These mechanisms
not only preclude the healthy development of all human
faculties but also create a tension between the repressed faculties in the unconscious and the expressed
faculties of consciousness that culminates in the evil
of neuroses. Although Fromm continues to maintain that
the unpredictable faculty of reason constitutes the indispensable cause of transcendence, he also indicates
that certain social factors may be conducive to transcendence. Specifically, a marginal position in the social stucture provides a more objective and detached
perspective from which to view and evaluate one's society. Similarly, there is the possibility that unexpected individual experiences may so traumatize a person that he or she is shocked out of complacency, begins to speculate, and to doubt the validity of his or
her heretofore unquestioned assumptions about the
world. The culmination of these innate faculties and
social experiences is the discovery of universal
ideals, commitment to those ideals, critical evaluation
of one's own society in the light of these higher
ideals, and if necessary, individual and collective
action to reorganize society according to transcendent
ideals.

The process by which evil becomes manifest, as
previously indicated, originates with the inculcation
of the instruments of repression—the social character,
social filter, and social unconscious. Secondly, the

tension which arises between the many repressed faculties within the social unconscious and the few expressed faculties of consciousness undermines through
distortion the permitted contents of consciousness,
leading finally to neuroses. Thus, the usual processes
of an insane society signify that human thought and behavior are greatly determined by forces of which humans
are not aware, and in the case of neuroses, they are
almost completely determined such forces.

The process of transcendence of societal evil
requires the enhancement of rationally deduced insights
by external events such as the insecurities of marginal
social position, or the shock of unexpected traumatic
individual experiences. The added evidence of such external events both supports the conclusions of reflection, and lends further impetus toward continued critical reflection, commitment, and constructive action in
service of universal ideals.

As in The Sane Society, the final consequenes
of evil are here conceived in terms of the deterioration of human faculties. In an insane society the human being becomes an automaton exhibiting above all
obedience and mindless conformity to the dictates of
society—which by repressing and perverting human potentials, is also destroying itself. Similarly, the
consequences of transcendence are conceived in terms of
the maximum development and realization of human faculties which serves to preserve society through the
creative interaction of individuals and society, and
through the reorganization of the society in line with
rationally perceived human values.

CHAPTER 8: Concluding Remarks on the
Perspective of Psychoanalysis

Both of the psychoanalysts considered in
this section conceive of mental illness as the ultimate
evil and mental health as the ultimate good. Subsequently, their definitions of evil are given in terms
of forces which undermine mental health and precipitate
mental illness, whereas trancendence is defined in
terms of forces which prevent the decline into mental
illness and which preserve mental health. Freud identified as evil the predispositions in human nature and
conditions of social reality which interfered with or
precluded the satisfaction of innate biological needs
which constituted the necessary condition of mental
health. Fromm perceived as evil the predispositions of
human nature and conditions of social reality which inhibited or prevented the full realization of the human
being's specifically human qualities, which constitutes
the necessary condition for mental health. Conversely,
Freud identified as transcendent the factors in human
nature and social reality which opposed the subversive
factors conducive to mental illness and which facilitate the satisfaction of innate biological needs.
Similarly, Fromm perceived as transcendent the factors
in human nature and social reality which counteract
the subversive factors conducive to mental illness and
which facilitate the development of the human qualities.

That each identifies factors of evil or
transcendence within both the realms of human nature
and social reality indicates their common perception of
the dichotomous nature of causality--that both human
nature and social reality are realms of causality,
though each emphasizes the primacy of a different
realm. That is, Freud stresses the primacy of cultural
causality, whereas Fromm stresses the equal dynamism of
human nature and social reality. Consequently, the
sources of evil and transcendence are similarly identified as components of human nature and/or social
reality, or the action of human nature on social

95

reality or of social reality on human nature. Specifically, Freud traces the sources of evil to certain elements in the human's biological constitution, and to the repressive influence culture exerts on the personality, while Fromm traces evil to the interaction of the regressive tendency arising from the contradiction in human nature and the possibilities of satisfaction of ontological needs in social reality. Conversely, the sources of transcendence, according to Freud, consist of several elements of the human's biological constitution, and the interaction of some of these elements with the external sanctions of the moral code. According to Fromm, the sources consist of the interaction of the progressive tendency arising from the contradiction in human nature and the existing possibilities in social reality for satisfaction of ontological needs in a progressive fashion.

In accordance with their definitions of evil and transcendence, both authors delineate the manifestations of evil as symptoms of mental illness involving a deterioration of the specifically human qualities--i. e., reason (Freud); and, reason, freedom and love (Fromm). In each case also, the process through which evil and transcendence becomes manifest is conceived as an interaction of individual consciousness and the social construction of reality. Evil for Freud, is manifested in the internalization of societal repression in the formation of the superego. For Fromm, evil is manifested in the evocation and maintenance of the regressive tendency according to the hostile conditions for the satisfaction of needs in social reality. On the other hand, transcendence for Freud, is manifested as the repressed contents of the unconscious are brought to consciousness--for Fromm, the process of transcendence similarly involves the overcoming of control by irrational forces in the unconscious through the combined activity of reason, effort and will. For both authors, the consequences of evil are specified as the decline into mental illness with the concomitant deterioration of distinctive human qualities--reason (Freud), reason, freedom and love (Fromm). Similarly, the consequences of transcendence are specified as the preservation of mental health, and the concomitant development and realization of the distinctive human qualities.

With regard to the central issue of human judgment, within Freud's theory there is no evidence for a natural, perhaps biologically-grounded, awareness

of good and evil. Indeed, it appears that the forces
of evil which preclude the exercise of human judgment--
the internalization and rigid enforcement of an arbitrary moral code by means of the superego--prevail over
the embryonic forces of transcendence given in the
faculty of reason. The exercise of human judgment cannot become a reality until individuals are liberated
from the pressures of societal repression through the
exorcism of irrational influences in the unconscious,
and whether or not this can be accomplished, in Freud's
pessimistic view, is doubtful.

Within Fromm's more optimistic perspective,
the potential for ethical behavior derives from the
innate faculty of reason and the individual sense of
self:

> Ethics...is inseparable from reason. Ethi-
> cal behavior is based on the faculty of
> making value judgments on the basis of
> reason; it means deciding between good and
> evil, and to act upon the decision. Use of
> reason presupposes the presence of self;
> so does ethical judgment and action (Fromm,
> 1955:155).

Although both the sense of self and the exercise of
reason are stimulated by social interaction, their development can be impeded by distortions in social relations triggered by pernicious changes in the mode of
production, and social and economic organization. Yet
Fromm contends that reason, by nature a creative and
emergent process, is also therefore transcendent.
Reason is applied to socially determined concepts, but
in the process of combining these given concepts in new
ways and drawing the logical conclusions from such
combinations, reason transcends the limitations of the
concepts, and allows perception of universal meanings
and values common to all humanity. If reason is an
innate faculty which is animated through interaction—
despite the various distortions in social relations—
and through which it is possible to conceive of universal values, then ethical awareness is an invariable facet of human existence. The actualization of
this awareness in ethical behavior depends upon the
greater strength of an individual's feeling of solidarity with the human race than with his or her particular
society. Ethical awareness is invariable, but ethical
behavior is variable.

To that degree to which a person—because of
his own intellectual and spiritual development—feels his solidarity with humanity,
can he tolerate social ostracism, and vice
versa. The ability to act according to one's
conscience depends on the degree to which
one has transcended the limits of one's society and has become a citizen of the world
(Fromm, 1971b:127-128).

PART FOUR: THE PERSPECTIVE OF

SOCIAL PSYCHOLOGY

CHAPTER 9: Rollo May

Introduction

The basic question is how the individual,
in his own awareness of himself and the
period he lives in, is able through his decisions to attain inner freedom and to live
according to his own inner integrity....
But no "well-integrated" society can perform for the individual, or relieve him
from, his task of achieving self-consciousness and the capacity for making his own
choices responsibly. And no traumatic world
situation can rob the individual of the
privilege of making the final decision with
regard to himself, even if it is only to af-
firm his own fate...each individual must come
to his own consciousness of himself, and he
does this on a level which transcends the
particular age he lives in (May, 1967:233).

Man is the "ethical animal"—ethical in potentiality even if, unfortunately, not in,
actuality. His capacity for ethical judgment—like freedom, reason and the other
unique characteristics of the human being—
is based upon his consciousness of himself
(May, 1967:150).

What is this element? It is the capacity to
sense injustice and take a stand against it
in the form of I-will-be-destroyed-rather-
than-submit. It is a rudimentary anger, a
capacity to muster all one's power and assert it against what one experiences as un-
fair. However it may be confounded or
covered up or counterfeited, this elemental
capacity to fight against injustice remains
the distinguishing characteristic of human
beings (May, 1972:220).

No, the dragon and the Sphinx are not in themselves the problem. The problem is only whether you project them or confront and integrate them. To admit them in ourselves means admitting that evil and good dwell within the same man, and that potentialities for evil increase in proportion to our capacity for good. The good we seek is an increated sensitivity, a sharpened awareness, a heightened consciousness of both good and evil (May, 1972:217).

Of all the social scientists reviewed in this study, Rollo May addresses most directly and explicitly the moral problems of evil and ethical judgment. It is his provocative contention that human beings are ethical animals—that ethical sensitivity, as well as reason, freedom, and responsibility, are innate and distinctively unique qualities of human nature. That humans are "ethical in potentiality, even if, unfortunately, not in actuality"—(May, 1967:150) indicates that May believes the capacity for ethical judgment can be taken for granted, but its utilization in the construction of behavior cannot. Considering this elemental sensitivity to injustice to be the most profoundly significant human attribute, May explores the issues of evil and transcendence of evil in terms of their consequences for the function of human judgment. Drawing from his professional experiences and his personal observation of catastrophic world events, he concludes that the dignity of human life is violated when the exercise of human judgment is denied by the individual or suppressed by society.

Definitions of Evil and of Transcendence

In Man's Search for Himself, May argues that ethical sensitivity is a function of the human being's original form of consciousness. That is, human consciousness is reflexive, reflective, and empathetic. The reflexiveness of consciousness refers to the fact that the human being can be an object to himself or herself, that he or she can perceive himself or herself—as an object—as others perceive him or her, and as he or she perceives others. Human beings can become self-conscious just as they are conscious of others, and, indeed, this consciousness of self derives from consciousness of others. Through the internalization of others' perceptions of him or her the human is enabled to perceive himself or herself.

102

Thus, in imagination, humans can observe themselves
and their actions in relation to others. The re-
flectiveness of consciousness refers to the fact that
humans can live through, and observe the course of an
act before the act is carried out in reality. This
imaginative construction of the act allows the individual to determine its probable consequences, and
hence to alter or previse the act in accord with his or
her intentions before it is completed. The empathetic
aspect of consciousness refers to the fact that humans
are able, in the imagination, to put themselves in the
place of the other, to take the role of the other.
Human beings anticipate the behavior of others, by
imaginatively taking the role of the other, and determining what their own thoughts and feelings would be
in the situation of the other. Human beings thus
have the ability to observe themselves in relations
with others, to interpret the meanings of the actions
of others, to previse their activities according to
their own intentions and the predicted intentions of
others, and to perceive and understand the attitudes
and needs of others.

          The reflexive, reflective, and empathetic
characteristics of human consciousness signify that
humans have the ability to recognize beforehand the
probable consequences of their actions not only for
themselves but for others as well. The actions of
each individual implicitly and irrevocably involve
other persons, and the inescapable recognition of
this interrelation, according to May, is the source of
ethical sensitivity. In this context, then, the meaning of good and evil is a function of the primal fact
of interrelation: that is, goodness consists of
acting toward others as one would have them act toward
oneself, and evilness consists of acting toward others
as one would not have them act toward oneself. Since
ethical awareness is, therefore, an implicit and immanent potential of human consciousness, consciousness is, in effect, equivalent to conscience. Thus,
On the basis of this evaluation of ethical awareness
as the most important human quality, May consequently defines evil as whatever—either tendencies
in human nature or conditions of social reality—is
inimical to the development and expansion of consciousness and ethical awareness. Conversely,
transcendence is defined as whatever—either tendencies in human nature or conditions of social reality—is conducive to the development and expansion of
consciousness and conscience. "The good we seek is an

increased sensitivity, a sharpened awareness, a
heightened consciousness of both good and evil"
(May, 1972:217).

Locus of Causality

The notions that the self is born in a social context, that consciousness arises from social
interaction, and that the social interaction of human
beings arouses the uniquely creative potentials of
human beings indicate that May assumes a primary and
integral interdependence of self and society. This
interdependence, moreover, signifies that self—i.e.,
(human nature) and society (social reality) are
mutually determinative. That is, the self that society creates possesses a dynamic and creative consciousness which is more than the sum of its constitu-
ent roles, which is cognizant of itself, of its role-
playing activities, of others, and of its social environment. As such, it is the nature of the self not
only to reflect the society that creates it, but also
to react back upon that society, to reverse the causal
process, and in effect, to create society.

On the one hand, it is clear that human nature is to a great extent a function of social reality,
since the self arises in a social context. As such,
the self internalizes and reflects two basically antithetical aspects of society—i.e., a tendency toward
stability and a tendency toward change. Through
the socialization process individuals internalize the
concepts, definitions, and values contained in their
society's social construction of reality. The pattern of individual thought and behavior derives from,
and is consequently supportive of societal requirements. The individual develops a tendency to conform
to the dictates of society, and hence contributes to
the stability of society. On the other hand, however,
the societal tendency toward change is also incorporated into the individual self through the arousal
and development of rational, reflective, and critical
consciousness. The experience of interpersonal interaction stimulates development of the reflexive, reflective, and empathetic aspects of consciousness.
The invariable exposure to situations of conflict—
i.e., of values—evokes doubt concerning the given
concepts, definitions and values of society, which
prompts development of critical consciousness. The individual is thus informed also with a tendency to

question the dictates of society, and becomes an agent of social change.

The incorporation of these antithetical societal tendencies—of stability in the form of conformity, and of change in the form of critical reflection—signifies that the individual is indeed a reflection of society, that human nature is a function of social reality. But this incorporation, given the dynamic nature of the second tendency, means also that the individual is considerably more than merely a reflection of society, that his or her reaction against society also constitutes a causal process, and that social reality is in part a function of human nature. Human nature and social reality both comprise realms of causality, and in their interaction, each determines to a great extent the other. The intrinsic creative potentials of human nature direct the destiny of society, whereas the challenging, conflictual conditions of social reality that stimulate these potentials direct the destiny of human nature. And May, moreover, emphasizes the transformative potency of the human's higher mental faculties, thus indicating the causal priority of human nature over social reality.

> We do not mean to imply that there are not an infinite number of deterministic influences in anyone's life.... But no matter how much one argues for the deterministic viewpoint, he still must grant that there is a <u>margin in which the alive human being can be aware of what is determining him.</u> And even if only in a very minute way to begin with, he can have some say in how he will react to the deterministic factors (May 1967:139).

Sources of Evil and of Transcendence

As indicated above, through assimilation of the social construction of reality, individuals receive a specific set of concepts, definitions, and values which constitute a necessary frame of reference for orienting and guiding their thoughts and actions. It is against the background of these crucial definitions of situations that individuals evolve their own personal meanings and values. That is, society provides the initial contents of consciousness with reference to which individual reflection and judgment are exercised and developed. These given definitions

105

of situations also necessarily structure the process
of interpersonal interaction. In the process of this
interaction, two significant events occur: the interaction calls forth the reflexive, reflective, and
empathetic aspects of consciousness, and simultaneously evokes an awareness of the societal definitions and
values which structure social relations. As individuals interact with others, they are thus capable of and
are impelled to evaluate the validity of the
societally-determined givens of their world-view.
Reflecting on the consequences for themselves and
others which ensue from these givens, they can evaluate the validity—the goodness or evilness—of assumptions which they had heretofore taken for granted.
Awareness of the consequences for all those implicated
in an act, within the context of the intrinsic solidarity of human life, constitutes the foundation for
individual judgment of societal definitions and
values.

Individuals are hence enabled to react back
upon their society through this evaluation of societal
values. By means of this evaluation, they may choose,
on the one hand, to accept the society's values as
their own, or to use those values as a basis for evolving similar values pertinent to their particular life-
styles. On the other hand, they may choose to reject
those values completely, to use their own experience
and understanding of others, and their imagination to
evolve an original constellation of values. The interdependence of individual and society signifies that
societal definitions and values are an essential pre-
requisite for the exercise and development of individual judgment.

However, May's analysis of contemporary society discerns that in an era of transition such as
the present, it is precisely such necessary values
which are lacking in the social construction of reality:

> The upshot is that the values and goals
> which provided a unifying center for previ-
> ous centuries in the modern period no longer
> are cogent. We have not yet found the new
> center which will enable us to choose our
> goals constructively, and thus to overcome
> the painful bewilderment and anxiety of not
> knowing which way to move. (May, 1967:49).

Essentially, the individual discovers in an era of transition that the acquired societal values are neither functional nor relevant to contemporary situations, and furthermore, that these values are totally useless in the construction of new and pertinent value-systems. In effect, the task of developing individual judgment becomes considerably more difficult as the individual—having lost the benefit of societal guidance—is thrown back completely on his or her own resources. The absence of a definite, initial frame of reference as a point of departure for reflection and evaluation, indicates that the individual must rely entirely on the first-hand evidence of personal experience, and the gradually and painfully won understanding of this experience. In a period of transition, the process of interaction continues to stimulate an awareness of societal values—such as they are--but these values are no longer definite and ascertainable, but rather unstable, uncertain, and confusing, and offer no material for critical reflection.

This is not to say that critical reflection and judgment become impossible—certainly not, given the nature of human consciousness, but it is to say that these faculties encounter greater obstacles in the course of development. The absence of stable societal guidelines effectively removes a part of the internalized motivation to develop the critical faculties. Instead, individuals internalize the confusion of values that prevail in society, and exhibit a tendency of mindless conformity to this bewildering state of affairs. Even so, May contends, eventually, through the inevitable exposure to situations of conflict, and stimulation of social interaction, individuals will become aware of the confusion of values and the need for a personal construction of values. In the last analysis, then, the experience of the anxieties and unhappiness ensuing from a societal confusion of values and surrender to mindless conformity is a matter of individual choice—and a manifestation of personal irresponsibility. The evil restriction of consciousness and numbing of ethical sensitivity fostered by a society in transition is aided and abetted, as it were, by the individual denial of an integral element of being, by a willful abrogation of personal responsibility to express and expand the immanent human potentials—

Having the capacity to experience the world, one has at the same time the responsibility for not closing one's sensibilities to that experience (May, 1972:211),

and:

But our society...has this power because we as individual capitulate to it.... To that extent, we victimize ourselves (May, 1972: 205).

That this process of the evil constriction of consciousness does indeed involve an interaction of human and social reality is evident also in May's identification of ambivalent tendencies in human nature toward the extension and quiescence of consciousness— i.e.:

...is it not the conflict between every human being's need to struggle toward enlarged self-awareness, maturity, freedom and responsibility, and his tendency to remain a child and cling to the protection of parents or parental substitutes? (May, 1967:166).

This latter tendency, which he calls "pseudoinnocence" (May, 1972:49-50) entails a voluntary blindness to the facts of reality, a willful disregard of the effects of one's actions on others, an egoistic failure to take into account—in the construction of one's acts—the welfare of others involved. According to May, exposure to conflictual situations which reveal inadequacies of societal values, the awareness of values which structure interaction and which is aroused in interaction, and the foreknowledge of the consequences for self and others of actions ensuing from societal values, all are conditions endemic to human life, and which are inevitable in every person's life. Therefore, the failure to evaluate and if necessary, to reject given social values, the failure to recognize the beneficial or harmful effects on others of one's own actions as guided by the social values, the failure to take the welfare of others into account in the construction of one's own acts, constitute voluntary negligence of ethical imperatives emanating from the very structure of the self. Thus, the essence of the innate tendency to pseudoinnocence consists of a willful abrogation of the implicit ethical awareness culminating in the ultimate evil of the construction of consciousness, and

the dulling of ethical sensitivity. In times of
transition, then, the pernicious inhibition of the
growth of consciousness effected by the confusion of
values is exacerbated by the self-willed manifestation
of pseudoinnocnece.

The sources of transcendence of evil likewise involve a combination and interaction of factors
in human nature and social reality. Within human nature, there is, first of all, an elementary sensitivity to injustice, energized by the ability to assert
oneself against perceived injustices. Within social
reality, there are inevitably, situations of conflict
which generate critical reflection by arousing problematic doubt, by bringing into question a portion of
the world-view. In the interaction of human nature
and social reality, the incorporation into the self of
the societal tendency to change manifested as the impetus to critical reflection provides an indispensable
condition for transcendence. Similarly, the interaction of self and other elicits the exercise of this
impetus to critical reflection by arousing the reflexive, reflective, and empathetic aspects of consciousness. Further, the awareness of societal
values which underlie interaction is also provoked by
social interaction and provides material for the exercise of critical reflection. Finally, the situations of conflict encountered in social reality—i.e.,
between individuals or between the individual and
society—not only imperatively require the exercise of
reflection and judgment in regard to basic values, but
further necessitate an individual decision regarding
those values or possible alternative ones, and the
assertion of that decision in the construction of actions, an actualization of personal commitment to the
chosen values.

In May's view, then, ethical insight and
self-awareness are coterminus, and thus, although any
society may facilitate or interfere with this development, it is, in the last analysis, a matter of individual decision. Each individual develops his or her
in-born capacity for self-awareness through processes
that transcend the particular age he or she lives in
and which are indigenous to human existence. The
authentic innocence of transcendence involves the
recognition that self-consciousness is implicity
other-consciousness, and that evil arises from a sur-
feit of egoism through which the welfare of others is
neglected in the construction of one's own acts.

By virtue of self-consciousness, no person can claim
ignorance of societal evil, and no person is exempt
from complicity in evil—as May states it:

> To admit frankly, our capacity for evil
> hinges on our breaking through our pseudo-
> innocence. So long as we preserve our one-
> dimensional thinking, we can cover up our
> deeds by pleading innocent. This anti-
> diluvian escape from conscience is no longer
> possible. We are responsible for the ef-
> fects of our actions, and we are also re-
> sponsible for becoming as aware as we can of
> these effects (May, 1972:259).

Manifestations of Evil and of Transcendence

Having given the generic sources of evil
and of transcendence, it is next necessary to identify
the specific causes and effects of evil and transcendence subsumed under these sources. For the most
part, May concludes that evil is caused by hostile
conditions in the social environment which either directly—through the pressure of external threat, or
indirectly, through the internalization of threatening
conflicts—block the development of consciousness and
ethical sensitivity. For example, periods of social
change may generate threatening situations to which
individuals who feel unable to cope will react by developing anxieties, hostilities, and all manner of
neurotic symptoms. He identifies the conditions most
likely to produce such trauma as changes in societal
values. He specifically notes that catastrophic consequences have ensued from the following changes in
values in contemporary Western society: (1) loss of
viability of the ethic of competition (May, 1967:41-
49); (2) loss of the sense of the worth and dignity
of the human being (May, 1967:49-56); (3) failure of
language to convey personal meanings (May, 1967:56-59);
(4) loss of relatedness to nature (May, 1967:59-65);
(5) loss of the sense of the tragic significance of
human life (May, 1967:65-69).

The effect of this loss of a center of values in society is to rob individuals of their crucial
frame of reference for reflection and judgment, leav-
ing them subject to confusion, uncertainty, and self-
doubt, which if exacerbated by the proclivity to
pseudoinnocence culminates in nullification of ethical sensitivity. Feelings of emptiness, powerlessness,

despair, fear of loneliness, and an excessive dependence on others for the sense of self are corollary effects of this loss of values which contribute to the constriction of consciousness and psychological impoverishment. Other societal conditions outside of social change which May identifies as causes of evil include: the denial of social power, i.e., socially-enforced impotence (May, 1972:97); denial of a sense of significance (May, 1972:138-139); lack of genuine parental love (May, 1972:113-114); denial of personal responsibility in society (May, 1972:225-231); and, most importantly, the blocking of all avenues of expression for the human's healthy aggressive tendencies (May, 1972:149). The effect of these restrictions is to provoke explosions of destructive violence, as well as "...a zombielike deadening of consciousness, neurosis, psychosis..." (1972:42-43).

Conversely, the social conditions conducive to transcendence of evil consist of: the stability of a definite center of values which serves as a basic frame of reference for reflection and judgment; equal distribution of social power; experiences that support a sense of personal significance; experience of parental love in childhood; social recognition of the individual's personal responsibility for his or her actions; the existence of avenues of expression for the human's healthy aggressive inclinations. The effects of transcendence are specified as the individual recognition, confrontation, and integration of the inner capacity for evil; the exercise of critical reflection in regard to oneself, others, and society; a rationally directed rebellion against societal injustices; and action toward social reform—all in all, a radical expansion of consciousness and conscience—"...a heightened consciousness of both good and evil" (May, 1972:217).

Processes of Evil and Transcendence

The process of the manifestation of evil, in accordance with May's dichotomous conception of causality, requires an interaction of factors in human nature and social reality. On the one hand, there must be a growth of societal conditions which impede the expansion of consciousness-conscience, principally, a loss of the center of values in society. On the other hand, there must be an individual choice between the innate tendencies to authentic innocence and pseudoinnocence, where the individual chooses the latter. The fact that the interaction of self and other necessarily arouses the reflexive, reflective, and empathetic aspects of consciousness through which individuals are able to anticipate the consequences of their actions for others as well as themselves, that interpersonal interaction and exposure to conflictual situations bring to awareness the values which structure interaction and subject those values to the scrutiny of problematic doubt, and that exposure to conflictual situations necessitates ethical decisions and choices of values, signify that the ethical awareness of good and evil is an inexorable fact of human existence rooted in the very structure of the self.

Although the lack of a center of values in society makes more difficult the intensification of this awareness, it cannot prevent it. The loss of a center of values simply removes the basic frame of reference of societal concepts, definitions, and values which in normal times constitute the object of individual reflection and judgment. The individual thus internalizes the confusion of values prevailing in society instead of a definite and ascertainable value system. He or she becomes subject to the perilous uncertainty of the times. However, the person does not become a victim of the times since the experiences of interaction and conflictual situations stimulate an awareness of the societal confusion of values, and of the consequent necessity for an individual determination of values. The victimization of the person—in terms of the constriction of consciousness and ethical sensitivity—occurs only at the point of choice, where the individual, realizing the uncertainty and instability of societal values and the need for an evolution of new values, and aware also of the antinomic tendencies to expand or to fail to expand his or her own consciousness, willfully chooses the latter course, thus participating in and precipitating the deterioration of his or her unique ethical potential. The individual chooses to surrender to the uncertainty and bewilderment of the times, refuses to use the personal resources of consciousness and experience to create new values, and voluntarily assumes the blindness of pseudoinnocence which ignores the consequences for others of his or her actions. This self-determined and self-imposed conformity to the confusion of the times eventually "...undermines the development of an individual's ethical awareness and inner strength. ...he loses his real powers of ethical, responsible choice" (May, 1967:170).

Similarly, the possibility for the manifestation of transcendence—even in a period of historical
transition—is activated at precisely the same point
of individual decision between authentic innocence and
pseudoinnocence. The choice of authentic innocence
entails above all a constructive and positive response
to the anxieties evoked by the trauma of social
change. This positive response takes the form of ac-
knowledging the potential for evil within oneself—
that is, the realization that evil arises from mindless conformity to unexamined values, and from the
deliberate neglect of the welfare of others in the
construction of one's own acts. Moreover, authentic
innocence involves a deliberate and active attempt to
expand the awareness of one's own needs and desires,
of one's irrational resentment and hate, and the perception of the universal values that emanate from the
primal unity of self and other, the solidarity of the
human race. With regard to the latter perception, in
May's perspective, the transcendent consciousness of
authentic innocence is predicated on the innate ability
of human beings to reach a level of consciousness un-
contaminated by the dichotomy of subjectivity and objectivity, and thus to intuit objective truth. The
realization of objective truth and universal values
attained in the ecstatic level of consciousness instills in the individual a commitment to a higher
cause, an ideal against which the prevailing values
and practices of contemporary society can be evaluated.
The person who chooses the course of authentic innocence transcends the societal upheavals peculiar to
his or her time, and evolves a critical consciousness
that impels and guides his or her judgment of the
goodness or evilness of society, and serves as a crucial base for the possible rebellion against and reform of an evil society.

Consequence of Evil and Transcendence

In conclusion, it is May's fundamental contention that the sources of evil arising from social
reality—i.e., the loss of a center of values, are always and invariably opposed by an inexorable personal
awareness of good and evil. The triumph of the forces
of evil or the forces of transcendence depends, finally, on the unpredictable individual choice for
pseudoinnocence or for authentic innocence. The triumph of evil derives from the combination of societal
evils and the personal choice of pseudo-innocence,
whereas the triumph of transcendence ensues from the

113

conquest of societal evils made possible by the choice
for authentic innocence. May designates as the consequences of the triumph of evil the deterioration of the
unique human faculty of ethical sensitivity and thus
psychological impoverishment of the individual, and on
the collective level, the manifestation of unquestioning obedience to the dictates of society, resignation
to fate and historical destiny, and finally and most
importantly, the degeneration of society into some
form of authoritarianism or totalitarianism. Conversely, the consequences of transcendence consists of
the intensification of ethical awareness, a concomitant
realization that one is responsible for the effects as
well as the intentions of one's actions, and a corollary assumption of personal responsibility for whether
one is right or wrong. Finally, evaluation of the
goodness or evilness of society, individual and collective rebellion against societal injustices, and the
active attempt, individually and collectively, to
eradicate injustices, and to transform an evil society
into a good one, are the ultimate consequences of
transcendence.

CHAPTER 10: George Herbert Mead

Introduction

...the view here maintained is that human
nature is not something existing separately
in the individual, but a group-nature or
primary phase of society, a relatively simple and general condition of the social
mind.... Man does not have it at birth; he
cannot acquire it except through fellowship,
and it decays in isolation (Cooley, 1970:
157-158).

Man comes to himself, becomes truly a person,
in a dialogue, not in a monologue. The feeling of selfhood, self-worth, self-identify
comes when one stands over against another.
One cannot become a human being, that is to
say, he cannot acquire that core of personality which we call the self-conscious,
responsible, moral self without contact and
interaction from other human beings. Not
just action, nor even reaction, but interaction (Pfuetze, 1954:80).

...neither the "single one" nor the social
aggregate is the fundamental fact of human
existence. The fundamental fact is man
with man. What is uniquely characteristic
and constitutive of the human world is something that takes place between one person
and another (Pfuetze, 1954:131).

...a theorist is not interested in making
traditional institutionalized values clear,
with the implied contention that an answer
to the question What ought I do? is to be
found in precepts, whether known through
revelation, handed down from the past, or
found by experience to have been satisfactory

in the past. Ethical theory is analogous to
scientific method. It is a statement of what
is involved in the solution of moral problems, that cannot be solved by resorting to
institutionalized and previously universalized ways of acting (Miller, 1973:230-
231).

Science does not attempt to formulate the end
which social and moral conduct ought to pursue, any more than it pretends to announce
what hypothesis will be found by the research
scientist to solve his problem. It only insists that the object of our conduct must
take into account and do justice to all of
the values that prove to be involved in the
enterprise, just as it insists that every
fact involved in the research problem must be
taken into account in an acceptable hypothesis (Mead, 1964:256).

The founder of symbolic interactionism,
George Herbert Mead, was concerned first and foremost
with explicating the social origins of human life. To
this end he focused his analysis on the development
of mind, self, and society from the seminal process
of social interaction. The symbolic nature of communication involved in social interaction accounted,
in his view, for the emergence of the distinctively
human characteristics of both individual and collective life—for self-consciousness and the faculty of
reason on the one hand, and for the organization of
human society on a basis other than physiological differentiation on the other. Moreover, he was concerned
with determining the implications and consequences for
moral conduct ensuing from the fountainhead of social
process. In this respect, he identified the fundamental interdependence of human beings as the origin of
moral consciousness, and the faculty of reason as the
principal means of constructing moral action. Assimilating also the tenets of pragmatism to his social
and ethical philosophy, he developed a theory of social reform based on the conception of utility as the
prime criterion of value, of the phenomenon of evil
as the object of problem-solving activities, of reason
as the most successful problem-solving activity, and
of scientific method as the highest development of
reason. Hence, he advocated the application of scientific method to the solution of moral and social
problems. With regard to the ultimate destiny of

the human race, he optimistically envisioned the establishment of a unity of humanity as the feliticious inevitable culmination of the interaction process's ever-expanding integration of individuals.

Given these conceptions of the socially-derived capacity for moral consciousness and conduct, of the intrinsic tendency of social interaction to universalize personal interrelations, and of the phenomenon of evil as constituting a challenge inviting the reconstructive activities of reason and science, it is not surprising that Mead's philosophy as a whole evokes an optimistic image of human society progressing toward perfection. In contrast to Freud and Solzhenitsyn's sensitive and painful intuition of the intensity and extensity of the capacity for evil in human nature and social reality, it is indeed difficult to imagine how Mead—with his idealistic vision—would have attempted to account for the atrocities perpetrated by stormtroopers, the SS, the Gestapo, the NKVD, the KGB, for forced labor camps, prison camps, and concentration camps, for Nazism, Stalism, and the atom bomb. But then, Mead, unlike Freud or Solzhenitsyn, never personally encountered evil in its modern forms. The product of an earlier and perhaps more secure era, Mead escaped the psychological trauma of the Second World War, and hence his philosophy, understandably, exhibits an overestimation of the forces of good and progress, and an underestimation of the forces of evil and barbarism. Consequently, although this examination of Meadian philosophy will derive and clarify the conceptions of evil and of transcendence implicit in his theoretical assumptions—as with the other scholars considered—it will, furthermore, draw from critics of Mead to augment his somewhat inadequate account of evil.

Definitions of Evil and of Transcendence

The point of departure for Mead's ethical theory—for definitions of evil and transcendence—is the fundamental fact of:

> ...the common social dependence of all these individuals upon one another (or from the fact of the common social dependence of each one of them upon that society as a whole or upon all the rest of them)... (Mead, 1967: 320),

117

originating from and sustained by the social interaction process. This interdependence is demonstrated
in the emergence of minds and selves from the interrelations of self and other stimulated by the significant symbol, and in the organization of human society
on the basis of the interpretive activity generated
and maintained by social interaction. Since self and
society derive from and depend upon social interaction,
it follows that the ethical constructs of evil and
transcendence must be defined in relation to that process. That is, evil must therefore be conceived as
whatever is detrimental to or destructive of the social interaction process—and by extension also undermines the welfare of self and society. Conversely,
transcendence must be conceived as whatever is beneficial and conducive to social interaction—and
hence also contributes to the welfare of self and
society. In terms of individual conduct this indicates that evil is manifested as behavior which hinders
or disrupts social interaction, whereas transcendence
is manifested as behavior which facilitates interaction. Mead expresses this view as follows:

> Every human individual must, to behave ethi-
> cally, integrate himself with the pattern of
> organized social behavior which, as reflected
> or prehended in the structure of his self,
> makes him a self-conscious personality.
> Wrong, evil, or sinful conduct on the part of
> the individual runs counter to this pattern
> of organized social behavior which makes him,
> as a self, what he is, just as right, good,
> or virtuous behavior accords with this pat-
> tern...ethical and unethical behavior can
> be defined essentially in social terms: the
> former as behavior which is socially benefi-
> cial or conducive to the well-being of so-
> ciety, the latter as behavior which is so-
> cially harmful or conducive to the disrup-
> tion of society (Mead, 1967:320-321).

By saying that individual conduct must be
integrated with the "pattern of organized social behavior" to be ethical, Mead is not proposing a moral
justification for blind conformity, but is rather
suggesting that moral conduct is conduct in accord with
the intrinsic principle of the social interaction
process—that is, the ever-expanding integration of
self and others. Drawing from his social theory—
according to which the individual is realized as a

118

social being through the integrating relations to others—he constructs an ethical theory according to which, analogously, the individual is realized as an ethical being through the integration of self-interest and the interests of others, or the expanding of narrow self interest to include the interests of others with whom one is involved. Being vehemently oppposed to doctrinaire moral systems which stipulate inflexible rules for conduct, Mead proposes only this one general guiding maxim, and he derives it from the fundamental interdependence of human beings. Moral action is thus action predicated on the recognition of the social origins of human life—which takes into account the interdependence of human beings, according to which self-interest is identified with the interest of others, and self-interest is served by incorporating the interests of others. From the example of the operation of the social interaction process, then, Mead extrapolates an ethical maxim which stipulates, in the first place—that since in interaction self-interest becomes identified with the interest of others, individuals should therefore consider the interests of others in the construction of their own behavior. Secondly, since the integrating activity of interaction is in principle universal, the implication follows that individuals should attend to or consider every interest or value involved in a particular situation.

> The only rule that an ethics can present is that an individual should rationally deal with all the values that are found in a specific problem (Mead, 1967:388).

The validity of Mead's propositions that moral ends must be social ends, and that self-interest is identified with other-interest can be illustrated in terms of self-actualization and by the conversation of gestures. With regard to self-actualization, since the individual self can only be realized through the integrating relations to others, those who act solely on the basis of self-interest actually work against their own interest as they inhibit the fullest development of their self potentials. Secondly, in terms of the interaction between self and other, Mead's theory specifies that the mechanism of role-taking enables individuals to put themselves in the other's place and to understand the other's reactions—i.e., thoughts and feelings, and the mechanism of reflexive role-taking allows individuals to perceive themselves from

119

the standpoint of the other. Therefore, when individuals act in selfish or harmful ways toward others,
they are acutely aware of the pain inflicted on the
others since their own implicit response anticipates
the others' actual response (through role-taking).
Secondly, they perceive themselves through the reflected appraisal of the others as selfish, hostile,
or aggressive people (through reflexive role-taking).
In this fashion, selfish or aggressive people are
themselves subject to the painful experience they inflict on others, and their own self-image suffers from
the reflected negative appraisal of the others. Thus,
Meadian social and ethical theory concurs with the
Biblical injunction to "Do unto others as you would
have them do unto you," because, in essence, you do to
yourself what you do to others.

     A final consideration on the topic of Mead's
ethics concerns the moral ramifications of the relation of reflective consciousness to overt conduct.
The faculty of reflection signifies that human behavior is subject to individual control through the
prevision and construction of acts. That is, human
beings determine the course of their acts by imaginatively initiating and completing the act mentally
prior to its actual manifestation which allows for
anticipation of the possible consequences of an act,
the examination of alternative acts and consequences,
and hence the aligning of intentions and consequences
of acts. When human beings act, they have already
decided upon the end they wish to achieve, and that
end is incorporated in the construction of the act itself. Human beings do anticipate the consequences in
their intentions, and by virtue of the control which
they thus exercise over their acts, they are morally
responsible, not only for their intentions, but also
for their actual consequences. Reflective consciousness enables human beings to utilize past knowledge and
imagination to anticipate the future effect of present
acts—to know in advance the beneficial or harmful
consequences of their intentions—and hence they are
responsible for their intentions, their ends, and their
use or failure to use their reflective ability. As
Dr. David Miller has summarized Mead's strong position
on this important point:

          Probably every person at some time or
          another acts immorally. If one acts im-
          morally unwittingly, it is only because he
          should have known better; that is, he is

120

responsible for not knowing better. If a person acts immorally unwittingly, he commits an offense against society, of which he is a member (Miller, 1973:242).

A person who acts immorally, ostensibly unwittingly, is morally culpable for possessing the reflective ability to determine the right act, and yet neglecting to exercise that faculty. Human beings are morally culpable therefore for both their witting and unwitting immoral actions.

Locus of Causality

As indicated previously, Mead perceived the social interaction process as the primary locus of causality from which emerge mind (reflective activity), self (self-consciousness), and society (society organized on the basis of symbolic communication). Within the context of an evolutionary perspective, he traces the development of these uniquely human phenomena from earlier, simpler forms. Specifically, - this development presupposes two predisposing conditions: (1) that there is a primitive society composed of biologic individuals, (2) that these biologic individuals are endowed with the physiological attributes of the cortex and a highly developed nervous system. Furthermore, this development presupposes the essential precipitating condition of interaction at the non-symbolic level—as Charles W. Morris phrases it:

> The transformation of the biologic individual to the minded organism or self takes place, on Mead's account, through the agency of language, while language in turn presupposes the existence of a certain kind of society and certain physiological capacities in the individual organism (Mead, 1967:xx).

Interaction or communication at the non-symbolic level among biologic individuals occurs through the medium of gestures, including the vocal gesture. From the vocal gesture—which affects the speaker much as it affects the individual to whom it is addressed—emerges the significant symbol or gesture. The significant symbol stimulates the speaker to respond implicitly to his or her own gesture in the same manner as it stimulates the other to whom it

121

is addressed to respond explicitly. The functional identity of the covert and overt responses of the interacting participants constitutes the shared meaning represented by the symbolic gesture. Since "The social process relates the responses of one individual to the gestures of another, as the meanings of the latter...." (Mead, 1967:78), the advent of the significant symbol indicates that the individual's experience now encompasses both the gesture which he or she makes, and the meaning of the gesture as given by his or her own implicit response which anticipates and reflects the other's overt response. That is, by virtue of the mutual stimulation of self and other effected by the significant symbol, the individual internalizes the sequence of gesture and response—the conversation of gestures—occurring between himself or herself and the other, and this internalization enables the individual to conduct a dialogue with another within his or her own imagination. The individual gains the ability to initiate and to respond to a gesture in the imagination before manifesting the gesture in actual behavior—the ability to previse his or her actions in accord with personal intentions, to construct his or her actions rather than merely reacting to external stimuli, in other words, the ability to reflect. The biologic organism is transformed into a minded individual.

As a second consequence of the significant symbol's reciprocal stimulation of self and other, the individual's tendency to respond to his or her own gesture as does the other constitutes reflexive role-taking according to which the individual enters the other's perspective from which he or she turns back, as it were, and perceives himself or herself as an object as the other perceives him or her. The individual experiences himself or herself indirectly, from the vantage-point of the other, becomes an object to himself or herself, and in Mead's view, attains self-consciousness, becomes a self. In this fashion, the human phenomena of minds and selves emerge from the transformative action of the significant symbol on the biologic organism—in Morris' words:

> Mead's endeavor is to show that mind and
> the self are without residue social emer-
> gents; and that language, in the form of
> the vocal gesture, provides the mechanism
> for their emergence (Mead, 1967:xiv).

The transformation of the biologic organism into a minded self has the further consequence that human society attains a unique form of social organization. Its organization, that is, derives from the ability of individuals to enter into each other's perspectives, to take the role of the other, and by this means to ascertain the intentions of others, and thus to align their own actions with those of others. In sum, then, the process of development generated by social interaction begins with a primitive society of biologic organisms interacting at the non-symbolic level. This interaction becomes symbolic with the emergence of the significant symbol from the vocal gesture. The dual effect of the significant symbol stimulates reflexive role-taking which enables individuals to internalize the conversation of gestures, and thus to acquire a mind, and to perceive themselves indirectly from the perspective of others, thus acquiring a self. Finally, the appearance of the minded self engenders the organization of human society on the basis of interpretive activity. Thus the social interaction process functions as the primary locus of causality in the human world.

The newly created self and society, however, also manifest the attribute of causality in the sense that they constitute secondary and interdependent realms of causality. Specifically, the individual self exerts a decisive influence on society by means of the critical and reconstructive activities of reflective consciousness. In return, society exerts a determinative influence on the individual self through the provision of a necessary frame of reference for reflective activity in the form of the generalized other. On the one hand, then, the individual's reflective consciousness—represented by the "I"—acts upon society: "The 'I' is the principle of action and of impulse; and in its action it changes the social structure" (Mead, 1967:xxv), and, on the other hand, society—in the form of the generalized other—acts upon the individual:

> It is in the form of the generalized other that...the community exercises control over the conduct of its individual members; for it is in this form that the social process or community enters as a determining factor into the individual's thinking (Mead, 1967: 155).

Individual critical reflection contributes to society's dynamic adaptability, and the generalized other
sustains individual reflective activity. Self and society are thus mutually determinative second-order
realms of causality, and both derive from the first-
order realm of social interaction.

Sources of Evil and of Transcendence

Meadian ethical theory, as stated above,
defines evil as phenomena disruptive of social processes. In terms of this definition, three distinct
sources of evil can be discerned within Mead's cos-
mology, though he himself referred to only one of
these. Specifically, these are: (1) the processual
or mutable nature of reality; (2) the asocial aspect
of the self (identified by Mead), and (3) the unconscious internalization of the existing social construction of reality as an absolute.

The first source reflects Mead's position as
a "process" philosopher, meaning that his theories
incorporated the concept of evolution, i.e., the notion of the dynamic potential in all the natural
world for the emergence of more complex and novel
forms from simpler and earlier (older) forms. Applied to reality, the evolutionary principle indicates
that the nature of the existing world that is there is
not given as a static eternal essence but rather as a
dynamic mutable process. The given reality of the
world that is there—which is taken for granted by individuals since it provides the necessary frame of
reference for their thought and behavior—is subject
to unpredictable change. At any time, novel dimensions may arise from any aspect of the old order, and
these novel dimensions are necessarily incomprehensible within the old order. For the human beings who
must rely on the stability of the given reality in order to orient their thought and conduct, the emergence
of novel dimensions renders part of the given problematic. The human activities predicated on the now
problematic aspects of the old order are interrupted
and cannot be resumed until a new order of the world
that is there emerges which encompasses and renders
comprehensible both the older order and the novel
dimensions that arose from it. As David Miller summarizes this phenomenon: "A situation is a problem
simply because a part of the old past, the world that
was there, is no longer reliable in our contending
with that situation" (Miller, 1973:204-205), and
again: "...moral problems arise at the very point
where institutionalized, universalized ways of acting

124

are found to be inadequate" (Miller, 1973:234). Thus, the mutable nature of reality—the possibility for the transformation of the given into the problematic—engenders disruptions of human social processes, and hence functions as a source of evil. According to the classification scheme of this essay, this source of evil is constituted by the action of one system—social reality—on another system—social interaction.

Secondly, Mead identified the "asocial aspect of the self" as a source of evil:

> The asocial or personal aspect of the self... differentiates it from, or sets it in distinctive and unique opposition to, the other members of the social group to which it belongs; and this side of the self is charac-terized by the individual's feeling of su-periority toward the other members of that group.... the "asocial" aspect of human society... is responsible for the rise of ethical problems in that society (Mead, 1967: 321).

Relating this conception of the asocial aspect of the self to Mead's definition of evil reveals that this asocial self functions as a source of evil by disrupt-ing the process of interaction through behavior which is in opposition or antithetical to the integrating principle of interaction. There are two possible avenues for such hostile behavior, and there are therefore two corresponding dimensions of the asocial self. Specifically, the asocial aspect may appear in the form of individual egoism or selfishness, i.e., in behavior predicated on the basis of self-interest to the exclusion of the interests of others, or in the form of group eogism or ethnocentrism, i.e., in be-havior predicated on the basis of group-interest to the exclusion of the wider system of interests (the uni-versal group of humanity) in which the group is in-volved. Both dimensions of the asocial self's egoistic orientation entail a refusal or failure to integrate narrow interests with a broader system of interests, and are thus diametrically opposed to, and disruptive of the operation of the interaction process. Since the asocial aspect of the self, according to Mead, is just as much a product of social interaction as is the so-cial aspect of the self, this source of evil must be classified as the action of a component of one system (asocial aspect of the self/social interaction system)

125

upon another component of the same system (integrating activity/social interaction system).

The third source of evil in the Meadian world is comprised of the social control of the pattern of individual thought and conduct which results from the individual's unconscious internalization—through socialization—of the established social construction of reality as an absolute. Socialization refers to the process by which each individual is integrated into the common life of the group, and learns his or her role within that common life. This process takes place principally through the individual's unconscious internalization of society's established conception of reality. The individual thus receives from the group a predetermined world-view—a system of socially approved definitions of situations, concepts, values, attitudes, expectations—as the essential frame of reference for reflection and conduct. This preordained definition of the given—of the world that is there—which is internalized as the "Me" component of the self structure—comes to the individual and is experienced by him or her as an a priori to his or her own existence. It is, in other words, perceived and assimilated unconsciously, arbitrarily, as an indubitable absolute. Since this societal world-view constitutes the orienting framework for individual thought and behavior, its unreflected acceptance generates an unconscious individual conformity to societal requirements. Although such conformity is necessary as a basis for much of the human being's routine and habitual behavior, it becomes dysfunctional for both self and society when it blocks or prevents individual critical reflection. The internalized societal world-view thus comprises a form of social control which detracts from the well-being of self and society by disrupting the social process of critical reflective activity. In terms of the classification scheme, this source of evil may be identified as the action of a component of one system (socialization/social interaction system) upon another component of the same system (the self/social interaction system).

Turning to the alternative issue of transcendence of evil, this is defined in Meadian ethics as phenomena which are conducive to or supportive of the process of social interaction—which accord with and facilitate its operating principle: the ever-expanding integration of self and other. According to

126

this definition, three separate sources of transcendence may be discerned: (1) the self as a social
being, (2) the social aspect of the self, and,
(3) the faculty of reflection. The first of these,
the self as a social being, refers to the fact that
the distinctively "human" nature of human beings is
socially constituted, that the self-conscious, minded
organism is a social construct. The biologic organism which precedes the human being acquires a mind
and a self, becomes a human being, only through the
transformative action of the social interaction process. The dual stimulation of the significant symbol
generates, on the one hand, incorporation of the dialogue between self and other which comprises the mind,
and on the other hand, induces reflexive role-taking
by means of which the individual acquires a self
through the experience of himself or herself as an
object from the perspective of the other.

The self-conscious minded individual emerges
from the biologic organism as a result of interaction
with others through which the perspectives of others
are assimilated into personal experience—the organism becomes a self by first becoming others: "...the
self has become the other, and the values of the
other are his own" (Pfeutze, 1954:99). The composi-
tion of the self in terms of others signifies that the
values of the self accord with, and reflect the opera-
ing principle or value of the social interaction process:

> ...the self has taken the values of others
> into itself; its values are indeed the
> values of the social process. There is then
> no problem as to how the self can take others
> and the values of others into account
> (Pfuetze, 1954:238-239),

and:

> ...to the degree that the self has taken
> the attitudes of others into itself through
> the language process, it has become the
> others, and the values of others are its
> own; ...its values are the values of the so-
> cial process itself (Mead, 1967:xxxii).

This correspondence between the intrinsic values of the
self and the social process indicates, significantly,
that human nature is, from its very inception, oriented

127

toward the transcendence of evil. That is, from the very beginning the self is involved with others. It arises by internalizing the interests of others, it becomes identified with the interests of others, and most importantly, it is sustained by the continual integration of self-interest and the interests of others. Transcendence of evil is thus built into the very structure of the self, and, consequently, transcendence can be avoided only through an abrogation of selfhood. In terms of the classification scheme for sources of transcendence, the self as a social being constitutes the action of one system—social interaction—upon another system—human nature (i.e., the biologic organism).

Secondly, Mead himself identified the "social aspect of the self" as a source of transcendence:

> The social or impersonal aspect of the self integrates it with the social group to which it belongs and to which it owes it existence; and this side of the self is characterized by the individual's feeling of cooperation and equality with the other members of that social group.... The "social" apsect of human society...is the basis for the development and existence of ethical ideals in that society... (Mead, 1967:321).

From this it appears that Mead conceives of the social aspect of the self as providing the inner motivation for individual conduct in accord with the operating principle of social interaction—for actions predicated on an integration of self and other interest, of self-interest and the wider system of interests in which the individual is involved. As the source of this "altruistic" motivation, the social aspect of the self must be grounded in an intuitive or affective awareness of the nature of the human self as a social being, of the primary social dependence of human beings. The altruistic attitude emanating from this recognition may be manifested on either an individual or collective level—that is, in individual conduct constructed on the basis of the integration of self-interest and the interests of others, and in individual conduct predicated on the integration of one's narrow group-interest with the wider system of interests in which the group is implicated (the universal group of humanity). In both cases, the actual behavior arising from the social aspect of the self accords with and reflects the operating principle or value of social interaction, and consequently functions to sustain the interaction process. As a source of transcendence the social aspect of the self—as in the case of the asocial aspect of the self as a source of evil—is classified as the action of a component of one system (social aspect of self/social interaction system) upon another component of the same system (integrating activity/social interaction system).

The third discernible source of transcendence in the Meadian world is given in the faculty of reflection which functions as the medium for the implementation of the motivation for ethical action provided by the social aspect of the self into actual conduct. The altruistic inclination to take into account the interests of others and the wider system of interests implicated in a social situation is translated into ethical conduct by means of the reflective prevision of the consequences of intended acts. Through the internalization of the dialogue between self and other, human beings acquire the ability to step outside of themselves, as it were, and to observe in the imagination the probable course of an act from initiating gesture to the answering response, to compare the courses and consequences of alternative acts, and hence to select from among the imagined alternatives the most desirable act. As Mead describes this ability to control the course of an act through prevision of the future:

> More specifically, the central nervous system provides a mechanism of implicit response which enables the individual to test out implicitly the various possible completions of an already initiated act in advance of the actual completion of the act— and thus to choose for himself, on the basis of this testing, the one which it is most desirable to perform explicitly or carry into overt effect (Mead, 1967:117).

Moreover, since the mechanism of role-taking enables human beings to enter the other's perspective, and to perceive and understand the reactions of the other, human individuals are thus also capable of determining before the fact the probable beneficial or harmful effect of their own actions on the others involved. By virtue of the control which human beings thus exercise over their own conduct through the imaginative prevision of the future and anticipation of the consequences for others through role-taking, they are endowed with responsibility for the morality of their acts, for the beneficial or harmful consequences of their consciously chosen and directed acts. Reflective consciousness insures that human beings are cognizant of the good or evil nature of their acts, that moral and immoral behavior is pursued wittingly. By means of the reflective faculty, then, human beings consciously and willingly choose to manifest in behavior either the evil inclination arising from the asocial aspect of the self, or the transcendent inclination arising from the social aspect of the self. As a source of transcendence—a means for implementing moral action--the reflective faculty may be classified as the action of one system—social interaction—upon another system—human nature (the biologic organism).

Manifestations of Evil and of Transcendence

The fact that George Herbert Mead never published a systematic account of his sociological and ethical theory, that his theory must therefore be reconstructed from the notes and commentaries of his students, lends a certain obscurity to the finer points and details of his system of thought. In terms of the examination of evil and transcendence, this unfortunate obscurity is particularly evident in the area of the causes and effects of evil and transcendence. Hence, in the following sections there will be a relatively greater emphasis on the contributions of his students and critics in order to delineate the more subtle aspects and implications of his social behaviorism.

With regard to the first of the above-mentioned sources of evil—the processual nature of reality—the specific cause of evil is clearly given in the principle of emergence. The destabilizing and disruptive characteristic of reality follows from the ever-existent potential throughout nature for the evolution of totally novel forms—"...from unique combinations of pre-existing elements of older forms...." (Theodorson, 1970:137). The principle of emergence refers to the unpredictable appearance of unique forms which are qualitatively distinguished from antecedent forms, and which cannot be accounted for in casual terms by the world that was there prior to their appearance:

> The emergent, being unpredictable in principle, does not follow logically from the

conditions necessary for its emergence, from what is traditionally called its cause (Miller, 1973:41).

The emergent itself exhibits a causal dimension in that its appearance necessitates adjustments in both the past—in the world that was there as a condition for its appearance, and in the present—in the world that is there as a condition for its existence:

> The world that was there, the past conditions for the emergent, as well as the newly selected future, must take on new characters; and these characters, of course, emanate from emergents, due to the adjustments that are made. Both the living form and its environment are what they are because of adjustment (Miller, 1973:41).

The emergent comprises a problematic phenomenon, unpredictable and incomprehensible in terms of the old world order in which it arose, which renders problematic a segment of that given order, and undermines the continuity of the social processes predicated on that particular segment. The return of this problematic dimension to the given order, and the restoration of the rationality of the world and the continuity of social processes becomes possible only through a reconstruction of the old past—the conditions in which the emergent arose, and of the new present—the conditions in which the emergent now exists—which emanates from the novel nature of the emergent and renders it intelligible. The emergent—like the scientific discovery of an unknown phenomenon in nature—changes the world as it generates adjustments in the givens of past and present which confer a new character on the world by revealing a hitherto unknown aspect of the world. Similarly, a scientific discovery revolutionizes the world by calling forth a new theory which encompasses and explains the nature of the universe preceding the discovery and the transformed universe which ensues from the discovery. The fact that reality—as well as the rest of the natural world—is subject to transformations in the given initiated by emergents—signifies that it conduces to evil in the form of temporary disruptions of social process during the transitional period of adjustment to the novel features of emergent phenomena.

Turning to the second of the identified
sources of evil—the asocial aspect of the self—the
attempt to discover the specific causes of the two-fold
egoistic inclination to disregard the interests of
others (selfishness) and the wider system of interests
(ethnocentrism) is hindered by the obscurity of
Meadian theory with reference to the origins of the
asocial aspect of the self. Although Mead indicates
that this aspect of the self must also be a product of
social interaction, and furthermore, that there are
several possible modes of interaction between self and
others, he does not specify which particular phase of
the interaction process or which mode of interaction is
responsible for the appearance of the asocial self.
For this information it is necessary to examine the
theoretical elaborations of Mead's disciples and
critics. First of all, sociological theory differen-
tiates two general types of relations evoked by the
interaction process, i.e., primary and secondary relations. The former is characteristic of informal
groups, and refers to personalized, long-lasting social relations which are based on frequent contact and
a wide variety of shared interests and activities, in
which individuals perceive and relate to the total personality of the other, value each other as ends rather
than means, and are closely emotionally attached to
each other (Theodorson, 1970:313). The latter is
characteristic of formal groups and refers to impersonal, short-term social relations which are based on
infrequent contact in the interest of performing specific functions, in which individuals perceive and
relate to the other only in terms of the role performed, value each other as instrumental means rather
than as ends, and are devoid of emotional attachment
(Theodorson, 1970:372).

These two distinct types of relations involve, correspondingly, two distinct modes of interaction between self and other. The mode of interaction which induces and sustains primary relations has
been analyzed and classified by Edward Tiryakian as
"authentic" comportment, and by Martin Buber as the
"I-Thou" relation; the mode of interaction which induces and sustains secondary relations has been analyzed and classified by Tiryakian as "inauthentic"
comportment and by Buber as the "I-It" relation.
Following the theoretical formulations of Tiryakian
(1968:75-85) and Buber (1970:56-85)—which effectively
extend and substantiate Meadian concepts—it is proposed that, on the one hand, the "authentic"

132

interaction between self and other in the I-Thou relation is the causal process responsible for the development of the social and altruistic inclination to take
into account the interests of others. On the other
hand, it is suggested that the "inauthentic" interaction between self and other in the I-It relation is
the causal process responsible for the development of
the asocial and egoistic (selfish) inclination to
disregard the interests of others in the construction
of conduct.

Tiryakian considers interaction in the I-It
mode as inauthentic (authentic interaction will be
explained in the section on the causes of transcendence) because it is founded on the a priori definition of the other as an It, a thing, an object, an
alien entity fundamentally different from the perceiving subject or self (Tiryakian, 1968:77). The I
and the It do not relate to each other as equals,
for the a priori definition of the other as something
less than the transcendent I determines the objectifying course of perception and relation. The I-It
mode is a partial relation in which the objectified
other is partitioned into a number of dimensions each
of which is perceived as either relevant or irrelevant
to the purposes of the I, and the discerning I relates
only to the dimensions relevant to its purpose. The
It is defined, perceived, and related to by the I only
in terms of its instrumental value in furthering the
purposes of the I:

> The I-It is a psychological object-relation
> marked by relating to the other in terms
> of and only in terms of functional speci-
> ficity (since an object-for-me is determined
> by specific properties which are instrumen-
> tal for my ends) (Tiryakian, 1968:78).

Since interaction in the I-It mode of secondary relations presupposes and is predicated on the primal dis-
similarity and ontological inequality of I and It,
the personal experience and internalization of such
interaction insures that the conduct of the I will be
constructed on the basis of self-interest only to the
exclusion of the interests of the objectified, depersonalized, alien other. The experience and perception of the self as a transcendent subject over against
the non-transcendent objectified other precludes consideration of other-interest on an equal level with
self-interest. And thus, the asocial aspect of the

133

self with its concomitant egoistic inclination may be considered as a function and manifestation of the de-personalized interaction of the I-It mode.

The causal origins of the second dimension of the asocial aspect of the self—i.e., the ethnocentric attitude which neglects to incorporate the interests of humanity in the construction of behavior on the basis of group-interest—are illuminated by Paul Pfuetze's critical examination of the "generalized other." According to Mead, the generalized other is a product of social interaction, in that it develops in the individual as a generalization of the attitudes of significant others internalized through the process of taking the role of the other. Through the medium of role-taking, the individual internalizes the attitudes of others with whom he or she is involved toward him-self or herself, toward each other, and toward the common group activities in which they all participate. The total configuration of all those attitudes, values, expectations, and definitions comprises the generalized other and represents the world-view common to the group as a whole.

The very significant function of the gen-eralized other is to provide the essential frame of reference for orienting individual thought and be-havior. In this function as the frame of reference, the generalized other acts as an agent of social con-trol—of community control over the individual, since individual thought and conduct is necessarily founded on the given community world-view. The individual perspective consists of an internalization of the group perspective, and conduct constructed on this basis accords with the values of the community. How-ever, as Pfuetze argues, conduct which accords with the values of the community does not also and neces-sarily accord with the universal values of humanity, since the isolated or individual community is not synonymous with the entire human community. Or, from another point of view—and in contrast to Charles W. Morris's interpretation: "...to the degree that the self assumes the role of the generalized other, its values are the values of the social process itself" (Mead, 1967:xxxii)—the generalization of the values internalized by means of role-taking is not synonymous with a generalization of the role-taking process, with the intrinsic value underlying social interaction— i.e., the ever-expanding integration of self and other. As Pfuetze perceptively observes, the world-view and

134

concomitant values received from a community are characteristic of that particular community and reflect and support its unique configuration of interests (Pfuetze, 1954:239-240). The significance of this observation is evinced by the fact of group-conflict—that is, the interests of different communities are frequently antagonistic, and the clash of these interests results, more often than not, in an intensification of group hostility rather than in a harmonious synthesis of competing interests. In fine, although the tendency of the process of interaction is to evoke an expansion of interest from an isolated to a universal basis, Pfuetze contends that the function of the generalized other is to reify the system of isolated interests, and to preclude incorporation of the wider system of interests in which every human group is involved.

Thus, individual internalization of the community perspective in the form of the generalized other imbues the individual self with the isolated interests and values of a particular community, and evokes a commitment to the realization of those interests and values in preference to those of other groups, or of the universal values of the community of humanity. By virtue of the operation of the generalized other, the ethnocentric orientation develops as a second dimension of the asocial aspect of the self, and hence: "Mead's self is not more ethical than the social group which molds the self" (Pfeutze, 1954:355).

Lastly, the third source of evil—the social control of individual reflection and conduct originating in the unconscious assimilation of the established social construction of reality—is manifested in the limiting or restraining influence exerted by the "Me" over the "I." In the dialectical relation between these two dimensions of the self structure, the Me initially makes possible the creative activity of the I through provision of the contents of consciousness or the orienting frame of reference upon which the I's reflective faculty is exercised and developed. The Me furnishes the established community perspective against which the I reacts in a critical fashion. The critical reaction of the I to the existing world-order is given as a tentative hypothesis suggesting partial reconstruction of the status quo in order to redress current injustices of the system. However, the I's critical appraisal and recommendation in turn elicits a modifying or qualifying response from the community,

from the Me. That is, the value or validity of the
revision suggested by the I is determined by testing
the hypothesis within the context of the given reality—the individually-derived recommendation is
subject to the approval or disapproval of the community to which it is addressed. Consequently, if the
implicit assumptions and values of the proposed revision are antithetical to or conflict with the intrinsic assumptions and values of the socially approved status quo, the judgment of the community given
in the response of the Me will be to reject or modify
the proposed revision. Whereas, if the configuration
of values in the recommendation and the status quo
concur, the judgment of the community will be to accept the suggested revisions. The I can, of course,
again react against the negative judgment of the community and the limitations set by the Me, but in any
case, the fundamental process consists of critical
acts initiated by the I in reaction against the status
quo which come under the control of, and are subject
to the limitations imposed by community standards
represented in the Me:

> Every act begins in the form of an "I" and
> usually ends in the form of the "Me." For
> the "I" represents the initiation of the act
> prior to its coming under the control of the
> definitions and expectations of others (the
> "Me").... The "I," being spontaneous and
> propulsive, offers the potentiality for new,
> creative activity. The "Me," being regula-
> tory, disposes the individual to both goal-
> directed activity and conformity. In the
> operation of these aspects of the self, we
> have the basis for, on the one hand, social
> control and, on the other, novelty and inno-
> vation (Meltzer, 1970:11-12).

The I provides the motivation toward critical
reflection and social change which is countered by the
motivation toward mindless conformity and social control provided by the Me. The revolutionary fervor of
the I—which disposes the individual to thorough-going
social change—is tempered by the conservative orientation of the Me—which disposes the individual to
gradual piecemeal social reconstruction. Thus, the
intensity of reflection and the extensity of advocated
social change is regulated by the censoring activity
of the Me representing the existing community standards
and interests.

136

Turning to the alternative issue of the causes of transcendence, the first to be considered are the factors which determine the nature of the self as a social being. As explained in preceding sections, the self is a product of the social interaction process which constitutes the self by means of and in terms of the internalization of the attitudes and values of others, and as such, the values of the self are identified with others, and reflect the underlying values of the social process itself. The internalization of the others takes place by means of reflexive role-taking which is in turn generated by the reciprocal stimulation of self and other characteristic of the significant symbol. The significant symbol is a special type of gesture, and, according to Mead, the function of all gestures—whether symbolic or nonsymbolic—is to stimulate responses and adjustments among the participants in a social act which facilitate completion of the act. Since the significant symbol evokes shared meanings among the participants in an act, it is most effective in expediting the cooperative activity necessary for completion of the act. The facilitation of co-operative social behavior, the arousal of the tendency in individuals to enter each others' perspectives, and to ascertain the intentions of others', and the evocation of shared meanings are functions of the unique nature of the significant symbol. That is, it arouses implicitly and covertly in the individual making it a tendency to respond to his or her own gesture in the same way that the other to whom it is addressed tends to respond explicitly and overtly. The arousal of these analogous responses in the experienced of both self and other constitutes the shared meaning of the symbol or the aspect of the other which is brought into the experience of each participant:

> The means by which the individual "gets outside himself" and takes the attitudes of the other is the language gesture (Miller, 1973:50),

and;

> The content of the other that enters into one personality is the response in the individual which his gesture calls out in the other (Mead, 1967:161).

137

The singular propensity of the significant symbol to evoke similar tendencies to respond in both self and other is, then, the causal factor which makes possible the internalization of others, and the constitution of the self as a social being.

With regard to the causal origins of the altruistic inclination to integrate self-interest and other-interest, and isolated interests with universal interests of the social aspect of the self, it was suggested earlier--following the formulations of Tiryakian and Buber—that the "authentic" interaction between self and other in the I-Thou mode of primary relations is the causal process from which this altruistic tendency develops. According to Tiryakian, the I-Thou mode is authentic because it is grounded on the a priori definition of the other as a transcendent subject like the self, as a being with the same ontological status as the perceiving self (Tiryakian, 1968:77). This a priori recognition of the other as an equal entity determines the self- and other-actualizing course of the ensuing interaction, for in that interaction each participant perceives, responds, and relates to the total being of the other rather than to a selective dimension of the other: "...authenticity is genuine action, or 'depth behavior' which is reflectively carried out in response to the totality of the person..." (Tiryakian, 1968: 77). Each actor perceives and relates to the other as an end-in-himself or herself rather than, as in the I-It mode, as an instrumental means for furthering the actor's purposes. Each actor enters into the other's perspective with the intention to understand the other, and assimilates the other's perspective into his or her own. The reflected appraisal of the other reveals each actor to himself or herself as a transcendent subject—which validates and confirms the self-conception—and the incorporation of the other's experience and perspective expands, enriches, and actualizes each actor's self. Interaction is thus predicated on and proceeds through—not manipulation—but identification with the other. Hence, the interests of the other become an integral part of each actor's perspective, self-interest is identified with other-interest, and narrow interests are expanded to encompass wider interests. The experience and internalization of interaction in the I-Thou mode of primary relations—which presupposes and is constructed on the basis of identification of self and other—ensures that the conduct of each participant will

138

manifest an integration of self-interest and the interests of other, an integration of narrow interests with the wider system of interests, and thus the social self and its altruistic inclinations may be considered a function of the authentic interaction between I and Thou.

In searching for the causal origins of the third source of transcendence—the reflective faculty—it becomes apparent that the creative component of the self—the I—furnishes the crucial impetus to reflection. As noted previously, it is the critical reaction of the I against the Me which counterbalances the tendency to mindless conformity. The I is the medium which enables and motivates individuals to question, criticize, and reform their society. The I as well as the Me is a product of socialization into the societal world-view, and it "...develops as a response to the attitudes of the social community, internalized as the 'me'" (Theodorson, 1970:193). The creative and crucial nature of the I's impulsive and spontaneous response to the societal world-view is a function of two things: (1) the unique individuality of every human being, and (2) the unpredictable or emergent character of the reflective process. That is, although every individual self reflects the general social process from which it derives, the constellation of interactions surrounding any individual self is unique to that self, and hence its internalization and reflection of the whole social process is given in terms of a specific and unique vantage point within that process.

Individuality is thus socially constituted, and the reflective response of any individual to the world-view or activities of the community arises from a distinctive vantage-point unique to that individual. Secondly, although the reflective faculty represented in the I is exercised and developed in relation to the pre-determined context of the societal world-view embodied in the Me, the direction of reflection—or the response of the I to the community—is unpredictable, unique, and novel. The evaluative examination of the community in terms of the logical and intuitive projection of its potentials and alternatives for development in the imagination bypasses and goes beyond the community's existing boundaries, limitations, and injustices. In this imaginative projection, the existing community is compared to the potential community, which comparison indicates the nature of

necessary reforms. Every individual thus perceives and responds to the given world-view of the
community from a unique vantage-point within the community. On the basis of this particular perception,
he or she reflectively anticipates possibilities for
the community which could not occur to any other individual in the same community, and in this fashion, reflection on the given transcends the restrictions imposed on reflection by the given.

Moving to the subject of the effects of
these several causes of evil and of transcendence,
Meadian theory specifically designates only one such
manifestation, i.e., the phenomena of impulses. Mead
observes that there are two kinds of impulses:

> ...those which lead to social co-operation,
> and those which lead to social antagonism
> among individuals; those which give rise to
> friendly attitudes and relations, and those
> which give rise to hostile attitudes and
> relations... (Mead, 1967:303-304).

As such, these good and evil impulses reflect and constitute the manifestation of, on the one hand, the altruistic orientation of the social aspect of the self
toward integration with others, and on the other hand,
the egoistic orientation of the asocial aspect of the
self toward opposition to others. Evil impulses are
those which are self-defeating, which diminish and
inhibit the expression of other impulses, which detract from our social relations through the exclusion
of other-interest in self-interest, which inhibit
self-actualization as objectification of the other
eventually becomes self-objectification, and which
thus are destructive of the well-being of society.
Good or transcendent impulses, conversely, are those
which are self-reinforcing, which strengthen and
stimulate the expression of other impulses, which enhance our social relations through assimilation of
other-interest into self-interest, which are conducive
to self-actualization as the self is confirmed in the
reflected appraisal of the other, and which thus contribute to the welfare of society.

According to Mead, then, the manifestations
of evil and transcendence appear as phenomena which
are, on the one hand, antithetical and destructive of
the operating principle of the social interaction
process (i.e., evil), and on the other hand, accord

with and support the operating principle of social interaction (transcendent). Likewise, the effect of the significant symbol—through which the self is constituted as a social being—appears as a continuing identification and integration of self and other which sustains social relations, and conduces to the well-being of society. The effect of the I's impulse to critical reflection is manifested in moral actions directed toward the reconstruction of the social order which maintains society's dynamic adaptability. Conversely, the effect of the evil emergence of the problematic from the given appears as a temporary but troublesome disruption of the continuity of social life. The tendency to thoughtless conformity to the established societal world-view diminishes and undermines society's vital adaptability, thus conducing to stagnation and decay. The manifestations of evil and transcendence also and necessarily reflect the social origins of human life.

Processes of Evil and of Transcendence

Within the context of Meadian theory, it is evident that the social interaction process or one of the derivatives thereof (i.e., the self, the I, the me, the reflective faculty, etc.) is the principal medium through which any phenomenon emerges. In the case of evil, the process of its manifestation begins with the individual experience and internalization of the inauthentic I-It mode of interaction of secondary relations from which arises the asocial aspect of the self and its intrinsic egoistic orientation. This, in turn, forms the base for the construction of actions contrary to the implicit integrating principle of social interaction—of actions in accord with self-interest to the exclusion of other-interest, and which are thus the means for the expression of evil impulses.

When an individual acts in this fashion, the imaginative prevision of his or her gestures entails: (1) visualization of the other as a depersonalized object whose inconsequential interests are to be disregarded, and which is only important as a means of achieving the actor's own aims or self-interests; and (2) observation of the sequence of gestures conducive to manipulation of the other in accord with self-interest. The other becomes aware of the meaning of the actor's manipulative intentions and gestures through the responses evoked in himself or herself, and thus he or she is revealed to himself or herself as an instrumental object, whose own interests are insignificant or negligible. This depersonalized and devalued reflected appraisal reduces the other's self-esteem, decreases awareness of self as an active, volitional, and significant agent, and hence diminishes the capacity for authentic interaction. When the onto- logical significance of his or her own being, and the value of personal interests are thus diminished for the other, he or she ceases to pursue personal goals, and withdraws from active participation in the co-operative social activities which sustain the community life. Moreover, the other's now depersonalized and devalued self-conception interferes with and distorts also his or her perception of the actor, so that the actor is likewise reflected back to himself or herself as an objectified entity with inconsequential interests, and is also inclined to withdraw from the essential co- operative activities of community life. Paradoxically, but in consonance with the social origins of human na- ture, the egoistic pursuit of self-interest is self- defeating, is injurious to the self as well as the other, and undermines the coordination of individual activities necessary to the harmonious functioning of community life.

With regard to the transcendence of evil, the reflective faculty figures as the crucial factor. That is, when individuals examine and evaluate the probable consequences of their intended actions—selfish or altruistic—or the probable consequences of society's activities--ethnocentric or universalistic--the imaginative completion of an intended act reveals to them the injurious and undesirable consequences of selfish or ethnocentric actions, and the beneficial and desirable consequences of altruistic or univer- salistic actions. Reflective prevision exposes the essential functionality of integrating self/narrow interests with other/wider interests. This beneficial integration of interests--or from another view, escape from a traumatic and debilitating conflict of interests in terms of either individual or collective life--is achieved by the individual through a reflective con- struction in the imagination of a social system (self with other, or group with other groups) in which all the competing and conflicting interests are integrated and harmoniously achieved. That is, individuals imaginatively anticipate what a social system would have to be like in order to include and attain all the divergent interests, and this reflective construc- tion indicates to them the ways in which their

personalities or their society must be reconstructed
to implement a maximum integration of interests.

Imaginative reflection upon the given
system—of personality or society—exposes the existing deficiencies or injustices of the system, and
designates the reconstructions necessary for transcendence or elimination of the system's limitations.
Individuals who recognize and accept the implications
of such a revealing vision construct their conduct
with reference to that vision—their lives are grounded
in, and guided by belief in a better society. Mead
contends that individuals are the agents of social
change and moral progress—that it is through their reflective responses to the community that the community
itself is improved. Transcendence of individual egoism and societal ethnocentrism takes place through individual reflective projection of a wider and better
social system:

> The group advances from the old standards
> toward another standard; and what is im-
> portant from the standpoint of morality is
> that this advance takes place through the in-
> dividual, through a new type of individual...
> this new individual appears as the represen-
> tative of a different social order...he con-
> ceives of himself as belonging to another
> social order which ought to take the place
> of the old one (Mead, 1967:386).

Consequences of Evil and of Transcendence

With respect to the ultimate destiny of the
human race as it is decided in the struggle between
the forces of evil and of transcendence, Mead optimistically anticipated the triumph of the forces of
transcendence. However, an objective review of the
various contending powers indicates instead a relative
balance between evil and transcendence. Specifically,
forces of transcendence are manifested in: (1) the
incorporation of the integrative universalistic value
of the social process into the constitution of the self
as a social being; (2) the inclination toward co-
operative and integrative behavior arising from the
social aspect of the self; and (3) the conscientious
exercise of critical reflection generated by the I.
Conversely, the countervailing forces of evil are
manifested in: (1) the internalization of the par-
ticularistic values of the community into the Me and

143

the generalized other; (2) the inclination toward egoistic and antagonistic behavior arising from the
asocial aspect of the self; (3) the control and restriction of critical reflection imposed by the Me as
the agent of the community.

Thus, a catalogue of the identifiable sources
of evil and transcendence does not substantiate Mead's
happy vision with a greater weight of power on the
side of transcendence, but neither does it portend the
apocalypse with greater power on the side of evil. A
fortuitous deadlock seems best to summarize the existing balance of power. But assuming that this balance
were to shift in the direction of transcendence, then,
according to Meadian theory, the consequences for the
human race ensuing from the universalizing tendency
of the social process would be manifested as the emergence of a unity of humanity. In this case, every individual, reflecting the integrative value of social
interaction in the structure of self, would be able,
and would in fact understand and identify with his or
her neighbor, and would value the interests of others
as much as his or her own. Every self would be actualized through authentic interaction with others.
Responsible moral conduct in regard to other individuals
and society as a whole would be considered a privilege
as well as a duty. Finally, critical reflection
on the givens of personality and society would be con-
scientiously utilized to remedy the deficiencies of
either system, and to expedite the correlative maximum
development of self and society. Thus, the integrating operation of the social interaction process culminates in the realization of a universal community
founded upon every individual's "...conscious identification with and participation in the society of man as
such" (Mead, 1967:xxxiv).

On the other hand, were the balance to shift
in favor of evil, the consequences for humanity, in
Mead's view, would include an inhibition or decrease
in the possibilities for self-actualization ensuing
from inauthentic interaction with others. A disastrous disruption of the social activities of community
life would arise from intensification and predominance
of antagonistic attitudes. Community life would be
disrupted by the egoistic pursuit of self-interest to
the exclusion of other-interests, and by irresponsible
and immoral conduct in the form of deliberately uncritical conformity to societal dictates. Finally,
abrogation of the moral obligation of critical

reflection would culminate in an absorption of individual will into the collective will, destruction of society's vital adaptability, and the decline of society into barbarism. As Paul Pfuetze succinctly observes: "We have established the fact that without free, responsible selves society itself withers at the roots" (Pfuetze, 1954:348).

CHAPTER 11: Concluding Remarks on the Perspective of Social Psychology

Though it may seem somewhat unusual to juxtapose a psychologist and a social psychologist in one section, the comnination of Rollo May and George Herbert Mead is justified on the ground that their respective theories are based on similar domain assuptions. Specifically, both assume a causal interdependence of self and society. Secondly, both perceive the unique nature of human consciousness as an ethical consciousness. Thirdly, on the basis of their scientific theories, each seeks to develop an ethical theory. Briefly reviewing the basic tenets of their respective theories, it is evident that since both consider the development and exercise of ethical consciousness as the ultimate good, each defines evil and transcendence in terms of phenomena either detrimental or conducive to that development. For Mead, according to whom the social is the source of the ethical, evil is defined as phenomena destructive of the process of social interaction, and transcendence as phenomena conducive to that fundamental process. For May, according to whom ethical awareness is an innate though latent quality of human nature, evil is defined as predispositions in human nature and social reality which interfere with the expansion of consciousness/ethical sensitivity, and transcendence as factors in human nature and social reality which facilitate this expansion. Both assume the causal interdependence of self and society, though May emphasizes the primacy of human nature (self), whereas for Mead the social interaction process has causal priority.

Regarding the sources of evil, both emphasize a transaction between systems of reality or the components of systems although the specific demensions involved vary considerably. That is, May identifies as the source of evil the interaction of a component of human nature (the tendency to pseudoinnocence) and a component of social reality (the loss of a center of values in society), and the source of transcendence, similar-

ly, as the transformation of inimical conditions in
social reality (component of social reality) effected
by the manifestation of authentic innocence (component
of human nature). In the Meadian world, there are
three discernible sources of both evil and of transcendence. The sources of evil are: (1) the mutable nature of reality (action of one system—social reality—
on another system—social interaction), (2) the asocial
aspect of the self (action of component of one system
—asocial aspect of the self/system of social interaction—upon another component of the same system—integrating operation of interaction process), (3) unconscious internalization of the given social construction
of reality (action of component of one system—socializa-
tion/social interaction—upon another component of the
same system—the self/social interaction system). The
sources of transcendence are: (1) the self as a social
being (action of one system—social interaction—upon
another system—human nature), (2) social aspect of
the self (action of component of one system—social aspect of self/social interaction—upon another component
of the same system—integrating operation of interaction process), (3) the faculty of reflection (action of
one system—social interaction—upon another system
(human nature).

The manifestations of evil and transcendence
are again identified in terms of phenomena relating to
the development of ethical awareness. According to
May, evil is mainfested in the symptoms of mental illness which entail a deterioration of ethical consciousness, and transcendence is manifested as an increase in
ethical sensitivity. According to Mead, evil appears
as behavior contrary to the integrating principle of
social interaction, and transcendence as behavior
which accords with that principle. The processes by
which evil and transcendence become manifest, for both
May and Mead, involve individual decision as a crucial
factor. May contends that evil results when the individual chooses to assume the attitude of pseudoinnocence, and voluntarily becomes a victim of the societal
confusion of values, where as transcendence occurs when
the individual chooses to enact the attitude of authentic innocence, and transcends the upheavals of values
peculiar to his or her time. Mead maintains that evil
results from the individual's deliberate manipulation
of the other which eventually leads to the objectification of self as well as other, and that transcendence
follows from the individual's conscientious critical
reflection upon the givens of personality and society.

Finally, both May and Mead identify the consequences of evil and transcendence in terms of the fate of the distinctly human ethical awareness. That is, May predicts as the consequences of evil the decline into mental illness with its noncomitant deterioration of ethical sensitivity, and the consequences of transcendence as the preservation of mental health with the concomitant amplification of ethical sensitivity. Similarly, Mead predicts the culmination of evil in the inhibition and minimization of self-actualization with a concomitant decline of society into barbarism, and envisions the culmination of transcendence in the maximum correlative development of the potentials of self and society culminating in a unity of humanity.

With regard to the central issue of human judgment, both May and Mead are genuinely optimistic, since both conceive of ethical consciousness as an intrinsic component of the self structure. According to May, this ethical sensitivity arises from the reflexive, reflective, and empathetic aspects of consciousness. Ethical awareness and behavior is thus predicated on the imaginative perception and understanding of the effects of one's actions on the other—as one identifies with the other and feels the meaning of one's own action toward the other—and the construction of action in accord with the welfare of others. May summarizes this ability as follows:

> Man can "look before and after." He can transcend the immediate moment, can remember the past and plan for the future, and thus choose a good which is greater, but will not occur till some future moment in preference to a lesser, immediate one. By the same token he can feel himself into someone else's needs and desires, can imagine himself in the other's place, and so make him choices with a view to the good of his fellows as well as himself. This is the beginning of the capacity, however imperfect and rudimentary it may be in most people, to "love thy neighbor" and to be aware of the relation between their own acts and the welfare of the community (May, 1967:151).

This ethical awareness—the recognition of the beneficial or harmful effects of one's actions on others—according to May, is invariably aroused in interpersonal interaction—a process which essentially consists of the coordination of individual action with the actions of others. This coordination of activities necessarily requires an identification with the other in order to anticipate his or her intentions, to judge the effects of one's actions toward him or her, and thus to previse one's activity in line with the activity of the other. Thus, awareness of the benefit or harm the other experiences as a result of one's action ensues from taking the role of the other, the necessary identification with the other. Social interaction not only stimulates awareness of moral consequences of actions, but also awareness of the societal values which implicitly structure the interaction by informing the construction of individual acts. The recognition of these values and the consequences which follow allows for, and impels individual evaluation of the validity of the values. Additional impetus for such evaluation is provided by conflictual situations which generate problematic doubt in regard to the values and assumptions that comprise the "givens" of one's world-view.

Since, as may contends, social interaction and conflictual situations are inevitable experiences endemic to human existence, ethical awareness is likewise inevitable. The existence and exercise of human judgment, therefore, is unavoidable and can be taken for granted, but whether the aroused ethical awareness is actually used to guide conduct is a matter of individual decision—the moral choice between innocence and pseudoinnocence. Human beings are intrinsically responsible for the good and evil that ensue from their own actions and from their society, but whether they accept and live according to this responsibility depends upon a personal decision, and is a function of the dynamics of individual personality. Nevertheless, according to May's perspective, ignorance is not an excuse but a reflection of deliberate negligence:

> The future lies with the man or woman who can live as an individual, conscious within the solidarity of the human race. He then uses the tension between individuality and solidarity as the source of his ethical creativity.... We must accept responsibility for whether we are right or wrong (May, 1972:254),

and:

We are responsible for the effects of our actions, and we are also responsible for becoming as aware as we can of these effects (May,
1972:259).

Thus, the faculty and function of human judgment can
be taken for granted as an innate quality which is
brought to fruition by invariable and universal social
processes. Human beings are responsible and can be
held accountable for the evil effects of their actions
and of their society's actions--to the extent that they
have been able to become aware to those effects. But,
the unresolved question is thus, what is the extent of
their awareness? and further, how can this be determined, for instance, in a court of law?

        In a similar fashion, Mead constructed a de-
manding ethical theory based on the crucial assumption
that human consciousness is inherently and inescapably
ethical consciousness. Essentially, he contends that
the ethicality of human beings is a function of their
sociality--that ethical awareness arises inevitably
from universal and fundamental social processes--from,
that is, reflexive role-taking, role-taking, and reflective activities. Through reflexive role-taking
individuals come to perceive themselves through the
eyes of others as objects, are enabled to observe themselves in interaction with others, and learn to evaluate themselves in a positive or negative (good/tran-
scendent or evil) fashion according to this reflected
appraisal. Through role-taking they enter into the
other's perspective, and become aware of the effect of
their own actions upon the other by experiencing the
other's cognitive and affective reactions. Through re-
flection--or the imaginative prevision of action, they
realize before the fact the probable consequences of
their intended actions. By virtue, then, of this knowledge of the other, and foreknowledge of the ends of
their acts, humans are able to predict, and know in
advance the beneficial or harmful effect they will direct toward others.

        The control which they thus exert over their
own behavior signifies that humans are morally responsible for the effects of their actions on others, for
the goodness or evilness of their motives toward others,
and moreover, for the conscientious utilization of the
reflective faculty as a guide to moral conduct. That

151

is, having the ability to reflect--to consciously construct moral action--they are morally obligated to exercise that faculty. Mead does not naively assume that people always and necessarily apply this reflective faculty, but contends that people are ethically obligated to do so--for the welfare of both themselves as individuals, and for the well-being of society. Thus, Mead assumes that human beings possess free will in this respect--they do necessarily become aware of their ethical sensitivity, but whether or not this sensitivity is used as a guide in the construction of conduct is a matter of individual choice and decision. Nevertheless, because of the social dependence of all individuals and of self and society, human beings are morally culpable for the failure to exercise this faculty: "It is as social beings that we are moral beings" (Mead, 1967:385).

Thus, Mead agrees with May that the faculty and function of human judgment can be taken for granted. Moreover, because human beings possess the reflective faculty, they are morally cupable for the evil which they perpetrate unwittingly as well as wittingly, since the former constitutes a deliberate negligence or abrogation of moral responsibility.

PART FIVE:

THE PERSPECTIVE OF SOCIAL PHILOSOPHY

CHAPTER 12: Herbert Marcuse

Introduction

It is from Marx that the sociology of knowledge derived its root proposition—that
man's consciousness is determined by his
social being (Berger and Luckmann, 1967:5-6).

He emphasized that human knowledge is given
in society as an a priori to individual experience, providing the latter with its order
of meaning. This order, although it is relative to a particular socio-historical situation, appears to the individual as the natural way of looking at the world. Scheler
called this the "relative-natural world view"
... of a society... (Berger and Luckmann,
1967:8).

You say that science itself will then teach
man...that as a matter of fact he possesses
neither will nor uncontrollable desires, and
never has done, and that he himself is nothing more than a sort of piano-key or organ-
stop and that, in addition there are the laws
of nature in the world; so that whatever he
does is not done of his own will at all, but
of itself, according to the laws of nature.
Consequently, as soon as these laws of nature
are discovered, man will no longer have to
answer for his actions and will find life
exceedingly easy. All human actions will
then, no doubt, be computed according to
these laws, mathematically, something like
the tables of logarithms, up to 108,000 and
indexed accordingly. Or, better still, certain well-intentioned words will be published, something like our present encyclopaedic
dictionaries, in which everything will be
calculated and specified with such an

exactitude that there will be no more independent actions or adventures in the world
(Dostoevsky, no date:129-130).

...the piracy theory served only to dodge one
of the fundamental problems posed by crimes
of this kind, namely, that they were, and
could only be, committed under a criminal law
and by a criminal state (Arendt, 1973:262).

"I'm afraid I don't understand again," Alyo-
sha interrupted. "Is he being ironical, is
he laughing?"
"Not in the least. You see, he glories in
the fact that he and his followers have at
last vanquished freedom and have done so in
order to make man happy" (Dostoevsky,
1958:294).

...You want to go into the world and you are
going empty-handed, with some promise of
freedom, which men in their stupidity and
their innate lawlessness cannot even compre-
hend, which they fear and dread—for nothing
has ever been more unendurable to man and to
human society than freedom! And do you see
the stones in this parched and barren desert?
Turn them into loaves, and mankind will run
after you like a flock of sheep, grateful and
obedient, though forever trembling with fear
that you might withdraw your hand and they
would no longer have your loaves (Dostoevsky,
1958:296).

As the preceding quotations from Berger and
Luckmann indicate, the discipline of Sociology is
grounded in the principal domain assumption of the causal and explanatory primacy of society or social reality. The multitudinous manifestations of human nature
are considered to be functions of various societal
forces. According to the sociological world-view, human nature arises within a social context, and the direction of its development depends upon the vicissitudes of that context. The potentialities which may be
implicit in human nature are maximally or minimally realized according to the facilitating or inhibiting influence of catalytic societal conditions. Thus, the
final destingy of human beings, in terms of the complete realization of the species' uniquely human qualities, or the fatal elimination of these qualities—as

Dostoevsky illustrated in the polemical Notes from the Underground—is determined by the predominace of antithetical social forces. If the progressive humanization of human beings is defined as the ultimate good, and their utter dehumanization as the ultimate evil, and if society is indeed the decisive determinant of human destiny, then society as a whole can be evaluated in terms of good and evil, as conducive to good and evil, and finally, as good or evil in itself.

The possibility, moreover, the reality of society as evil, has been demonstrated in this century in the destructiveness of "a criminal state"—i.e., the Nazi regime (Arendt, 1973:262). Whatever the source and manifestation of societal evil—whether it arises from the mode of production prevalent in a society, or from a specific societal institution such as bureaucracy, whether it is expressed as the surrepticious psychological dehumanization of a total population—as Marcuse (1966) observes to be the case in advanced industrial society, or in the physical destruction of a specific group of people—as in the Nazi extermination of the Jews—it is imperative to recognize that the moral concepts of good and evil, and the legal implications of these concepts which apply to individual behavior apply also to the society which condones or which generates evil behavior. That is, in Berdyaev's words, "Society itself stand in need of moral evaluation and presupposes the distinction between good and evil" (Berdyaev, 1945:21). Yet, according to the logic of the sociological perspective, individual moral evaluation of society is precluded by the societal determination of human nature. If individuals in fact receive the value-laden precepts and knowledge of the world from society as an a priori to individual experience, then their own existence is identified with and constitutes a replica of the collective life, and transcendence of society is therefore rendered impossible. Thus, apparently, if the society is good, individuals will consequently be good, and if the society is evil, individuals will be evil. The means of transition from the societal determination to the societal destruction of human nature was revealed by Dostoevsky in his "Legend of the Grand Inquisitor" (1958:288-311). According to this legend, the Inquisitor and his followers corrected Christ's work by rejecting the miracle of the human's divine free will in order to establish universal happiness on earth. The creation of happiness at the expense of the sacrifice of freedom was the theme of Dostoevsky's passionate denunciation of the Catholic

157

Church, and this is also a main theme of Herbert Marcuse's critique of contemporary society.

Definitions of Evil and of Transcendence

With the concept of one-dimensionality, Marcuse symbolizes the debilitating effect of an evil society on human nature. He defines evil in the modern world in terms of the societal domination of human beings effected through socialization into a dehumanizing one-dimensional mode of being which inhibits the "free development of human needs and faculties" (Marcuse, 1966:ix), subverts the creative and critical reflective process, and reduces humans to the ontological status of things, instrumental automations in service of existing institutions. This form of societal determination and eventual destruction arises from, and is maintained by the institutions of domination, the interests of which, Marcus contends, are served by the perpetuation of scarcity, poverty, the servitude of humans in the struggle for exitence, and the transformation of the individual from a free, creative agent to a veritable puppet of society. Thus, Marcuse identifies the predominant mode of being generated by modern society as one-dimensional, and defines this phenomenon as evil because

> ...it does not lead to the greatest rational use of productive forces, to the elimination of war, to the "pacification of the struggle for existence," to the maximization of emotional and cultural values (Marks, 1970:90).

Given his perception of the dehumanization ensuing from societal domination, Marcus defines the transcendence of evil, by contrast, as liberation from servitude in an unnecessary struggle for existence imposed by the institutions of domination. This liberation is effected through the rational utilization of technological resources to abolish scarcity, poverty, and superfluous labor, which would thus free human beings to develop and expand their unique needs and faculties.

Locus of Causality

In agreement with the sociological perspective presented in the Introduction, Marcuse assumes the distinctively social context of human life to be the origin of human nature, thus identifying social reality

158

as the primal locus of causality. While granting, on the one hand, that social life constitutes the essential condition for the progressive humanization of the species, Marcuse focuses his analysis on the antithetical potentiality of modern society to dominate, and eventually destroy the species' embryonic humanity. He traces this destructive potential to invisible institutions of domination which covertly undermine and redirect the ostensibly humanizing process of socialization. According to Marcuse, the inimical influence of societal domination is responsible for the contemporary version of the final socialization, the perversion of human nature in the form of one-dimensionality. This conception of societal causality has been summarized by Robert Marks:

> Private disorder today, reflects the disorder of society as a whole; and the cure of personal disorder requires, more than ever before, a cure of the general disorder (Marks, 1970:41).

Sources of Evil and of Transcendence

Although the institutionalization of rationality has been perhaps the most remarkable attainment of industrial society, Marcuse contends that the rational development of technological resources in such societies becomes irrational precisely at the point where it creates new and greater possibilities for the progress of humanization. At that point, it becomes possible to greatly reduce or even to eliminate much of the human involvement in the labor process, and consequently, to free people to explore, and pursue other avenues of advancement. However, such an achievement, Marcuse argues, is detrimental to the vested interests of those who control the various institutions of domination. On the contrary, these interests are served by the perpetuation of the struggle for existence. The defensive reaction of those who control the institutions to the emerging freedom from the economy is manifested in the establishment of an irrational organization of the means of production. This mode of organization is irrational in the sense that it inhibits the immanently liberating technical innovations, and promulgates instead the continuation of human labor. This dichotomous goal is implemented through the generation of false needs which can be satisfied by the products of the irrational mode of production. Technology is transformed into an instrument of domination as it is used to create the false needs, to inculcate

159

these needs in individuals, to provide for the satisfaction of these needs, and in this fashion to promote psychological and material happiness while simultaneously undermining individual freedom.

Despite its inevitably harmful consequences for human beings, the system of the irrational organization of production is both self-validating and self-sustaining. That is, by virtue of its impressive record of increasing productivity and the creation of affluence, the system satisfactorily provides for the (false) needs of more and more individuals, and thus binds them affectively to the system and the society. The creation and extension of affluence not only demonstrates the beneficial efficiency of the system, but further, eliminates the overt evidence of societal inequality, poverty, and misery which in previous times stimulated the recognition and rebellion against societal evils. Thus, the evil society protects itself against the awareness of destructive domination, and assimilates the potential sources of conflict into the irrational system by cultivating the tantalizing vision of "an ever-more-comfortable life for an ever-growing number of people" (Marcuse, 1966:23). The source of evil, then, according to Marcuse's analysis, is identified as the action of the irrational organization of production—which is a component of the social structure—upon the mode of thought and feeling—which is a component of human nature.

With respect to the phenomenon of transcendence of the evil one-dimensionality, Marcuse is conspicuously vague—and it is difficult to determine whether this ambiguity derives from deficiencies in theoretical construction, or from an inadequate understanding of his analysis, or whether it reflects accurately a genuinely problematic aspect of social reality. It seems logically paradoxical that Marcuse, on the one hand, exposes the disastrous subversion of rational and critical thought as as integral aspect of the socially induced one-dimensional mode of being, and then contends, on the other hand, that this subversion is to be counteracted by an expansion of rational and critical consciousness—as Robert Marks phrses it: "Marcuse's remedy is to oppose one-dimensionality with negativity" (Marks, 1970:128). This is, to say the least, logically inconsistent, since it is precisely the capacity for negative thinking or critical consciousness which is being eliminated by the development of one-dimensionality. It may be, however, that

Marcuse assumes this apparent inconsistency will be resolved as a result of an ever-increasing disparity between the potential technological resources of a society and the actual uses of these resources. That is, as one of Marcuse's critics observes:

> Industrial society is highly rational in the development of its technological resources; it becomes irrational when the success of these efforts opens up new dimensions of social well-being. This is the internal contradiction of the civilization (Marks, 1970: 68).

Perhaps the increase in this internal contradiction between the development of technological innovations which could render human labor unnecessary and the actual restricted and distorted utilization of these resources to perpetuate human labor is to function as a material, structural stimulus of critical consciousness, of negative thinking. If this material contradiction does indeed expose the discrepancy between the actuality and the potentiality of the society, it may thus raise doubt concerning the established givens of the society, generate reflection on the given, and eventually lead to the recognition of societal domination, and the evil consequences of such domination. If this is the case, then the function of negative thinking will be to cease to rationalize the irrational. That is, negative thinking must stimulate recognition that the irrational organization of production is the source of evil, and that this mode of production provides happiness at the price of freedom through the inculcation of false needs. Such an understanding would lead to a reorganization of the means of production that maximizes societal rationality through the utilization of available technological resources to eliminate unnecessary labor, and liberates people to pursue other avenues of humanization. Thus, the emergence of negativity facilitates the rational use of technology in the interest of freedom. The source of transcendence of evil, then, is conceived as the action of negative thinking (a component of human nature) on the mode of production (a component of social reality).

Manifestations of Evil and of Transcendence

Marcuse distinguishes several characteristic aspects of one-dimensional thought. First of all, it

161

entails an inability to perceive beyond the overtly functional features of an evil society to the hidden dysfunctional elements. Secondly, one-dimensionality involves a cognitive immunity to the possibility of alternatives to the status quo. Thirdly, this mode of thought includes an unquestioning and uncritical acceptance of societal givens, which is supported by an affective identification with the existing system. Finally, these several components of one-dimensionality culminate in a thorough-going conformity to the requirements of society. One-dimensionality, thus, involves a radical subversion of the reflective processes, and a transformation of consciousness. While this subversion originates in the irrational organization of the means of production, the specific factors of social life which are conducive to one-dimensionality are many and diverse. With regard to the false needs already mentioned, Marcuse cites as examples:

> ...the overwhelming need for the production and consumption of waste; the need for stupefying work where it is no longer a real necessity; the need for modes of relaxation which soothe and prolong this supefication; the need for maintaining such deceptive liberties as free competition at administered prices, a free press which censors itself... (Marcuse, 1966:7).

The creation and inculcation of these false needs—which expedite human servitude to labor—is directed by the institutions of politics, business, and the mass media. Marcuse emphasizes the significance of this psychological manipulation as a means of social control: "The very mechanism which ties the individual to his society has changed, and social control is anchored in the new needs which it has produced" (Marcuse, 1966:9). The promulgation and satisfaction of such false material needs displaces and represses the awareness of the true need for freedom. Similarly, the diffusion of affluence and the prospect of an ever-improving life reduces the utility of freedom, undermines the position of the socially disenfranchised as the negation of the society, and with this the usefulness of conflict or protest, thus facilitating the assimilation of all sectors of the population into the "good" society, Indeed, the very awareness of being in a negative positon with respect to the society is obliterated by the conditions of labor in modern society which induce passivity rather than sensitivity:

162

The rhythm of production in a semi-automated
factory, the nature of skilled work, the increase in the proportion of white-collar
workers all destroy any consciousness of being
in opposition to the work system (MacIntyre,
1970:73).

Another development which Marcuse cites as
significant in promoting one-dimensionality consists of
the "liquidation of two-dimensional culture" (Marcuse,
1966:57). He conceives of culture, specifically art
and literature, as implicitly transcendent—as providing an "other dimension" in contrast to the reality of
the status quo. Traditionally, art and literature symbolize, and evoke the awareness of ideals antithetical
and alternative to the given reality, functioning as an
impetus to critical relection, protest, conflict, and
social change in the interest of improving the human
condition. However, in advanced industrial society, the
transcendent power immanent in the antimony between the
other dimension of culture and social reality, and symbolized in the evocative ideals, is obliterated as
these ideals are incorporated into the established social construction of reality. The refusal of culture
to come to terms with existing reality is negated
as the cultural ideals are assimilated into the established reality, and as this assimilation is justified
on the grounds of the progress of the society in ameliorating human life through technological advancement.
Consequently, one of the primary sources of transcendent consciousness, of negative thinking, is thereby
eliminated.

In a similar vein, Marcuse argues that a nullification of transcendent consciousness ensues from
the "functionalization of language" (Marcuse, 1966:87),
and a trend toward rigid empiricism in scientific method—manifested as operationalism in the physical sciences, and behaviorism in the social sciences (Marcuse,
1966:12). Both of these trends entail an emphasis on
the unambiguity, clarity, and exactness of concepts,
the result of which is a narrow restriction of meaning
to the given facts, and the exclusion of implicit alternatives. These trends in language and in science
are both conducive to a "...concreteness (which) prevents reflective, critical thoughts about the realities
referred to" (MacIntyre, 1970:76), and which hence sustains the uncritical attitude and mindless conformity
of one-dimensional people. The final effect of these
various mechanisms of social control is, of course, the
institutionalization and maintenance of one-dimension-

163

ality which Marcuse summarizes as "a more progressive stage of alienation" (Marcuse, 1966:11). Individuals willingly participate in the irrational system of production which satisfies their needs, and offers the prospect of an even better future. They identify with the society which exhibits as its own the ideals falsely appropriated from the other dimension of culture. They conform happily to the irrational requirements of the society which has undermined the consciousness of opposition. They accept without question or doubt the social construction of reality which has been emptied of all its antagonistic, antithetical, transcendent concepts.

In attempting to trace the specific causes of transcendence of evil in Marcuse's analysis, the validity of Martin Jay's succinct comment:

> ...the key problem of how change might occur in a society that controlled the consciousness of its members remained a troubling element in much of Marcuse's later work, especially One-Dimensional Man (Jay, 1973:59)

has become ever more apparent. That is, Marcuse does not identify a single structure or process which can effectively oppose and overcome societal evil. He does designate a few developments which may, possibly, perhaps in combination, exert sufficient opposition— but even these are susceptible to the pernicious influences emanating from the irrational organization of production. As has been stated above, transcendence of evil—within the framework of Marcuse's analysis—consists of human liberation from slavery in the work world, and from the one-dimensional mode of thought and being this world imposes. Whereas the labor which ensues from the irrational organization of production is oriented toward the satisfaction of false needs, Marcuse contends that the true function of labor—rationally organized—should be to satisfy vital human needs. At base, freedom from want—in terms of the satisfaction of vital needs—is the essential precondition for freedom. Thus, if human beings are to be freed from labor in order to develop their human qualities, these vital needs must somehow be provided. This provision is possible, he argues, with the expansion of automation. Automation constitutes a catalytic force which can effect the transformation of the irrational organization of production which satisfies false needs into a rational organization of production which satisfies vital needs.

The transformation through automation of labor will occur as the advancement of technology reaches a dialectical turning point. At that point, the continuation of technological development will require a thorough-going reorientation and redirection of the utilization of technology. Specifically, further progress will depend upon a radical reconceptualization of labor as a function of machines rather than of people, and a consequent application of technology to the mechanization of labor. According to Marcuse, this drastic reconceptualization and automation of labor necessitated by the progress of technology will reinstitute the rationality of the system, release people from the servitude of superfluous labor, provide for the universal satisfaction of vital needs, alleviate scarcity, poverty, and misery, and allow for the optimal realization of human resources. In addition to this qualitative change in the mode of production, Marcuse proposes that a transcending and transformative force arises from the negative position—though not the negative consciousness—of those who exist outside the system. The real life situation of these marginal people exposes the irrationality of the system with all its concomitant inequalities and deficiencies. Apparently, then, some sectors of the population remain immune to society's assimilating forces, and the blatant disparity between the life of the many insiders and those on the periphery of the system exposes the hidden evil of the system itself. The consequences of the qualitative change in the mode of production, of the transformation of technology from an instrument of domination to an instrument of freedom, include the release of human beings from slavery in the work world and from an alien and alienated existence, the emergence of individual autonomy and self-determination, the alleviation of inhuman conditions of existence, and progress toward the maximization of individual human development.

Processes of Evil and of Transcendence

In delineating the process by which the evil of one-dimensionality becomes manifest, Marcuse begins with the observation that the high level of productivity in advanced industrial society is detrimental to individual freedom of thought and action. That is, when the level of productivity in a society is not sufficient to provide for all individual needs, then the freedoms of independent thought, autonomy, and political protest have the valuable function of generating

165

social change and movement to a higher, sufficient level of productivity. However, when such a higher level of productivity is reached—through the advances of technology—and a great many if not all of people's needs can be satisfied, then the former freedoms are emptied of their critical content, and their usefulness declines. In the comfortable society, the need for qualitative change vanishes, and so do the freedoms which facilitate change. When the existing system fosters happiness by providing desired goods and services, the need for qualitative change is eliminated, and so are the personal political freedoms which traditionally initiate transcendence through the opposition to domination, and the advocacy of human development. The superficially efficient productivity of the society is self-validating, and renders people willing subjects of domination.

The erosion of political freedom is complemented and reinforced by an elimination of personal freedom and self-determination which ensues from the production and satisfaction of false needs by the irrational organization of production. Socialization into these false needs for labor, production, and consumption binds individuals to the dominating labor process, blinds them to the reality of domination, and eradicates awareness of the vital need for freedom. The conditions of labor in modern society lull the workers into a state of passivity, while the products of the system—which embody values, ideals, and attitudes supportive of the system, becoming available to more and more people, demonstrate in concrete terms the system's beneficial efficiency, and hence foster identification with the system. This indoctrination promoted by means of the intrinsic ideological nature of the products gradually subverts and reduces the sense of self as a separate and unique entity, which is the psychological origin of negativity, of the individual's unique reaction against the "given," the internalized definitions of the society. Automatic acceptance of and identification with the society that provides a good life displaces individual critical reaction to and evaluation of established reality. This covert psychological subversion of critical faculties is further reinforced by the "functionalization of language" (Marcus,1966:87). That is, the identification of things with their functions, the substitution of images for concepts, the reduction and restriction of meaning to the immediate, the concrete, and the given—all prevent perception of alternatives to the established reality, and militate against

reflection. Finally, while these diverse tendencies combine to undermine the capacity for critical
thought, the very impetus or motivation for negative
thinking is destroyed through the elimination of the
transcendent tension between culture and social reality. As the dimension of culture—which evoked and
sustained the consciousness of contradiction, of the
divergence between the ideal and the real—is incorporated into social reality, the ideal is identified with
the real, established social reality is recognized as
the "best of all possible worlds" (Voltaire), and the
idealistic motivaton for critical reflection disap-
pears. Thus is critical consciousness absorbed and
dissolved in the consciousness of one-dimensionslity.

With respect to Marcuse's analysis of the
process of transcendence, Robert Marks comments:

> In attempting to supply an answer to the
> "How?" Marcuse is as much at a loss as all of
> the earlier social critics. Break the bonds
> of domination and surplus repression, he ad-
> vocates. But how? He himself concedes that
> simply changing the external forms of the
> means of production is not enough (Marks,
> 1970:124-125).

This apparent deficiency in his theory seems to reflect
his pessimistic conclusion that the possibility of
transcendence of evil in advanced industrial society is
extremely tenuous since it is precisely the potential
sources and causes of transcendence which are undermined by the forces of one-dimensionality. Thus, for
example, the consciousness of domination is counteracted by the happy consciousness of conformity, and the
material contradiction between the potential and the
existing resources of society is counter-balanced by
the diffusion of affluence. Yet Marcuse argues that
transcendence may ensue from a combination of objective
material and subjective mental conditions. That is,
although changes in the means of production may not be
sufficient to eliminate irrational domination, nor even
to generate an awareness of domination in the majority
of the population, these changes may be conducive to a
transcendent consciousness in sectors of the population
which are not assimilated into the system. That is, as
technological development continues, and the internal
contradiction of the society between the possiblilities
for liberation immanent in technical innovations and
the rigid domination which is sustained by the

167

irrational and minimal usage of technical improvements
increases, this disparity between the ideal and the
real may be perceived by the unassimilated marginal
sector of outcasts and socially dislocated. The reality of the divided world may thus become subjectively
perceptible to those whose objective social position
and real life situation embodies all the inequalities,
injustices, and evils of the irrational system. The
emergence of this dual recognition of domination in labor as a function of the irrational organization of
production, and of the possibility of liberation
through a rational reconceptualization and reorganization of production will lead, Marcuse contends, to the
institutionalization of automation in the labor process.

Thus, once the internal contradiction explo-
des the one-dimensional consciousness and reawakens the
critical faculties, and the critical consciousness perceives the necessity of transforming the irrational
mode of production, the rational application of automation will abolish the mechanisms of domination, provide
for the satisfaction of vital needs, and release people
from the servitude in labor to freely explore, and develop the many dimensions of their embryonic humanity.

Consequences of Evil and of Transcendence

Within the context of Marcuse's analysis,
then, what are the prospects for human destiny as it is
determined by the conflict of forces for evil and for
transcendence of evil? On the one hand, it is clear
that the potentially liberating factors in technological progress are nullified by the containment of qualitative social change engineered by the irrational organization of production. The need for freedom is suppressed and displaced by the satisfaction of false
needs. The consciousness of being in opposition to the
system is dissolved by the conditions of work and the
spread of affluence. The liquidation of culture removes the motivation for reflection. The capacity for
perceiving the hidden reality of domination is undermined by the removal of transcendent elements of concepts in the language. On the other hand, however,
Marcuse argues that the inimical consequences of these
forces for evil can be refuted through the emergence of
a critical consciousness in unassimilated sectors of
the population. That is, if there remains a social
group whose objective total life situation symbolizes,
and constitutes a living negation of the evil society's

false promises, and if, psychologically, this group has not been incorporated into the system, then it is possible for a critical consciousness of the society's internal contradiction between real conditions and ideal potentials to emerge as a result of the ever-increasing disparity between real and ideal technological achievements. Once this awareness of domination, and the concomitant recognition of the need for a reconceptualization and reorganization of labor has emerged, then the abolition of irrational domination and the liberation of human beings from labor by means of automation becomes a realistic possibility. Transcendence of evil appears to be a tentative chance, but a chance nevertheless.

Finally, the ultimate consequences of the triumph of evil—of a total socialization into one-dimensionality—are indicated by the fact that the containment of qualitative social change implicitly entails a containment of qualitative change in human nature. In this respect, it is the progressive humanization of people which is contained, as they are reduced to the ontological status of things, unthinking automatons. This process eradicates the crucial social and psychological bonds of a common humanity, and eliminates the essential internal barriers against genocidal aggression, destruction, and nuclear holocaust. Conversely, the final consequences of the triumph of transcendence —of a qualitative change in the means of production which succeeds in eliminating the struggle for existence and releases people from domination to freedom and creativity—also entails a qualitative change in human nature. People would be free to pursue the maximization of their human faculties, to optimally expand the bonds of humanity, and to firmly establish social and psychological barriers against genocidal aggression, destruction, and nuclear catastrophe.

CHAPTER 13: Hannah Arendt

Introduction

> What totalitarian ideologies therefore aim at
> is not the transformation of the outside
> world or the revolutionizing transmutation of
> society, but the transformation of human na-
> ture itself (Arendt, 1971:458).

As the introductory quote indicates, Hannah
Arendt concludes from her analysis of Nazi Germany and
Stalinist Russia that the modern-day phenomenon of
totalitarianism is inherently and inexorably directed
toward the liquidation of the distinctively human element in human beings. Totalitarianism, therefore, constitutes a novel and radically evil form of political
oppression which must be resisted by each and every
nation in the world, individually, and moreover by the
multilateral co-operation of all nations through the
medium of international law. This critical assessment
follows primarily from Arendt's discovery of the invidious conceptions of reality and power peculiar to
totalitarianism. Essentially, in this view, reality
is conceived and utilized as a means to the end of
power. Totalitarian movements and regimes excel in
the art of manipulating reality, in the deliberate
manufacture of a fictional reality designed to shatter
the bonds of interpersonal relations, confound rationality, and invalidate the perceptual experience of the
world. It is this strategically calculated assault on
human thought, perception, and the intersubjective
communication which confirms these processes that demolishes the crucial barrier to the totalitarian goal
of total domination, i.e., the human element in human
beings. In this context, power is conceived in terms
of absolute world dominion, and in terms of the terroristic oppression of each individual in every sphere of his
or her life which can only be executed through the destruction of human nature itself, and the transformation of human beings into mindless automatons.

171

Consequently, the nature of reality and of human nature become pawns in the quest for political power,
and as Arendt emphatically insists, the advent of
totalitarianism compels the world community to choose
between all or nothing. That is, the world must unite
against this common enemy in principle and in fact
through the establishment of international sanctions
and laws as deterrents to totalitarianism, or, by
failing to do so, will facilitate the process of universal dehumanization, concentration-camp style.

Definitions of Evil and of Transcendence

If the victory of totalitarianism is identified as the ultimate evil, it follows that evil should
be defined in terms of totalitarianism's intrinsically
pernicious purpose—the premeditated extermination of
the human being's essential humanness—an act which,
like genocide, violates the community of humanity, and
likewise rates the distinction of a "crime 'against the
human status'" (Arendt, 1973:268). The nature of evil,
then, as the evidence of Nazism and Stalinism reveals,
encompasses the permanent abolition of personal freedom
(Arendt, 1971:405), of individual identity (Arendt,
1971:314), of spontaneity—"...man's power to begin
something new out of his own resources..." (Arendt,
1971:455), and of the capacity to initiate action
(Arendt, 1971:455). By thus extracting the quin-
tessence of the human psyche while preserving intact
the physical exterior, the totalitarian version of evil
achieves an unprecedented transformation of human nature which reduces people to mindless "ghastly
marionettes with human faces" (Arendt, 1971:455) who
can then be conditioned or programmed to react automatically and identically in a fashion designed to
perpetuate total domination.

Thus, within the context of totalitarianism,
evil is constituted as a radical form of dehumanization
which eradicates not only individual uniqueness but also collective diversity, for the system "...strives to
organize the infinite plurality and differentiation of
human beings as if all of humanity were just one individual..." and to reduce every person "...to a never-
changing identity of reactions, so that each of these
bundles of reactions can be exchanged at random for
any other" (Arendt, 1971:438). Furthermore, the nature
of totalitarian evil signifies, conversely, that transcendence of evil must be defined in terms of the
deliberate protection, preservation, and continued

172

maturation of the unique human qualities—freedom, individual identity, spontaneity, the capacity to initiate action, and the infinite differentiation of human forms—which, according to Arendt, is most likely to succeed under the authoritative aegis of international law. Given the instructive precedents of Nazism and Stalinism, it appears that transcendence of evil must be constituted as a conscious and unrelenting resistance—through individual action and collective co-operation—to the stupendous forces of totalitarian dehumanization. The global scale of totalitarian designs testifies to the fact that individual resistance must necessarily be buttressed, reinforced, and legitimized by the indisputable authority and power of a unified international community. In essence, the momentum of totalitarian movements is so overwhelming that unless the outside world is mobilized against the movement, it may well be absorbed into, and mobilized within the movement's ever-accelerating vortex.

Locus of Causality

As indicated above, the crucial totalitarian goal of global domination depends upon a fundamental transformation of human nature which is implemented primarily by means of the manufacture of a fictional reality. To this end the propaganda and organizational structures of such movements are designed to capitalize on a population's dissatisfaction with the actual conditions of its world by creating the appealing illusion of a new separate reality unencumbered by the deficiencies of the real world, and which, gradually, imperceptibly, displaces and assumes the facticity of the real world in the minds of the discontent. The frightening effectiveness of such an illusion is vividly demonstrated in the case of Nazi Germany where, according to the rules of the new world, the concepts of the moral and legal order were redefined as immoral and illegal, and conversely, the conceptions of immorality and illegal actions were redefined as moral and legal. In this case, moreover, most members of the new regime apparently never thought to question the validity of this transvaluation, and hence were capable of committing blatantly criminal acts without ever recognizing them as such, or conceiving of themselves as anything but law-abiding citizens (Arendt, 1973:135).

The evidence of Nazi totalitarianism supports the view that the individual's consciousness

173

is indeed determined by his or her social being, that social reality is the locus of causality, and human nature the realm of effect. Furthermore, Arendt's analysis of the factors which led to the emergence of totalitarianism—i.e., that changes in the social structure initiated changes in human consciousness susceptible to the appeal of totalitarianism—also concurs with this sociologistic view. However, her emphasis on the instances of resistance to Nazism—by individuals and by nations (Denmark)—on the fact that not everyone was deceived, and that some people choose instead to follow their own judgment and resisted Nazism, supports the alternative view that human nature comprises a causal realm. It would appear, then, that Arendt's theoretical perspective presupposes a dichotomous conception of causality, according to which, on the one hand, the manifestations of human nature's innate potentials are determined by the conducive or repressive conditions of social reality, and, on the other hand, these innate potentials may react against, and perhaps overcome the repressive conditions of social reality. Finally, the fact that Arendt advocates the establishment of organizations to reinforce and implement the reaction of individual human judgment against totalitarianism signifies that causal priority belongs to the realm of social reality.

Sources of Evil and of Transcendence

Within the context of Arendt's monumental work—The Origins of Totalitarianism—the sources of evil may be identified as those changes and processes originating in the social structure which generated the one indispensable condition for the emergence of totalitarianism, that is, the phenomenon of mass society. In this regard, Arendt identifies the breakdown of the class system as the initial and central process. European class society, with its competitive structure, was itself characterized by a high degree of atomization and individual isolation, but these portents of mass society were alleviated by class membership. When, however, the class system disintegrated, the tenuous bonds of class identity dissolved, and the population experienced the full impact of pervasive social atomization and individual loneliness, the phenomenon of the masses appeared (Arendt, 1971: 316). The masses are defined as large groups of people whose lives are distinguished by "isolation and lack of normal social relationships" (Arendt, 1971: 317), and who "...are not integrated into any broad social groupings, including classes" (Kornhauser, 1959: 14).

Such people, according to the theory of mass society, are extremely vulnerable to mobilization by totalitarian-oriented elites, in the first place, because of the critical lack of autonomous organizations which represent and protect the social, economic, or political interests of different sectors of the population. Without such an avenue for expressing their interests, and exerting even a minimal influence on the established government, individuals are virtually estranged from the political decision-making processes that determine the quality of life in their country. They are hence favorably inclined toward totalitarian movements which promise not only to rectify existing injustices, but also offer the discontent a second chance for success in a radically restructured world. In addition to the absence of such organizational buffers between the masses and the elite, or as Kornhauser phrases it—the lack of "social insulation" against the elite (Kornhauser, 1959:22)—the loss of an integrating, stabilizing, and personally satisfying network of normal social relations—which also fell victim to the breakdown of the class system—exacerbates the isolation and concomitant alientation and anxiety of individuals. Such people are then attracted not only by the inducement of a new place in life, but also by the organized destructive violence of totalitarian movements as an opportunity to relieve these tensions, and give vent to their resentment against the inadequacies of the old regime (Kornhauser, 1959:32). As Kornhauser summarizes this aspect of Arendt's theory:

> The lack of autonomous relations generates widespread social alienation. Alienation heightens responsiveness to the appeal of mass movements because they provide occasions for expressing resentment against what is, as well as promises of a totally different world. In short, people who are atomized readily become mobilized. Since totalitarianism is a state of total mobilization, mass society is highly vulnerable to totalitarian movements and regimes (Kornhauser, 1959:33).

Expanding on the psychology of the masses— originating in the fall of the class system, and

175

intensified by the economic dislocation of military defeat, inflation, and unemployment—Arendt observes that they react to the disintegration of their world with feelings of individual failure, expendability, superfluousness, and a loss of self-interest (Arendt, 1971:315-316). These feelings, in combination with the loneliness and alienation ensuing from the disruption of integrating social relations, evokes a predisposition to give total loyalty to a movement that provides opportunities for a new identity, a new place and purpose in a meaningfully transformed world (Arendt, 1971:323). In essence, much of the appeal of the totalitarian vision derives from the expectation that existing banal and trivial social roles will be replaced with meaningful, heroic, and historic ones. Furthermore, and perhaps most importantly, the total disintegration of the world as they know and understand it, reveals to the masses an incomprehensible fortuitous aspect of reality which undermines their faith in that reality, and in their own perceptual experience of it. Unable to understand or accept either the chaos of their existence or the causal events that preceded it, the masses are attracted to the propaganda of totalitarian ideology because it offers appealing and therefore convincting causal explanations of hitherto incomprehensible events, and thus restores consistency and continuity to their disrupted lives (Arendt, 1971:351-352). This witting and deliberate escape from reality into fiction, "from coincidence into consistency" (Arendt, 1971:352) is made possible, moreover, by the previously mentioned dissolution of the network of social relations which, ordinarily, connects individuals to reality, and confirms or revises their perceptions and understanding of reality. Thus, it is totally irrelevant whether totalitarian propaganda blatantly contradicts the evidence of reality and sense perception, since what appeals to the alienated and confused masses is not truth but consistency.

Thus, in addition to the many other attractive allurements of totalitarian movements, the logical consistency of their ideology convinces the masses that such a risky escape into a fictional world is infinitely more desireable than the intolerable unpredictability of the real world. In terms of the classification scheme for sources of evil and transcendence, all of the above-listed sources of evil may be categorized as the action of components of one system

176

(social reality) upon a component (human consciousness) of another system (human nature).

Turning to the issue of transcendence of evil, there are in Arendt's theory fewer indications of sources of transcendence than for sources of evil. Though fewer in number, however, the evidence suggests—in contrast to the case of evil—that there are sources of transcendence originating in human nature as well as in social reality. Specifically, in Eichmann in Jerusalem Arendt argues for the existence of a moral instinct inherent in human nature (Arendt, 1973:294-295). Expounding upon "the nature and function of human judgment" (Arendt, 1973:294), she explains that even within the carefully constructed fictional reality of the Nazi regime—where the overwhelming majority of the populace had obediently, uncritically, and unreservedly adopted the prescribed reversal of moral and legal values—there were, nevertheless, a few individuals whose ethical judgment remained intact and impervious to the considerable pressure of the widespread transvaluation. Such people retained and demonstrated—usually to the detriment of their own well-being—the ability to distinguish right from wrong, and did so moreover, not only in spite of the approved prevailing standards, but also without the benefit of guidance by traditional values, and thus with only the evidence of their personal judgment to guide them.

Examples such as this suggest that human judgment (or conscience) is not merely, and perhaps not very much a product of socialization, but rather is a unique and innate quality of human nature, existing prior and external to the influence of social reality. Arendt's emphasis on the unprecedented nature of events which people encountered in the Third Reich indicates, furthermore, that human judgment is grounded not in an innate awareness of ethico-moral concepts or laws, but in an inherent ethico-moral consciousness—that is, a creative capacity to originate moral values and ethical judgments. The application in real-life situations of this capacity to create values ex nihilo requires, additionally, the complementary faculties of reflection—with respect to personal experiences, and decision-making—on the basis of individual reflection. Thus, according to Arendt's analysis of Eichmann and his world, the nature of human judgment is given as a combination of creative moral consciousness, logical reflection, and decision-making, and the function of human judgment

is to recognize and resist or transcend evil. Human
judgment, as a source of transcendence, may be classified as the action of a component of one system (human
judgment/human nature) upon components of another
system (conflictual situations in social reality).

While, on the one hand, Arendt argues per-
suasively for the existence of an innate moral instinct, she argues also, on the other hand, that this
instinct can be subverted, and even obliterated by inimical forces in social reality—as the Nazi experience
tragically demonstrates. In her view, then, the possibilities for transcendence must depend upon the existence and relative strength of societal factors antithetical to evil and conducive to transcendence, of
conditions in social reality which facilitate the
exercise of human judgment, and which reinforce and
sustain the individual's instinctive reaction against
evil. Since she conceives of totalitarian dehumanization as the ultimate evil, and identifies mass society as the necessary condition for the emergence
of totalitarianism, it follows that the societal
sources of transcendence consist of social conditions
which prevent or impede the transformation of populations into masses.

In this respect, judging from the previously
delineated deficiencies of social reality which contribute to and sustain the peculiar psychology of the
masses, it can be inferred, in the first place, that
integration into a broad framework of close personal
relationships—where the reflected appraisals of significant others evoke, confirm or revise, and sustain
the individual's sense of identify and self-esteem—
mitigates individual vulnerability to feelings of
isolation, alienation, and superfluousness fostered
by disruptions in the social order. Secondly, the
mutual expectations of obligation, responsibility,
trust, and dependency which bind individuals to each
other in the intensive personal relations of love,
family, and friendship provide and sustain the sense of
belonging, and of having a significant place in life
through fulfillment in meaningful social roles, which
effectively nullify the appeal of totalitarianism's
promised opportunities for a new historic place and
purpose in life. Thirdly, the extensive exchange of
information— experiences, values, opinions, and
perspectives—characteristic of such relationships
which initially stimulates and later preserves awareness of reality, while the emotive support of friends

and family strengthens individuals in times of crisis and chaos, reduce the incomprehensibility of reality, and guard against the temptation to escape into a comfortable and convincingly consistent fictional world. Finally, the establishment of voluntary associations for the express purpose of representing and advancing the social, economic, and political interests of various sectors of the population within the framework of the existing government may function as a protective buffer between the masses and totalitarian-oriented elites. The activities of such associations oriented toward redressing the grievances and rectifying the injustices that occasion dissatisfaction, serve to eliminate the need for destruction of the system, and the radical transformation of reality envisioned by totalitarianism. By this means a population may be protected or "insulated" against mobilization into totalitarian movements:

> For insulation requires a multiplicity of independent and often conflicting forms of association, each of which is strong enough to ward off threats to the autonomy of the individual (Kornhauser, 1959:32).

These several societal sources of transcendence may be classified as the action of components of social reality upon a component (human consciousness) of human nature, and, in the case of voluntary associations, as the action of a component of one system (social reality) upon another component (totalitarian movements) of the same system.

Manifestations of Evil and of Transcendence

Among the multitudinous specific causes and effects of evil, one of the more fascinating strategies utilized by totalitarian movements to attain the goal of universal dehumanization and global domination is the aforementioned manufacture of an alternative and "entirely imaginary world..." (Arendt, 1971:353). Deliberately designed to satisfy the peculiar needs of the uprooted masses, this alternative reality manifests a reliable causal structure, and a concomitant consistency, continuity, and predictability unequalled in the real world. A popular fiction, calculated to incite the masses for mobilization in the movement, constitutes the crucial cornerstone for the entire fabricated edifice. The convincing, but nevertheless superficial, validity of the

179

central fiction derives from the fact that it is initially drawn from the real world, and then distorted
or grossly exaggerated in order to suit the movement's
purposes. Such exaggeration, moreover, removes the
fiction from the realm of individual experience and
opportunities for verification or falsification, thus
transforming it from a problematic to a given or indubitable aspect of reality. Upon the base of the
chosen fiction, totalitarian movements then construct
a very real organization for the express purpose of
concretely implementing the fiction. Since within
the organization, the rules governing official roles
and duties are devised in accordance with the fiction,
the members act, in effect, as if the fiction were
true, and, consequently, the very operation of the organization proves prima facie the reality of the fiction.

The principal structural innovation of totalitarian organizations consists of the differentiation between party members and sympathizers, and the
incorporation of sympathizers into "front organizations" (Arendt, 1971:366). Front organizations, which
serve the dual purpose of deceiving both the non-
totalitarian world about the nature of the movement,
and the party membership about the nature of the outside world, are composed of the less radical and non-
fanatic admirers of the movement. To the party member, the front organization of fellow-travelers represents a sympathetic constituency outside the party
elite which holds the same beliefs though in a less
militant, more normal form. The disparity in strength
of convictions between the party member and the
fellow-traveler signifies to the former that the latter represents the attitude of the non-totalitarian
world. In actuality, the front organizations thus in-
sulate the party membership against contact with the
outside world—for such contact, by revealing the
truly great discrepancies between the fictional and
the real world, could undermine the party member's
faith in and devotion to the movement itself.

On the other side, the deceptive normality
of the sympathizers presents a harmless front to the
outside world, lends credibility to outrageous totalitarian lies, and allows for the surrepticious diffusion of totalitarian ideas to the outside world.
The necessity, moreover, for such isolation from the
real world, is evident in the fact that this protective relationship between front organizations and

party membership is constantly repeated throughout the entire hierarchy of the movement. That is, for each particular rank in the organization there is a corresponding lower and less militant rank which represents the nontotalitarian world, and thus every level is protected from encounters with the real world which might undermine the members' faith in the authenticity of their fictional reality (Arendt, 1971:367).

In contrast to this security function of the front organization structure, the function of the more militant ranks—especially the elite formations, which are entrusted with the dubious honor of committing crimes for the benefit of, and in the name of the party—is to demonstrate through such crimes that the movement has renounced completely the values of common morality, and that every member is hence implicated in, and accountable for the murderous activities of the elite (Arendt, 1971:372). Whereas the front organizations represent and preserve the members' sense of normality and respectability, the elite formations symbolize and sustain the awareness of withdrawal from the normal world, the rejection of universal values, and the necessity for total commitment to the movement.

In addition to the utilization of propaganda, front organizations, and elite formations to create and maintain the illusion of an alternative reality, totalitarian movements also employ the technique of duplicating, within the structure of the organization, the departments of the existing state administration in order to complete the image of a separate and autonomous world. This duplication, moreover, serves the further purpose of expediting the rapid transformation of a non-totalitarian country into a totalitarian state after the movement has succeeded in overthrowing the current regime (Arendt, 1971:372). Beyond this dual purpose duplication, totalitarian movements exhibit a curious multiplication of governmental agencies which generates a bewildering confusion and much conflict regarding jurisdiction and authority, thus precluding the development of professional expertise, competent performance, and productvie co-ordination of diverse activities. The net effect of this administrative bedlam, in combination with the Leader's unprecedented assumption of total responsibility for all activities of the movement—official and unofficial, criminal and legitimate—is to ensure, on the one hand, that the operation of the entire administrative apparatus hinges upon the will and the decisions of the Leader who alone possesses all the knowledge and authority necessary to understand and direct every aspect of the organization, and on the other hand, that the individual bureaucrat is relieved of the burden of responsibility for the consequences of his or her official activities. Moreover, as Arendt observed in the case of Adolph Eichmann, the individual bureaucrat is required to use, in pursuance of his or her criminal duties, a handy codebook of objective language rules which furnishes innocuous names for blatantly noxious actions. The result of this subterfuge is not to prevent the bureaucrat from realizing that within the context of traditional morality his or her official activities constitute crimes, but is rather to reinforce the conviction that within the context of the movement's higher morality such activities are not considered criminal and are expressly legitimized (Arendt, 1973: 86).

Thus, given the rules of the totalitarian reality—e.g., the total responsibility of the Leader, and the reversal of moral values and the legal order—it is conceivable that the individual bureaucrat of murder could quite sincerely deny responsibility for wrong-doing (Arendt, 1973:22), and moreover, believe that he or she only fulfilled the moral obligations of a law-abiding citizen—as Arendt describes Eichmann's attitude:

> As for the base motives, he was perfectly sure that he was not what he called an innerer Schweinehund, a dirty bastard in the depths of his heart; and as for his conscience, he remembered perfectly well that he would have had a bad conscience only if he had not done what he had been ordered to do—to ship millions of men, women, and children to their death with great zeal and the most meticulous care (Arendt, 1973:25).

Totalitarianism's usage of organization to supplement the deception of propaganda, and to objectify the ideology's central fiction is most concretely demonstrated in the establishment of concentration camps in order to exterminate those identified by the ideology as the enemies of the movement (Arendt, 1971:438). In terms of totalitarian logic, the purpose of the camps is to eliminate enemies of the movement. In the case of Nazi Germany, a

particular group of people, e.g., the Jews, were
killed in the camps; therefore, the Jews were the enemies of the movement who had to be eliminated. In
this fashion, the operation of concentration camps
translates a crucial element of the ideological fiction into an undeniable fact of reality. While the
camps thus provide physical proof to reinforce the
wtihdrawal from the real world initiated by propaganda, intellectual proof of the ideology's central
fiction is offered in the logic of ideology, i.e., in
a self-contained system of thought which does not depend upon the experience of reality for verification.
The ideology is predicated on the assumption that behind the given appearance of reality is hidden a true
reality--imperceptible to the senses--which contains
a causal law applicable to all historical events, and
it is this law which is represented in the single all-
encompassing idea of the ideology. This solitary
idea, then, represents the ultimate cause of all
things, and all things are comprehended in the evolution of the idea, through logical deduction from a
single premise. The understanding of true reality and
the historical process is contingent upon the idea as
the crucial "instrument of explanation" (Arendt, 1971:
469). This identification of historical process—
past, present, and future—with the logical development
of the idea renders superfluous the actual experience
of reality—of even unprecedented events. Consequently, reflection and understanding are divorced from the
evidence of reality perceived by the five senses, and
are instead dependent upon the logically consistent
evidence of ideological insight.

This totalitarian assault on the transcendent
creativity of human thought is completed with the institutionalization of terror, primarily through the
agency of the secret police in whose view—"Simply because of their capacity to think, human beings are
suspects by definition..." (Arendt, 1971:430). The
arbitrary and unpredictable exercise of terror by the
secret police produces an atmosphere of mutual suspicion that pervades the entire society, and eliminates
any remaining possibilities for genuine interpersonal
interaction. The elimination of such interaction signifies also that the vital medium of intersubjective
communication—which confirms and sustains contact with
reality—is at last abolished.

That human beings indeed become so thoroughly
estranged from the evidence of their own senses and

183

feelings, and so much puppets of invisible and invidious social forces is again illustrated in the case of Eichmann. For instance, Eichmann was ordered several times to inspect some of the killing installations, and each time he was sickened, repelled, and terrified by the illuminating experience. However, when he discovered that mass murder was vigorously approved by "...the Popes of the Third Reich" (Arendt, 1973:114), he swiftly overcame his own instinctive reaction, and willingly and unreservedly subordinated his judgment to the indisputably authoritative judgment of society. As ideological logic destroys the human being's relation to reality, so terror destroys the social interrelationships which confirm the perceptual experience of reality. Consequently, whatever is perceived by the senses and which contradicts the ideology takes on an appearance of unreality, and conversely, whatever is advocated by the ideology and confirmed by terror assumes the appearance of reality, even though it blatantly contradicts perceptual experience. Thus, for instance, in Nazi Germany, although the very real horror of the concentration camps was widely known, the terroristic activities of the secret police ensured that the subject was rarely discussed. As a result, this horror lost the aspect of facticity, and assumed instead the aspect of a nightmare, of unreality (Arendt, 1971:435).

In sum, totalitarian movements attempt to achieve the goal of global domination through a radical dehumanization of human nature effected by means of constructing an attractive alternative reality which is calculated to gradually displace the real world in the minds of a dissatisfied populace. Resocialization from the real world into the alternative fictional reality proceeds through the combined influence of propaganda, front organizations, elite formations, duplication and multiplication of governmental offices, concentration camps, ideological logic, and the institution of terror. The central fiction of the ideology disseminated through propaganda incites the populace against a specific enemy, and provides a motivation for mobilization in the movement. The propaganda promises of a new historic place and purpose in life in conjunction with the barriers to contact with reality provided by front organizations, ideological logic, and arbitrary terror induce total identification with the movement. The consciousness of irredeemable complicity in criminal actions aroused by the elite formations instills total commitment and

loyalty to the movement, even to the extent of voluntary self-sacrifice for the good of the movement. The
destruction of personal relationships through the arbitrary exercise of terror eradicates the ability to
take the role of the other, to identify and emphasize
with the other, thus eliminating psychological barriers to murderous aggression. The propagation of a
reversal of values essential to the success of the
movement undermines the validity of traditional values,
and hence eliminates social barriers to murderous aggression. The multiplication of offices, the Leader's
assumption of total responsibility, and the reversal
of values annihilate the sense of personal responsibility for the consequences of action, and thus facilitate voluntary compliance in destructive and
criminal activities. The legitimization of violence
induces the release of repressed hostilities against
the old world order, and directs these energies
against the enemies of the movement. The remoteness
from reality generated and sustained by the front organizations, the physical proof of the concentration
camps, the intellectual proofs of ideological logic,
and the absence of intersubjective communication enforced by terror, obscures the division between reality and unreality, the distinctions of true and false,
right and wrong. Ultimately, the experience of reality necessary for creative thought, and the formula-
tion of convictions and ethico-moral judgments which
transcend the inherent limitations of the given fictional reality are precluded. And thus, the final
consequence of totalitarian dehumanization is to exterminate the infinite diversity of human beings so
that its victims—as Hitler joyfully remarked:

> ...have outwardly become almost a unit, that
> actually these members are uniform not only
> in ideas, but that even the facial expression
> is almost the same. Look at these laughing
> eyes, this fanatical enthusiasm and you will
> discover...how a hundred thousand men in a
> movement become a single type (Hitler, as
> cited in Arendt, 1971:418).

As was found to be the case with respect to
the sources of transcendence, it is also true with regard to the particular causes of transcendence, that a
combination of factors in human nature and in social
reality is involved. In the first place, Arendt as-
cribes the greatest importance to the infinitely
creative and potent human capacity for thought which

she identifies as the one innate attribute most in-
flexibly resistant to the totalitarian assault on human nature, and as the most powerful antidote to the
manifold forces of dehumanization. This elemental
freedom of thought, in other words, is manifested as
the imagination and creation of the unknown and unprecedented from the given and known, in the in-
genious visualization of the totally novel which over-
comes existing limitations of verified knowledge and
material resources to transform the novel from a
vision of fantasy to a fact of reality. It is by virtue of this fountainhead of unpredictability within
human nature—which corresponds to the element of unpredictability in reality—that the human being's
natural relation to the real world is maintained despite the apparent authenticity of totalitarian il-
lusions. Moreover, it is this subversive unpredictability which has the power to explode the circumscription of thought imposed by the "tyranny of logicality" (Arendt, 1971:473), and, therefore, also, to
unmask the deception, vitiate the appeal, and impel
rejection of totalitarianism's infallibly consistent,
reliably predictable, and entirely fictional world.
Essentially, the intrinsic logicality of ideological
thought is the Achilles' heel of totalitarianism which
is necessarily vulnerable to a mode of thought that is
self-initiating and developmental rather than self-
validating and predetermined by and dependent upon a
given premise.

However, even though human thought is also
self-sustaining—in the sense that, for instance, one
can think creatively in complete solitude through the
medium of imaginative dialogue with a hypothetical
other—it is also true that such reflection eventually
requires the reinvigorating stimulus of a real other.
It is this aspect of the thought process which is
especially vulnerable to the totalitarian destruction
of the usual channel of intersubjective communication.
That is, the transcendent power of individual reflection ultimately depends upon, and must be replenished
by conditions in social reality which stimulate reflection, and such conditions consist primarily in the
exchange and discussion of ideas, values, and perspectives characteristic of the on-going dialogue between
self and other in interpersonal relations. Yet, as
the previous sections have made all too clear, it is
precisely the opportunities for the stimulating and
confirming dialogue of interpersonal relations which
are destroyed by the atmosphere of suspicion generated

by the institution of terror. However, it may be hypothesized, that even in the absence of interpersonal dialogue, the crucial element of exposure to unfamiliar concepts and different perspectives which necessarily calls into question the apparent validity of one's own world-view, and thus generates reflection, obtains also in confrontations with novel or unexpected situations. In this case, it is the shock of encountering the unexpected in a situation—rather than in a conversation—which disrupts the routine performance of behavior, and requires reflection on the intervening unknown before behavior can be resumed. Hence, the trauma of the encounter may stimulate reflection just as, ordinarily, exposure to another person's novel ideas does. Evidence in support of this hypothesis is given in the example of Denmark's resistance to the Nazi overlords. The effect of this opposition was to undermine the Nazi officials' confidence and faith in their prescribed world-view, so that they no longer took for granted as natural the mass extermination of an entire people (Arendt, 1973: 175).

Therefore, the ultimate consequence of exercising the unique human faculty of reflection—upon the given and the unknown—is the discovery of totalitarian deception, the rejection of its ostensibly alternative reality, and above all, the conscious and voluntary resistance and refusal to comply with or participate in evil.

Processes of Evil and of Transcendence

Drawing from the example of Nazi Germany, Arendt concludes that the one indispensable precondition for the manifestation of totalitarian evil, for the process of radical dehumanization which produces, on the one hand, armies of mindless, murderous robots, and on the other hand, masses of docile, unresisting victims, consists of the economic dislocations, and the disintegration of the social and political structures from which arises mass society, or the uprooted masses of isolated, alienated, bewildered marginal people who are, at one and the same time, inclined toward anxiety-releasing violence, and apathetic resignation to face (Arendt, 1971:447). It is these unstable and volatile masses, she argues, who are susceptible to the totalitarian transformation of human nature that destroys even the last vestiges of a common humanity.

According to her analysis, the actual administration of the official program for dehumanization begins with the murder of "the juridical person in man" (Arendt, 1971:447), or, in other words, the nullification of the human being's sense of justice, which is accomplished through measures which abolish all the civil rights of an entire population. Under the Nazi regime, such measures included the denationalization of entire sectors of the population, who, having thus been stripped of all civil rights were removed from the protection of the law, and hence liable to criminal prosecution. A second such measure is the establishment of the concentration camp as a unique type of prison establishment beyond the purview of the normal penal system, and in which the inmates are selected purely arbitrarily, without regard for innocence or guilt or any other element of judicial process. The fundamental principle of arbitrary arrest, incarceration, and extermination reveals the invidious criminality of the system, for here the ethico-moral concepts of "innocence," "guilt," and "justice" lose their meaning and practical significance. The innocent and the guilty, the law-abiding and the criminal, the victims and the aggressors are, for all intents and purposes, identical and interchangeable, all equally suspect, and liable to persecution. The institution of the arbitrary principle thus heralds the end of the rule of law, the dissolution of justice, and the disenfranchisement and subjugation of not only certain sectors, but the total population.

The second stage of the dehumanization process, Arendt asserts, entails the "murder of the moral person in man" (Arendt, 1971:451), which is achieved through the elimination of the social meaning of moral protest, and the invalidation of conscience as a guide to moral behavior. In the first place, for those among the subjugated populace who recognize the ultimately pernicious consequences of totalitarianism as well as the implicit evil of the system, and are moved to express their moral indignation in a courageous protest, the social meaning as well as the practical significance of their act is utterly annulled in a society where the mutual suspicion aroused by the reign of terror replaces personal relationships and intersubjective communication with solitude and silence. The moral protest would be performed in a void, and consigned to oblivion for among the anonymous masses there is no way to share or respond to it, and no one to acknowledge or appreciate the act as a testimony of

188

moral conviction. In the second place, the judgments
of conscience are invalidated under the reign of terror
when those inclined to protest or resist realize that
such an act will ensure not only their own death, but
the murder of countless other innocent victims who are
in one way or another associated with the protester.
And, moreover, the fact that totalitarian terror en-
meshes even the victims in criminal complicity, that
the victims are forced to make choices in which conscience can be no guide—choices not between good and
evil, but between murder (of relative strangers) and
murder (of friends or family)—renders conscience completely inadequate and invalid, and moral decisions
impossible. For instance: "Who could solve the moral
dilemma of the Greek mother, who was allowed by the
Nazis to choose which of her three children should be
killed?" (Arendt, 1971:452). Thus, with the nullification of conscience and moral protest, the murderers
and the victims become indistinguishable.

The third and final step in the program of
totalitarian dehumanization is to murder individual
identity, to eliminate the infinite differentiation
of human beings, and transform them all into one monstrous, faceless, anonymous, indistinguishable mass
(Arendt, 1971:453). In the case of those who are
chosen for the role of murderers, this is accomplished through rigorous resocialization into the fic-
ticious world of the movement—initiated by propagan-
distic indoctrination and sustained by terror—which
replaces individual identity with total identification
with the movement, and precludes the possibility of
life outside the organization. In the case of those
chosen for the role of victims, the same result is
achieved through the devices of arbitrary arrest, imprisonment and extermination, through the use of
brutality and torture to destroy human dignity, through
an efficient system of mechanized, impersonal murder,
and through a careful disposal of the evidence of mass
murder which finally establishes the anonymity of the
victims. By these means, totalitarian regimes liqui-
date the essential humanity of human beings, and transform them into obedient automatons superbly prepared
for existing under conditions of total domination.

As previsouly indicated, Arendt's conception
of transcendence as the recognition and resistance to
the multitudinous forces of totalitarian dehumanization
is predicated on the assumption of a trichotomous constellation of distinctively human qualities. These

189

qualities are: (1) an innate ethico-moral consciousness which exists prior and external to the influence
of social reality; (2) a mode of thought which is implicitly free, original, and unhampered by the necessarily consistent patterns of logic; and, (3) a capacity for formulating ethical judgments, and making
decisions on the basis of individual reflection on personal experiences. Each of these three interrelated
faculties is considered to be progressively developed,
and continually refined in the course of interpersonal
interaction which, moreoever, also sustains the vital
contact with reality, and confirms the authenticity
and validity of individual reflection. Ordinarily,
it is the provocative and on-going dialogue of self
and others, the day-to-day feliticious or melancholy
encounters with others, which provides countless opportunities for observing the beneficial or harmful
effect of other's actions upon oneself, and of one's
own actions for others. It is this dialogue which
therefore calls the critical faculties into operation,
brings them to the level of consciousness, and enables
individuals to formulate their own view of the world,
and to construct appropriate moral standards for
personal conduct.

The central and crucial factor in developing
the capacity for transcendence and in generating
transcendence in specific instances—as illustrated in
Arendt's description of Denmark's resistance to Nazi
demands, and in Eichmann's initial reaction to the concentration camps—consists of the unanticipated and
traumatic confrontation with novel and unfamiliar
ideas, perspectives or situations. The effect of such
encounters is to expose the relativity and/or provin-
ciality of one's own convictions and standards, to
reveal discrepancies or deficiencies in one's concepts, to undermine the assumed sanctity of personal
convictions, to render problematic the hitherto unexamined givens of one's world, and hence to provoke
reflection—i.e., consideration and evaluation—of
newly discovered aspects of the world, of alternative
and perhaps more inclusive perspectives than one's
own. Transcendence is thus primarily a matter of expanding and revising one's knowledge and understanding
of the world to encompass the manifold aspects of good
and evil which had not been previously foreseen or
encountered. Although this process accounts for the
recognition of evil, the further act of resistance to
evil—as the Eichmann case indicates—i.e., the fact
that the widespread social consensus in favor of the

190

Final Solution convinced Eichmann to overcome his own initial instinctive revulsion—apparently requires the affirmative sanction and support of some social group significant to the individual, such as a peer group or an association. Perhaps it is the idea of a greater commitment or the fact of the very real risk involved in active resistance to evil that accounts for this need for some means of social support. In the last analysis, the process of transcendence requires a truly fortuitous conjunction of individual and social factors.

Consequences of Evil and of Transcendence

In summing up the relative balance or imbalance of the forces of evil and for transcendence, those on the side of evil are as follows: economic dislocation and the disintegration of the political system and social structure; the absence of voluntary associations oriented toward the protection of political, economic, and social interests; the lack of normal social relationships; individual feelings of isolation, alienation, anxiety, and expendability; individual inability to understand or cope with the unpredictability of reality; the convincing and appealing illusion of an alternative reality; and the loss of contact with the real world sustained by propaganda, front organizations, the duplication of administrative offices, the logic of ideology, and terror. The factors of transcendence include: the triadic constellation of an innate ethico-moral consciousness, creative reflection, and decision-making; the existence of voluntary associations oriented toward the protection of political, economic, and social interests; integration into a stabilizing network of close personal relationships which preserves the sense of self-esteem, the awareness of a meaningful place in life, and sustains contact with reality; and traumatic and provocative encounters with the unknown which stimulate reflection on the given.

Unfortunately, it appears that the forces of transcendence—with the exception of the last one—are operable and effective only as long as they do not disintegrate into or are perverted into the corresponding opposite forces of evil. Therefore, it seems likely that once the factors of evil begin to prevail, the chances of transcendence are extremely remote. In other words, once totalitarian domination has been established in a particular country, it is extremely

unlikely that the regime will be resisted and ousted
from within, and much more likely that transcendence,
resistance, and opposition will have to come from the
outside, as was the case with Nazi Germany. The tenous
possibilities of transcendence thus signify that total-
itarianian evil is indeed the ultimate evil of the modern world. As Arendt emphatically states, the harrow-
ing, and perhaps therefore inconceivable final consequence of this ultimate evil which seeks total power at
the expense of human nature is to render human beings,
insofar as they are more than obediently functioning
interchangeable mindless marionettes, totally superfluous (Arendt, 1971:457). In a totalitarian world the
only matter of any consequence or value is the perpetuation of the regime, and for this end people are required
only in the role of instrumental functionaries, and
never as free, spontaneous, and creative beings. As
the Nazi experience demonstrates, the totalitarian ex-
perimentation with human nature is well on the way to
achieving this superfluousness when it successfully
conditions people to commit crimes for which there are
no humanly comprehensible motives.

Lastly, in terms of Arendt's theory of transcendence, the traumatic confrontation with this final
form of dehumanization promulgated under Nazism and
Stalinism should have shocked the world community into
the realization that human nature is itself at stake
in the battle against totalitarianism. The transcendent power of individual human judgment is not indes-
tructable against the invidious forces of dehumanization, but must be protected and reinforced by the authority and power of societal and international sanctions. The final consequence of our recognition and
painfully-won understanding of totalitarian evil must
be universal and unqualified opposition.

CHAPTER 14: Concluding Remarks on the
Perspective of Social Philosophy

In each of these two sections on the nature of
societal evil, the primary locus of causality has been
identified as social reality, and evil has been defined
as some form of dehumanization—either as socialization
into one-dimensionality (Marcuse), or socialization into superfluousness (Arendt). The concept of transcendence was defined by Marcuse in terms of freedom from
institutional domination—i.e., liberation from insti-
tutionally enforced servitude in an unnecessary struggle for existence through the rational and maximal use
of automation, whereas Arendt emphasized the actual act
of recognition and opposition to the process of dehumanization. In both cases the sources of evil and
transcendence were identified as the action of components of one system of reality upon components of another system. For Marcuse, the source of evil consisted
of the action of the irrational organization of production (component of social reality) upon the human being's mode of thought and being (component of human nature), and conversely, transcendence consisted of the
action of negative thought (component of human nature)
upon the organization of production (component of social reality). Similarly, Arendt found the source of
evil in the action of the disintegrating economic, political, and social structures (components of social reality) upon the human being's mode of thought and being
(components of human nature), and conversely, the principal source of transcendence in the action of human
judgment (component of human nature) upon dehumanizing
societal conditions (components of social reality).

Furthermore, each discovered the causes of
evil to be processes generated by the institutions of
domination—according to Marcuse, these included: the
promotion of false needs, the diffusion of affluence,
the elimination of two-dimensional culture, and the
concretization of language, science, and philosophy.
According to Arendt these included: the manufacture of
a fictional reality; the separation from the real world

193

enforced by front organizations, duplication of offices, the physical evidence of concentration camps, the intellectual proofs of ideological logic, and the mutual suspicion aroused by terror; the extension of complicity by the elite formations, and the destruction of the sense of responsibility generated by the multiplication of offices and the Leader's assumption of total responsibility. Marcuse identified the effect of these various casues of evil as the generation of a progressive alienation, i.e., one-dimensional thought and behavior. Arendt delineated the specific dimensions of totalitarian dehumanization as the destruction of individual identity, and the generation of total identification and commitment to the organization; elimination of the ability to empathize with others, and thus removal of psychological barriers to aggression; invalidation of traditional values, and the internalization of totalitarian values which removes the social barriers to aggression; and the transformation of human beings into a single uniform type. The causes of transcendence were specified in both cases as a combination of components or processes in the social structure and in human nature. For Marcuse, this combination involved the objective material condition of the increasing contradiction between the actual and potential use of technology and the recognition of this contradiction by persons marginal to the system. For Arendt, this combination entailed ethical consciousness, creative reflection and the encounter of conflictual situations in social reality. Similarly, the effect of transcendence in each case was identified as the recognition and opposition to inimical social conditions.

Marcuse and Arendt concurred in perceiving the process of evil as a corruption or destruction of the uniquely human qualities. The process of transcendence, according to Marcuse, entailed a dialectical reaction of human nature against the pernicious influences emanating from the institutions of domination, and in Arendt's analysis involved the societal reinforcement of the individual's instinctive inclination to transcendence. The consequences of evil in both cases were specified as the elimination of the psychological, social, and moral obstacles to social destructiveness which induces murderous aggression, whereas the consequences of transcendence were identified as the fortification of these obstacles, and the opposition to and prevention of destructive aggression.

194

With regard to the central issue of the function of human judgment, Marcuse and Arendt concur in the pessimistic conclusion that this attribute of human nature is not indestructible, and can be nullified or obliterated by antithetical social forces. Marcuse contends that the preservation of human judgment depends upon a forceful stimulation emanating from a society's increasing internal contradiction between the actual and potential utilizations of technology, and Arendt likewise maintains that its preservation is contingent upon reinforcement by affirmative societal sanctions. According to Marcuse it is the overwhelming evidence of society's internal contradiction that reawakens the critical faculties of human beings, and directs them toward the evil society. According to Arendt, it is the affirmative societal sanctions which provide the indispensable social meaning of transcendent acts that makes them worthwhile to the individual, and establishes their practical significance in the realm of political action. The function of human judgment cannot therefore be taken for granted since it is to such a great extent contingent upon exceedingly variable social conditions.

PART SIX: THE PERSPECTIVE

OF SOCIOLOGY

CHAPTER 15:   Evil and Transcendence
             Within Bureaucracy

Introduction

The objective indispensability of the once-
existing apparatus, with its peculiar "impersonal" character, means that the mechanism—in contrast to feudal orders based
upon personal piety—is easily made to work
for anybody who knows how to gain control
over it (Weber, 1963:74).

When we examine the world historical scene,
we may note that many times, in many coun-
tries, bureaucracies have launched the open-
ing phases of a destruction process...
(Hilberg, 1961:639).

The trouble with Eichmann was precisely that
so many were like him, and that the many were
neither perverted nor sadistic, that they
were, and still are, terribly and terrifying-
ly normal. From the viewpoint of our legal
institutions and of our moral standards of
judgment, this normality was much more terrifying than all the atrocities put together,
for it implied...that this new type of
criminal, who is in actual fact hostis
generis humani, commits his crimes under circumstances that make it well-nigh impossible
for him to know or to feel that he is doing
wrong (Arendt, 1973:276).

Whole societies or whole armies do not commit massacres. Certain men are always
singled out to do the work, and this commission of the act is the easiest of the
three forms of guilt to pinpoint. The men
do their work, however, in the name of the
society, the nation, the army, the police,

or the church. The subtle problems come in
determining final culpability and the location of conscience. Can whole societies
sense guilt? If organizational structures
are to be blamed, then what is the culpability of individuals within those structures?
Does it make any sense, indeed does it make
any difference, to talk about the location
of guilt in the Germany of the Third Reich?
(Duster, 1971:27).

...there is a moment in the human experience
when one's life itself no longer makes
sense when it is directed to the mutilation
and murder of his fellow man. There is a
demarcation line of morality beyond which no
man can cross and still claim membership in
the human race... (Uris, 1974b:419).

Genocide—carried out with the precision and
finality of a machine. At first the efforts of the Germans had been clumsy. They
killed by rifle. It was too slow. They
organized their transport and their scientists
for the great effort. Steel-covered trucks
were designed to lock in and gas to death
prisoners en route to burial grounds. But
even the gas vans proved slow. Next came
the crematorium and the gas chambers capable
of killing 2,000 people in a half-hour—
10,000 on a good day in a major camp. The
organization and planning proved itself and
genocide proceeded on an assembly-line
basis (Uris, 1974a:79).

    In the preceding chapter, the examination of
Marcuse and Arendt's theories revealed their analogous
perceptions of societal evil. According to Marcuse,
evil arises from an irrational organization of the
means of production, and according to Arendt, the to-
talitarianiam form of political organization generates
evil. Both scholars concur in identifying the principal manifestation of evil deriving from these sources
as the establishment of a radically dehumanized mode
of consciousness and being. In addition, both Marcuse
and Arendt intimate that societal evil may also arise
from a particular social institution, namely, the
organization of production known as bureaucracy.
While at first glance this proposition may seem paradoxical inasmuch as bureaucracy has generally been

regarded as a major organizational advance, and one which is indispensable in the modern world, it is also true that the manifest and constructive functions of bureaucracy have long tended to obscure its latent and perhaps destructive dysfunctions. The nature of these relatively mysterious and perhaps destructive dysfunctions of bureaucracy comprises the central concern of this chapter which offers the theory that the bureaucratic form of social organization is largely analogous to the totalitarian form of political organization. In other words, bureaucracy constitutes a smaller-scale version of the totalitarian state, and hence, bureaucracy, like totalitarianism, is conducive to dehumanization, and therefore also to various forms of social destructiveness, including—as the sequence of introductory quotes suggest—genocide. It is as an efficiency problem that the culmination of social destructiveness—genocide—comes within the purview of bureaucratic organization.

In the first quote, Weber points out that the impersonality of the bureaucratic apparatus insures that it will operate efficiently and effectively for whoever gains control of it. As a powerful and virtually indestructible instrument of domination, subordination, and coordination of activities, the bureaucratic structure furnishes those who know how to control and manipulate it, with the most effective means of transforming random collective action into rationally organized and efficient social action--directed toward either constructive or destructive ends. The ostensible objectivity of bureaucracy, as a technical means of social organization, is given in the fact that it contains neither any intrinsic structural components which guarantee that it can be used for constructive purposes only, nor any inherent structural safeguards against its utilization in destructive purposes. Thus, as Raul Hilberg has observed, there was nothing implicit in the German bureaucracy itself to prevent Hitler's rise to power in 1933, nor to prevent the transformation of the random violence of the early anti-Jewish pogroms into a systematic, rationally organized, and administered implementation of the "Final Solution to the Jewish Problem" (Hilberg, 1961:18). Hitler provided both the necessary control and direction from above as well as the essential initial impulsion that launched the destruction process, and culminated in the extermination of six million human beings. Obviously, then, this ostensibly neutral and objective means of organization can function just as

201

expeditiously in the perpetration of evil as of good. However, even beyond this potential utility as an instrument in the administration of evil, Hilberg suggests that the apparent objective neutrality of bureaucracy is deceptive—that there are certain integral components of the structure itself which are potentially if not implicitly "steppingstones to a killing operation..." (Hilberg, 1961:639). That is, the bureaucratic apparatus may not only expedite the implementation of social destructiveness, but may actually be conducive to social destructiveness.

If, indeed, specific social institutions such as bureaucracy can create conditions in which all normal moral guidelines are invalidated, and in which it becomes virtually impossible to distinguish right from wrong--as the quotations from Arendt, Uris, and Duster indicate—then difficult and critical problems arise in the determination of the nature of conscience and moral judgment, and of individual and collective responsibility and accountability for evi. For instance, even if it can be shown that institutions as well as individuals are not "beyond good and evil" but stand in need of moral evaluation, this does not automatically nor necessarily absolve individual guilt— for extraordinary circumstances do not mitigate the burden of guilt for complicity in evil—be it knowing or unwitting—when the actions involved constitute a crime against humanity. In the case of societal evil, the logical and ethical course—from the perspective of the sociologist—is to discover which particular structures are actually at fault, and either to devise practical and beneficial alternative structures, or to devise means through which the inimical components can be transformed into innocuous ones. That is, if evil is endemic to social reality as well as to human nature, then as long as human nature remains relatively more impervious to the calculations of scientific method than is social reality, it would seem adviseable to pursue societal reconstruction. In answer to Duster, it does make sense, and it could make a great deal of difference for future generations to "...talk about the location of guilt in the Germany of the Third Reich" (1971:27) if the detection of societal sources of evil is a preliminary step toward the elimination or transformation of those sources.

To this end, and in accordance with the view advanced in the Introductory Chapter that science should be reoriented toward investigating fundamental moral problems such as evil and transcendence, and that sociology in particular should examine and expose the covert societal determinants of human judgment, this chapter offers an original sociological analysis of bureaucracy as an inherently totalitarian form of social organization. This analysis is an attempt to determine, on the one hand, which of bureaucracy's components and processes induce dehumanization and social destructiveness through subversion and/or eradication of human judgment, and on the other hand, which of its components and processes generate transcendence of evil by evoking and sustaining the exercise of human judgment. The theory of evil and transcendence within the context of bureaucracy developed in this chapter draws selectively from and synthesizes into a novel framework the relevant and instructive contributions of several social science scholars, including: Sanford and Comstock's conceptualization of social destructiveness; the essential constituents of bureaucratic organization identified by Weber; the latent dysfunctions of bureaucracy identified by Merton; and the ultimate consequences for the aggressors and victims of bureaucracy's totalitarian features as these are delineated in Arendt's and in Hilberg's analyses of the Third Reich.

Definitions of Evil and of Transcendence

According to the sociological perspective, social reality is defined as the crucial locus of causality. In this view, the phenomena of good, evil, and transcendence are not matters of individual opinion, inclination, or action, but of societal predetermination. The moral conceptions of the individual consist of the internalized definitions of the society's normative order. If society is assumed to be the ultimate arbiter of good and evil, then it can be further hypothesized that good and evil may be defined in terms of what is beneficial or harmful to a particular society. Thus, good and evil may be construed in terms relative to the welfare of each society. On the basis of these assumptions, it is possible to conceive of a situation where the normative order of one society or group of people defines another society or group of people as detrimental or positively harmful to its welfare. Within the context of the first society's normative order, the removal of this threat through the destruction of the other society would be considered morally good, whereas toleration or peaceful co-existence with the other society would be considered morally evil. Thus, where moral notions are defined relative to the welfare of each society, genocide may be positively sanctioned. It goes without saying, however, that such relativistic standards are detrimental to the welfare of the world community of societies. On the basis of this judgment, such standards are interpreted as intimations of the nature of evil on the societal level. The term "social destructiveness" has been introduced by Sanford and Comstock in Sanctions for Evil as symbolic of societal evil on the basis of their analysis of similar situations in which "...members of one culture held the power of death or grievous harm over a people regarded as inferior and sometimes as subhuman..." (Sanford and Comstock, 1971:2). In consonance with their analysis and conclusions, societal evil will here be defined as "social destructiveness" which consists of the systematic and socially sanctioned perpetration of mental and/or physical injury on one group of people who are considered "inferior" or "subhuman" by another group of people (Sanford and Comstock, 1971:5).

Since individual participation in social destructiveness must thus be the consequence of socialization into the normative order, or the internalization of prescribed and habitual modes of thought and conduct, transcendence of evil will be defined as a conscious and unceasing individual endeavor to maintain an attitude of critical doubt, or skepticism toward the world, a diligent refusal to take for granted the socially sanctioned givens of one's world. That is, the induction into social destructiveness through the societal subversion of the critical faculties must be counteracted by a deliberate cultivation of the art of distrust of the given. It is such distrust that creates a perceptual and cognitive receptivity to experiences which negate or expose the falsity of the given, hence sustaining the latent potential of the critical faculties. Finally. transcendence through the art of distrust must be grounded in a rational recognition and an empathetic conviction of the inalienable humanness of all people which are manifested in conduct as universal and unequivocal respect for others.

Locus of Causality

As the scientific study of collective life, the discipline of Sociology focuses upon the social origins of and the group influences upon human thought and behavior. According to this world-view, individuals are born into a social world which fashions the content of their existence, and the individual life is construed as a minute replica of the collective life. The dependence of individual thought and behavior upon the social context is most strongly emphasized, and most clearly delineated in the subdiscipline of the sociology of knowledge which takes as its central proposition the Marxian thesis:

> It is not the consciousness of men that determines their existence, but on the contrary, their social existence that determines their consciousness (Marx, 1904:11-12).

It is the contention of the sociology of knowledge that the conception of reality is a social construct, originated, established, and maintained by group consensus, and that it is this aspect of human social existence which informs and fashions the content of consciousness. Thus, the varying patterns of individual perception, cognition, and behavior derive from the causal context of the social construction of reality. In the words of Karl Mannheim, one of the founders of the sociology of knowledge:

> Only in a quite limited sense does the single individual create out of himself the mode of speech and of thought we attribute to him. He speaks the language of his group; he thinks in the manner in which his group thinks. He finds at his disposal only certain words and their meanings...it is not men in general who think, or even isolated individuals who do the thinking, but men in certain groups who have developed a particular style of thought in an endless series of responses to certain typical situations characterizing their common position. Strictly speaking it is incorrect to say that the single individual thinks. Rather it is more correct to insist that he participates in thinking further what other men have thought before him. He finds himself in an inherited situation with patterns of thought which are appropriate to this situation.... Every individual is therefore in a two-fold sense predetermined by the fact of growing up in a society: on the one hand

he finds a ready-made situation and on the
other he finds in that situation preformed
patterns of thought and conduct (Mannheim,
1936:3).

This is not to say, however, that the sociology of knowledge denies that human beings possess the
unique and distinctively human attributes of reason
and imagination—a central assumption of psychologists
such as Erich Fromm and Rollo May—but rather stresses
that the contents of consciousness upon which these
critical faculties are exercised are predetermined by
society, and further and more importantly, that the
very pattern or direction of reflection itself is to a
great extent determined by social forces. That is, to
the extent that the routinized activities of a social
position pragmatically require and generate a functional and habitual mode of thought and behavior, the
emergent creativity of the critical faculties is
inhibited or reduced. To this extent, individual
thought and behavior is a product of the social inheri-
tence, human nature is a function of social reality,
and social reality constitutes the primary locus of
causality in human life.

Sources of Evil and of Transcendence

The provocative Marxian thesis that human
thought is grounded in activity, that a wide range of
human activities are determined by the predominant mode
of production in society, and that the specific set of
activities associated with a particular role or position in the productive process engenders a distinctive
pattern of thought and conduct has become a sociological truism. As Robert K. Merton phrases it:

Thus, it may be assumed that the various occupational
roles of the bureaucratic structure are informed with
a distinctive mode of consciousness and conduct generated by bureaucracy as one form of the organization of
productive activities. Recognizing also, however, that
every individual in society occupies a number of

206

diverse roles and activities, what are the distinctive features of the mode of consciousness and conduct characteristic of the bureaucratic role?

The distinctive features of the bureaucratic perspective are most vividly revealed through the comparison of this perspective with that which emerges in the basic process of socialization into social life. The process of socialization, according to the symbolic interactionists, typically instills in individuals tendencies toward two distinct modes of relation to others. On the one hand is the tendency toward the I-Thou mode of personalized interaction characteristic of primary relations, and on the other hand is the tendency toward the I-It mode of depersonalized interaction characteristic of secondary relations. In the I-Thou mode of relation, each participant perceives the other as a subject, like himself or herself, relates to the total being of the other, and incorporates the worldview of the other into his or her own, thus enriching his or her own subjective experience. Conversely, in the I-It mode of relation, each participant perceives the other as an object, unlike himself or herself, relates only to a particularized aspect of the other which is perceived as useful, selectively incorporates only a fraction of the other's world-view, and thus expands his or her own experience to a lesser degree than in the I-Thou mode.

Since the I-Thou mode of primary relations incorporates so much more of the other's total being into each participant than the I-It mode, it tends to maximize individual development or self-actualization. The I-It mode of secondary relations, conversely, because it incorporates so much less of the other's total being into each participant, tends to minimize individual development, and further, in the process of objectifying the other, also objectifies self, and hence tends toward dehumanization instead of self-actualization. This is not to say that the I-Thou mode is healthier or better than the I-It mode, for neither can be maintained exclusively and indefinitely without injuring the individual. Both are necessary to carry out the diversified activities of social life. The socialization process not only inculcates inclinations toward both of these modes, but moreover, induces a rational, and individually directed vascillation between the two modes in the interest of self-actualization and self-preservation. Thus, the pattern of thought and conduct promoted by socialization is oriented toward the

207

preservation and realization of the humanity of self and other.

However, such is not the case with the pattern of consciousness and conduct generated by the bureaucratic organization of production. The norm of relationship within the formal organization of bureaucracy requires strict impersonality. Both the relationships among the bureaucrats themselves, and between them and their clients are characterized by interaction in the depersonalized I-It mode of secondary relations to the exclusion of the personalized I-Thou mode of primary relations. The pernicious tendency of bureaucracy is thus to inhibit self-actualization, to induce objectification of self and other, and hence to promote dehumanization. The consciousness and conduct of the bureaucrat is characterized by a deleterious unawareness of the humanity of self and other.

A second critical difference between the generalized perspective instilled by socialization, and that ensuing from bureaucratic activities involves the faculties of critical reflection. According to Meadian theory, the self which arises through socialization consists of two antithetical components, the "Me" and the "I" (Mead, 1967:175). The "Me" aspect of the self is defined as the unconsciously internalized representation of the generalized attitudes of the community, of the existing social construction of reality. The "Me" embodies in the individual the predetermined givens of the world received from society. Received as a priori to individual experience, the social construction of reality defines the unproblematic aspects of the world which are therefore also unreflected. This uncritical acceptance of the established world-view binds the individual to society, and is manifested in unquestioning conformity of thought and behavior to the dictates of society. The "I" aspect of the self, which is also aroused in socialization, is defined, in contrast, as the unique personalized reaction of the individual to the given content of the "Me." The "I" is the original reaction of the individual against the established consensus of society. Whereas the content of consciousness is given in the "Me," the activity of consciousness is the function of the "I." As socialization proceeds, the societal givens are internalized in the "Me," the "I" responds to, and reacts against these givens, and the process of critical reflection emerges as the action of the "I" on the "Me." Thus, socialization imbues in the individual tendencies toward both mindless conformity and critical reflection.

208

Again, such is not the case in the internalization of the demands and expectations of the bureaucratic role. The contents of consciousness provided by the bureaucratic order consist of clearly delineated and restricted rights, duties, and regulations pertaining to a particular role. As Sjoberg and Miller (1973: 129) have observed, the bureaucratic order militates against reflection beyond the immediate requirements of the role functions through structural restraints against the free flow of information within the organization embodied in the hierarchial authority structure. The restrictions on the availability and adequacy of information about the goals, policies, procedures, and processes of the organization ensuing from the hierarchy of authority prevent the bureaucrat from developing a total picture of the situation, a comprehensive understanding of the organization, and its consequences for the public. Reflection on the organization as a whole, and its ramifications throughout the public domain is thus precluded by the inadequacy and unavailability of the data necessary for critical reflection and judgment. In contrast to the arousal of antithetical impulses to conformity and critical reflection characteristic of the socialization process, the bureaucratic structure tends to undermine the impulse to reflection, and generates instead an unwitting ignorance, or, more precisely, thoughtlessness.

Consequently, as opposed to the general perspective inculcated through socialization into collective life which is characterized by dual inclinations toward both the I-Thou and the I-It mode of relation, and tendencies toward both conformity and reflection, the distinctive features of the mode of consciousness and conduct engendered by bureaucracy include tendencies toward dehumanization ensuing from the norm of impersonality, and an inclination toward throughtlessness resulting from the hierarchial restrictions on the free flow of information. If this is indeed the case, then what is the significance of dehumanization and thoughtlessness with regard to the problem of evil? Dehumanization has been defined as a psychological state which:

> ...entails a decrease in a person's sense of his own individuality and in his perception of the humanness of other people. This misperceiving of others ranges from viewing them en bloc as "subhuman" or "bad human"...to viewing them as "nonhuman"....

209

As such, their maltreatment or even their destruction may be carried out or acquiesced
in with relative freedom from the restraint
of conscience or feelings of brotherhood
(Bernard et al., 1971:102).

Dehumanization, thus, ultimately constitutes a
sanction for social destructiveness, and conduces toward social destructiveness by removing the objectified victim from the realm of conscience and the unity
of humanity. Dehumanization effectively divides human beings into two groups: the human and the nonhuman, the good and the evil, the aggressors and the
victims, and finally, the survivors and the dead.
That dehumanization is incontestably a necessary condition of social destructiveness was demonstrated by
Nazi propaganda which defined the intended victim as
a criminal, a parasite, vermin a disease, and so on.
Such definitions eliminated the possibility of empathetic identification with the victims, and hence
effectively negated the psychological and moral obstacles to genocide.

Whereas dehumanization removes the objectified other from the considerations of moral judgment,
the relation of thoughtlessness to evil is given in
the fact that the restriction of information, and
the provision of inadequate or distorted data as in
the bureaucratic setting, renders the individual ignorant of the consequences and ramifications of his
or her own and the organization's actions, and thus
unaware of the perpetration of evil and his or her
complicity in evil. The individual becomes incapable
of perceiving or realizing the ultimately evil or
harmful effects of his or her own actions. The individual's reflections and judgments are, of necessity,
confined to the immediate situation in which he or she
functions, and beyond with he or she has no information. The structural limitations on information preclude thought beyond the immediate requirements of
the role, remove him or her psychologically from the
consequences of his or her actions, and transform him
or her into an unwitting participant in the perpetration of evil. That such thoughtlessness is conducive
to social destructiveness is also demonstrated by the
bureaucratization of genocide in the Third Reich—as
Hannah Arendt observed at the Eichmann trial:

Eichmann was not Iago and not Macbeth, and
nothing would have been farther from his

210

mind than to determine with Richard III "to
prove a villain...." He merely...never realized what he was doing.... It was sheer
thoughtlessness—something by no means identical with stupidity—that predisposed him to
become one of the greatest criminals of that
period (Arendt, 1973:287-288).

The pattern of consciousness and conduct typical of the bureaucratic setting are distinguished by
inclinations toward dehumanization—arising from the
norm of impersonality—and toward thoughtlessness—ensuing from the heirarchial distribution of information.
Since the evidence indicates that both dehumanization
and thoughtlessness are necessary if not sufficient
conditions for social destructiveness, the source of
evil on the societal level is identified—according to
the classification scheme given in the Introduction—
as the action of a component of the system of social
reality—bureaucracy—on a component of the system of
human nature, i.e., the mode of consciousness and conduct.

Having concluded that the source of evil is
none other than the predominant form of organization
and production in modern society, what, if any, are the
sources of transcendence of evil? As previously stated, transcendence of societal evil requires an awareness of and respect for the humanity of others, supported by the conscientious maintenance of an attitude of
distrust, of skepticism in regard to the world. Within
the bureaucratic setting, such a transcendence of factors which induce dehumanization may evolve from the
establishment of informal groups within the formal organization. Such groups exist outside the scope of the
rigid authority and requirements of the organization,
are founded on common interests and activities, are
characterized by interaction in the I-Thou mode of primary relations, and are sustained by the close personal
emotional involvements of members. In the relationships of informal groups, individual members value each
other as individuals—as ends rather than means—relate
to the total being of the other rather than to a specific aspect such as the function of the other, and are
attracted to each other, and become attached to each
other as fully human and uniquely individualized beings. The existence of such relations in informal
groups within the context of the bureaucratic organization sustains individual awareness and appreciation of
the humanness of self and other, and hence militates

211

against internalization of the dehumanized mode of consciousness fostered by the norm of impersonality.

Internalization of role requirements for dehumanized thought and behavior may also be counteracted by the experience of role conflict. Every individual occupies several social statuses outside of the occupational one, and performs the associated diverse role activities. Each status-role set contains distinctive values, expectations, and definitions of the situation relevant to that role. There may not necessarily be a consistency or congruency between the implicit values, expectations, and definitions of a person's several roles, but usually these discrepancies pass unnoticed due to compartmentalization of role activities. However, when a number of roles overlap—when the roles impinge or infringe on the territory of the others—the covert clash of contradictory values may be manifested externally in an inability to coordinate the inconsistent activities required by the roles. That is, disparities between the implicit values of dissimilar roles generate conflict in behavior, and impede conduct. The individual's attempts to resolve the conflict, and to coordinate the activities necessitate reflection on the assumptions, requirements, and consequences of the various roles. This reflection exposes the inherent discrepancies of values, as well as the functionality or dysfunctionality of the required behaviors. The individual is then in a position to accept or reject the roles accordingly, or to modify his or her performance of the expected behaviors. Thus, for instance, if a friend of the bureaucrat should become a client, the discrepancy between his or her personalized behavior required by the role of friend, and the impersonal behavior required by the role as bureaucrat may generate such a confusion in the performance of the bureaucratic function that he or she is literally forced by circumstances to reflect on the antithetical roles. This reflection may generate recognition of the dysfunctionality of dehumanizing the other as is demanded by the norm of impersonality, and hence recognition of the functionality of personalizing behavior as a bureaucrat. Thus, role conflict also may stimulate an awareness of the humanity of others, and counteract the internalized inclination to dehumanization.

With regard to the inclination to thoughtlessness generated by bureaucracy, transcendence of thoughtlessness as well as dehumanization may ensue from the establishment of informal groups. The openness, directness, and attachment of primary relations

212

within the group and outside the scope and requirements of the hierarchy of authority provides a forum for discussion, and promotes a free exchange of information about the organization and its role in society. Such an exchange of information among individuals from different levels in the organization promotes an accumulation of perspectives that makes possible a more comprehensive understanding of the inner workings of the organization as a whole, and its consequences for the public domain. This exchange of information provides more adequate data for reflection and judgment, stimulates the critical faculties, arouses an awareness of the need for knowledge, reflection, and judgment, and evokes a healthy distrust for the organization itself. Thus, the activation of the critical faculties resulting from the discussions in informal groups may counterbalance the factors in bureaucracy that foster thoughtlessness.

The psychological remoteness from the consequences of action which bureaucratic thoughtlessness entails may be mitigated by the continuing influence of modern education. Ostensibly at least, modern education is oriented toward awakening and developing the critical faculties of reason, logic, and imagination, rather than focusing on rote memorization of multitudinous facts. The constant exercise of the mind, learning to reason from given premises to logical but unknown conclusions, prepares the individual to cope with the unknown, unpredictable, and unusual aspects of social life. The inculcation of the habit of logical reasoning through education creates an active, inquisitive consciousness which is not likely to be susceptible to the bureaucratic decline into thoughtlessness. Secondly, modern education militates against one aspect of socialization into the bureaucratic role of thoughtlessness which entails the passive acceptance of the bureaucratic perspective as absolute truth. That is, as Mannheim observed:

> Modern education from its inception is a living struggle, a replica, on a small scale of the conflicting purposes and tendencies which rage in society at large.... This acquired intellectual heritage subjects him to the influence of opposing tendencies in social reality, while the person who is not oriented toward the whole through his education, but rather participates directly in the social process of production, merely tends to absorb the Weltanschauung of that particular group

213

and to act exclusively under the influence of
the conditions imposed by his immediate social situation (Mannheim, 1936:156).

The trend in modern education is to expose the student
to a diversity and multiplicity of world-views—all of
which seem equally valid. Such exposure demonstrates
the relativity of all perspectives, arouses a skepticism in the student and motivates him or her to doubt,
question, and critically examine his or her own perspective as well as those which he or she encounters in
later life. Thus, education reduces the possibility
for an unquestioning internalization of the bureaucratic perspective, and an unwitting socialization into
thoughtlessness.

Finally, the aforementioned mechanism of role
conflict—where the clash of values and expectations
intrinsic to the roles is manifested as an interruption
of behavior, a difficulty in conduct which necessitates
reflection on the roles to solve the problem—in the
case of bureaucratic thoughtlessness, induces an awareness of the hierarchially imposed ignorance, of the
dangers this ignorance entails, and of the unintended
but potentially harmful consequences for others ensuing
from actions calculated without consideration of possible effects. Thus, the awareness aroused by role
conflict may also mitigate the passive acceptance of
thoughtlessness as a role requirement.

In sum, the societal evil of the bureaucratic
mode of consciousness characterized by dehumanization
and thoughtlessness may be transcended by virtue of the
counteracting influences exerted by informal groups,
education, and role conflict. The sources of transcendence of evil are identified as the action of components of social reality which render problematic the
givens of the bureaucratic world-view, and require reflection as a medium of pragmatic problem-solving activity.

Manifestations of Evil and Transcendence

Turning to the particular causes of dehumanization and thoughtlessness in bureaucracy, it soon becomes evident that precisely those exceptional characteristics and components which insure its "...technical
superiority over any other form of organization"
(Weber, 1968:973) also give rise to the preconditions
of social destructiveness. Considering first the phenomenon of dehumanization, of the four characteristics

214

of the bureaucratic ideal type listed in the Dictionary
of the Social Sciences (Gould and Kolb, 1964:61) three
may contribute to dehumanization. In the first place,
rationality in decision-making insures a reliability of
judgments made on the basis of purely objective considerations, and not subject to the vicissitudes of whim
or fancy. However, a strict reliance on the conclusions of reason as dictated by the facts of a case, and
unmediated by a human concern and compassion for the
people involved, militates against recognition and consideration of all significant aspects of the case—such
as the subjective attitude and unique needs of the
clients—and tends to produce technically correct but
humanly inadequate decisions or solutions. Secondly,
it is true that impersonality in social relations expedites the performance and completion of specified
tasks. However, the definition and perception of the
client as an object deprives him or her of any claim to
the personal concern, compassion, or consideration of
the bureaucrat, and identifies him or her as a nonhuman
that can be ill-treated with impunity. Thirdly, while
the routinization of tasks promotes administrative continuity by allowing each similarly labelled case to be
dispatched in an identical fashion, it also prevents
recognition of the unique features of a case which must
be taken into account in order to formulate adequate
solutions (Gould and Kolb, 1964:61).

        Similarly, of the ten qualities Weber judges
to be eminently desirable in any form of organization,
and which are "...raised to the optimum point in the
strictly bureaucratic administration..." (Weber, 1968:
973),[1] four are potentially conducive to dehumanization. First, precision, which is defined as "exact
limitation," "accuracy," "definiteness," derives from
the Latin root "praecisio" meaning "a cutting off"
(Neilson, et al., 1956:1944). In the bureaucrat's
dealings with a client, the quality of precision may
entail a rigid attention and adherence to the bare
facts of the case, a "cutting off" of perception of aspects beyond the facts but relevant to the individual.
Hence, the bureaucrat develops a tunnel vision that

---

[1]My thanks to Professor Boyd Littrell for
suggesting the examination of the definitions and deri-
vations of key words as a method of approach to an unfamiliar topic.

ignores the special situation of the client, and admits
no alternative and perhaps more adequate solution to
the case than that which according to the general rules
is technically correct. Second, the emphasis on speed
—the rate of performance (rather than the quality of
performance) as measured by the amount accomplished in
a given time—encourages a tunnel vision detrimental to
the client in that the bureaucrat tends to restrict analysis of a case to its general rather than special aspects in order to dispose of it as quickly as possible.
Third, the quality of continuity "...signifies identity
with respect to a series of changes" and derives from
the Latin root "continere" meaning "to hold together,"
or "to repress" (Neilson, et al., 1956:577;576). The
stress on administrative continuity may detract from
the client's welfare by fostering an over-concern for
identicality of procedure in handling similarly defined
or categorized cases. This ritualization of procedure
suppresses the case's unique features, and precludes
comprehensive understanding and adequate resolution.
Fourth, reliance on knowledge of the files—on the
techniques which have been useful in the past, but are
not therefore necessarily applicable to the present—
supports administrative continuity, and hence exacerbates the detrimental restriction of vison and understanding with regard to individual cases.

        The net effect of each of these four quali-
ties is to insure that individual cases are perceived,
comprehended, and solved according to their identity
with the definitions, categories, and stipulations of
official rules, that the general aspects of cases are
emphasized to the exclusion of their special aspects,
and that the client is depersonalized and dehumanized
as his or her unique situation is transformed into a
common and ordinary one. The client is objectified and
ill-treated to the extent that his or her individuality
and exceptional situation are ignored. These several
qualities contribute to the extraordinary objectivity
of bureaucracy, which, according to Weber, constitutes
one of the significant improvements of bureaucracy as
opposed to other forms of organization, and is a major
cause of its increased efficiency:

        Bureaucratization offers above all the optim-
        um possibility for carrying through the prin-
        ciple of specializing administrative func-
        tions according to purely objective consider-
        ations.... "Objective" discharge of business
        primarily means a discharge of business ac-
        cording to calculable rules and "without

regard for persons...." Bureaucracy develops the more perfectly, the more it is "dehumanized," the more completely it succeeds in eliminating from official business love, hatred, and all purely personal, irrational, and emotional elements which escape calculation (Weber, 1968:975).

In contrast to Weber's obvious admiration for bureaucratic objectivity, Robert K. Merton points out its definite dysfunctions for the client:

> Another feature of the bureaucratic structure, the stress on depersonalization of relationships, also plays its part in the bureaucrat's trained incapacity. The personality pattern of the bureaucrat is nucleated about this norm of impersonality. Both this and the categorizing tendency, which develops from the dominant role of general, abstract rules, tend to produce conflict in the bureaucrat's contacts with the public or clientele. Since functionaries minimize personal relations and resort to categorization, the peculiarities of individual cases are often ignored.... Stereotyped behavior is not adapted to the exigencies of individual problems (Merton, 1968:256).

The distinctive feature of bureaucratic objectivity—which so efficiently expedites the transaction of business—thus arises from: (1) the institutionalization of impersonality as a role requirement, according to which the bureaucrat perceives, relates to, understands, and treats the client as an object, not a person, according to which the client does not exist except in so far as some aspect of his or her life constitutes a task for the official; and from (2) the organizational requirement that tasks be performed according to standardized rules which furnish abstract, generalized guidelines for categorizing cases, and for determining which aspects of the client and his or her situation are relevant or irrelevant, to be taken into consideration or to be ignored. The basic assumption underlying these two norms is that the total being of the client and all aspects of his or her life obviously are not pertinent to the specific task at hand, and consequently, that the awareness of such extraneous dimensions would impede the completion of the task. However, deliberately ignoring these other aspects of the

client effectively reduces his or her intrinsic person-
hood, and cultivates an incapacity to recognize the humanness of the other which ultimately disposes the bureaucrat toward maltreatment of the objectified other.

This psychological removal of the client from
the realm of humanity is exacerbated by a separation of
the bureaucrat's public and private life that has crucial moral implications. Weber observed that this separation comprises a fundamental characteristic of bureaucratic organization:

> In principle, the modern organization of the
> civil service separates the bureau from the
> private domicile of the official and, in gen-
> eral, segregates official activity from the
> sphere of private life (Weber, 1968:957).

That is, as the bureaucrat is socialized into the organization—internalizing the values, definitions, and
expectations of the role—he or she learns that the bureaucracy is a world in itself, apart from private
life. It possesses its own rules and regulations for
thought and conduct distinct from those of private
life. Whereas private life is characterized by the
personalized interaction of primary relations, and the
free exercise of individual critical and moral judgment, participation in bureaucratic life requires the
impersonal interaction of secondary relations, and imposes severe restrictions on independent individual reflection. The bureaucrat learns that the normative requirements of the public and private domains are mutually exclusive: the norms of public life are not suitable for private life, and should not be transposed to
it, and likewise, the norms of private life are not applicable to the public life, and should not be transposed to it. If he or she is to competently perform
official duties, the bureaucrat must rigidly abide by
the given rules, and resist the temptation to think and
act normally as he or she does outside the organization. Outside the organization he or she recognizes
that the laws of collective life arise from the bond of
a common humanity, according to which the unique individuality of others is of paramount significance, relationships are oriented toward the total being of
others, and are characterized by respect and humane
treatment of others. In contrast, within the organization, the normative regulations derive from the goal of
administrative efficiency, according to which the individuality of others is immaterial, the official

relates only to that aspect of the client's total being pertinent to his or her function, the relationship is characterized by indifference, and consequently, the moral bond of common humanity is negated. The other as client does not merit the status of human being, and hence is excluded from the moral requirements of just and humane treatment. Thus removing the client from the protective purview of morality, the segmentation of private and public life, intensifies the injurious effects of bureaucratic dehumanization.

Finally, the enactment of these role requirements—which are potentially and implicitly detrimental to the client's welfare—is insured by the inculcation of a sense of obedience and discipline in the official, buttressed by the inducements of various incentives. According to Weber:

> The discipline of officialdom refers to the attitude-set of the official for precise obedience within his habitual activity....
> Such compliance has been conditioned into the officials, on the one hand, and, on the other hand, into the governed (Weber, 1963:74).

Such conditioning, is to a great extent, a function of the secure existence offered in the form of "incremental salaries," pensions, a "graded career" through "promotion by seniority" (Merton, 1968:254), social prestige of the office, the absence of competition, and an affective esprit de corps among the officials themselves. The tantalizing prospect of a secure and materially rewarding career motivates the official to adopt the bureaucratic perspective, and to adapt his or her thought and behavior to the values, expectations, and requirements of the role. By appealing to the official's self-interest, the bureaucracy corrupts his or her human dignity, and seduces him or her into willing compliance with regulations and procedures detrimental to an other's—the client's—welfare.

The intrinsically invidious nature of these characteristics will be illustrated by means of examples taken from the Nazi regime which reveal their ultimate logical and evil end. First of all, the transformation in the definition (and perception) of the client from a unique individual personality to an undifferentiated object of official activity wrought by the factors of objectivity and segmentation removes from the client the essential humanness which is the source of psychological and moral restraints on

219

behavior harmful to others. The removal of these restraints constitutes, in effect, a positive sanction for, and a covert impetus to aggression against the other who has been surrepticiously defined as less than human. Such a redefinition not only makes possible, but calls for and calls forth destructive aggression. As Hilberg observed of the Nazi bureaucracy's redefinition of the Jews:

> Whatever their origins and whatever their destination, the function of these stereotypes is always the same. They are used as justifications for destructive thinking; they are employed as excuses for destructive action (Hilberg, 1961:8).

As a process, the transition from tacit dehumanization to manifest destructiveness may take place through the explicit legitimation of the dehumanizing definition of the other which constitutes both a positive sanction, and a legal justification for destruction of the victim. Further, such an explicit judicial ruling transforms the destruction of the victim into a moral obligation of the aggressor. Thus, in the Third Reich, the legal definition of the Jews progressively deteriorated to the point of "race-defiling Jewish habitual criminals" (Hilberg, 1961:602) which presented to the Nazis the historic mission of cleansing the Reich of the Jewish contamination. In accordance with this definition, the Jews became the victims of deportation, expropriation, extermination, and fatal medical experiments.

Secondly, the pernicious interrelation of bureaucratic objectivity and the compartmentalization of public and private morality is evident in the use of rigid language rules by the Nazis in order to maintain an impersonal, objective, and professional attitude toward the extermination process. The language rules consisted of objective code names for the destruction process. For example, the code name for the entire operation was the "Final Solution of the Jewish problem," and killing was alternately referred to as "evacuation" (Aussiedlung), "special treatment" (Sonderbehandlung) (Arendt, 1973:85), "special actions" (Sonderaktionen), "cleansing" (Säuberung), "cleaning up of the Jewish question" (Bereiningung der Judenfrage) (Hilberg, 1961: 216). The effect of the "objective" or more precisely, the deceptive, language system was to reinforce and maintain the bureaucratic division between private and public life, between private morality and professional

220

duty, and thus to exclude the extermination process from the domain of private moral judgment. The compartmentalization of morality allowed the bureaucrat to perform his or her professional duty, and function in the process of destruction without perceiving or evaluating his or her actions as murder. The bureaucrat's personal feelings were divorced from, and not relevant to his or her official duties. Thus many a devoted Nazi could claim that he or she was not anti-Semitic. The bureaucratic objectivity of the language rules sustained the separation of private morality and professional duty, preserved the official's sense of decency, and enabled him or her to murder or "cleanse" without compunction. The logical end of bureaucratic objectivity is the evasion of conscience and moral scruples.

The several causes of one precondition of social destructiveness—i.e., dehumanization—within bureaucracy have been identified as: (1) the tunnel vision engendered by the emphasis on the qualities of precision, speed, continuity, and knowledge of the files; (2) the learned incapacity to perceive or be aware of the humanness of others arising from the transaction of business impersonally and according to standardized rules; (3) the compartmentalization of personal morality and professional duty ensuing from the separation of private and public life; and (4) insensitivity to the harmful consequences of one's actions resulting from the incentive-induced devotion to duty and commitment to the organization's goals.

The cumulative effect of these several factors is initially manifested in a dualistic and mutually reinforcing dehumanization of self and other. That is, the bureaucrat's restricted perception of the other (i.e., client) as an object rather than a person not only dehumanizes the other, but further, dehumanizes the bureaucrat also since in interaction with the objectified other he or she perceives his or her reflection through the other as an object also. To the extent that individuals deny the humanness of others, the reflection of themselves in the others reduces their awareness of themselves as human beings, and conversely, to the extent that this sense of self decreases, their ability to perceive and relate to others as human beings also decreases. As Bernard and associates have summarized this relationship:

These two forms of dehumanization are mutually reinforcing: reduction in the fullness of one's feelings for other human beings...

221

impoverishes one's sense of self; any lessen-
ing of the humanness of one's self-image limits one's capacity for relating to others
(Bernard et al., 1971:104).

The destructive potential of such self and other dehumanization is exacerbated by the further fact that as
bureaucrats lose awareness of the humanity—of themselves and others—they lose also the ability to identify
with others, to take the role of others in order to understand and empathize with them, and subsequently manifest a callous indifference to the fate or the suffering of others. That is, the definition of others as
nonhuman, an objects alien to the self, dispel the previously ingrained inclination to take the role of
others, to identify oneself with others in order to understand them and expand one's own experience. The
failure to do so diminishes the bureaucrats' sense of
self and the intensity and extensity of their own affective capacities. This constriction of their affective capacities dissipates any motivation to be concerned
about the welfare or fate of others. The impenetrable
indifference generated by the failure to identify with
others predisposes the bureaucrats to inflict any manner of aggression or harm on the victim. As Bernard L.
Diamond succinctly summarizes this mechanism:

> ...a person who has no capacity to identify
> with others treats people and the objects
> people value as meaningless things that can
> be destroyed at will (Diamond, 1971:128);

and according to Bernard and associates:

> The magnitudes of annihilation that may be
> perpetrated with indifference would seem to
> transcend those carried out in hatred and an-
> ger. This was demonstrated by the imperson-
> al, mechanical efficiency of extermination at
> the Nazi death camps (Bernard, et al., 1971:
> 103)

Finally, among the consequences of the dehumanizing factors in bureaucracy conducive to social destructiveness, the segmentation of private and public
life evokes the most horrifying prospect of creating
conditions in which it is practically impossible to
distinguish right from wrong. The compartmentalization
of private morality and professional duty prevents the
bureaucrats from applying the moral principles

governing their private lives to the duties inhering in their official roles. The only guidelines allowed for evaluating their professional activities stem from the organizational goal of administrative efficiency. The judgment of official activities according to standards established by the organization of which the specific role is a part confines moral evaluation to the context of administrative efficiency, and excludes the "higher" morality of common humanity. The result is that the bureaucrats will simply not realize that the requirements of their offices violate the order of humanity. In private life the concepts of right and wrong are determined by the common bond of humanity. In professional life the concepts of right and wrong are determined by the context of the organization, and these two moral systems may be diametrically opposed, each antithetical to the other.

The descent into social destructiveness generated by bureaucratic dehumanization is demonstrated again by the informative example of Hitler Germany. In this case, while the goal of genocide initially arose from fanatic racial hatred, the bureaucratization of genocide tended to displace intense hatred with callous indifference. Indeed, such indifference proved essential to the rational and efficient systematization of the destruction process. Spontaneous but erratic acts of murder motivated by hatred disrupted the efficiency, and decreased the effectiveness of the destruction process as a whole. Therefore such acts were regarded as unworthy of the Nazis, and warranted disciplinary action. The administration of genocide depended upon rigorous performance of duty buttressed by identification with the goals of the organization, and a cultivated indifference to the suffering of the victims. It was precisely such an absence of feeling, an indifference to the fate of the Jews, which enabled Nazi officials like Adolph Eichmann to organize and administer the extermination of millions of people with assembly-line efficiency. That such indifference is causally related to the bureaucratic erosion of the ability to identify with others is supported by Arendt's observation that Eichmann displayed an "...almost total inability ever to look at anything from the other fellow's point of view..." (Arendt, 1973:49). Eichmann could not recognize the evil nature of his activities largely because he could not take the role of the victims, identify with them, and perceive the suffering that he inflicted upon them.

223

Finally, the conclusion that the conditions of bureaucratic dehumanization, specifically of the compartmentalization of morality and duty, render the individual bureaucrat incapable of moral evaluation in regard to his or her official role is supported by Eichmann's contention that the administration of his official duty—organizing the transportation of millions of people to the death camps—did not prey on his conscience. However, the failure to carry out his orders would have been ethically reprehensible (Arendt, 1973: 25). Given this division of realities, a normal person may willingly perform actions in the official realm which in the private realm are considered crimes, and which he or she would never think of committing as a private citizen, without ever equating these official duties with criminality. Remaining perfectly capable of moral judgment in personal life, he or she becomes incapable of distinguishing good and evil in the public realm. Bureaucratic dehumanization thus culminates in a devastating subversion of conscience and moral behavior that can plunge a whole society into unmitigated social destructiveness.

Turning to the causes of thoughtlessness in bureaucracy, there is evidence to indicate that all four of the characteristics of the bureaucratic ideal type listed in The Dictionary of the Social Sciences (Gould and Kolb, 1964:61) may be conducive to this second precondition of social destructiveness. The focusing of attention and analysis to the client's immediate situation and the pertinent facts of his or her case as these are established by the general rules of the organization which is promoted by (1) rationality in decision-making, (2) impersonality of social relations, and (3) routinization of tasks, prevents recognition or consideration of factors deemed irrelevent to the completion of the task at hand—solution of the client's problem—such as, specifically, the ultimate consequences of the bureaucrat's decisions for the infividual client. Such extraneous factors are normatively defined as beyond the scope of organizational activity in general and individual role performance in particular, and are considered detrimental to the swift and efficient operation of administration. Secondly, and more importantly, the (4) centralization of authority in bureaucracy which prescribes a limited sphere of official jurisdiction, competence, responsibility, and authority for each individual functionary, entails also a hierarchial distribution and restriction of information according to the limited area of activity in each official position. Each bureaucrat receives only information which is judged to be necessary and relevant to his or her role activities. Consequently, only the officials at the top of the hierarchy are fully informed about all aspects of the organization, and are in a position to perceive, recognize, and evaluate its consequences and ramifications for the general public, whereas the other functionaries in a graded hierarchy are prevented from developing a comprehensive understanding of the organization as a whole. Such a lack of information and understanding militates against recognition, reflection, and evaluation of the consequences of organizational activities for the general public.

Furthermore, this rigorous circumscription of thought and understanding is exacerbated by eight of the ten extraordinary virtues of bureaucratic organization. (1) The emphasis on <u>precision</u> in terms of a strict attention to detail, and a disciplined and methodical performance of duties in accordance with the stipulations of the general rules entails a narrowing of vision, a "cutting off" of perception or innovation of possible and perhaps better solutions alternative to those provided in the general rules. (2) The requirement for <u>speed</u> in the performance of functions encourages a superficiality in analysis of cases in terms of their general characteristics—as provided for in the general organizational rules, and to the exclusion of their special characteristics. Such a superficial or cursory analysis may well entail also a concentration on the immediate task—in order to dispose of it as quickly as possible—which tends to exclude or ignore the relation of one task to the many others, and hence detracts from comprehension of the total process or system. (3) The <u>unambiguity</u> of official directives specifying the acceptable modes of analysis and resolution of client problems militates against originality, and the creative innovation of alternative and more functional solutions to client problems. Departure from the given courses of thought and action is proscribed, and the bureaucrat's vision and understanding are restricted to the prescribed range of possibilities. (4) The call for administrative <u>continuity</u> fosters a rigid ritualization of procedure antagonistic to the recognition of changes in the social environment outside the bureaucracy which require revisions in archaic organizational perspectives and procedures. (5) The virtue of bureaucratic <u>discretion</u> may have negative consequences where discretion in service of the organization runs counter to the interests of the public it

serves. A policy of discretion with regard to outsiders may shield from public scrutiny illegal or undesirable practices, and may prevent an open conflict
of the bureaucracy and the public which discloses such
evils to both the uninformed outsiders and the ill-
informed bureaucrats themselves. (6) Reliance on the
knowledge of the files—on the methods and solutions
which were found to be functional in the past, but
which are not necessarily applicable to the present
social reality--inhibits both the recognition of significant changes in the social environment to which
the organization must adapt, and originality and
creativity in inventing more adequate solutions to
existing problems. (7) Similarly, while the reduction of friction in social relations within the bureaucracy enhances harmonious working conditions, it also
eliminates the constructive conflict of divergent
opinions that sometimes stimulates original invention
and creative innovations in problem-solving activities. (8) The strict subordination of lower eschelon
"inferiors" to higher eschelon "superiors" militates
against the critical examination of the organization
by "inferiors." The judgment and decisions of higher
officials who are in fact better informed about the
organization as a whole is not doubted or questioned
by those in the lower orders who are not sufficiently
knoweldgeable. The policies and processes determined
by the higher levels tend to remain unexamined.

        The generation of ignorance and thoughtless-
ness by these various role expectations is considerably reinforced by the normative requirement for the
objective discharge of business according to "calcu-
able rules." That is, the organization provides
generalized guidelines for analytic and problem-solving
activity which identify the relevant and irrelevant
aspects of the client and his or her situation, and
delimit the range of possible and acceptable solutions.
The structure of his or her thought is thus predetermined for the individual bureaucrat, and the rigidity
of the governing rules is not conducive to originality
or to thought beyond the immediate requirements of a
specific task. Secondly, the establishment of these
rules by higher eschelon officials constitutes a significant decision-making process in which most functionaries are not ordinarily involved. Hence, the individual bureaucrat's sense of responsibility for the
consequences of decisions he or she did not make is
considerably reduced. He or she is psychologically
detached from the consequences of his or her own

226

actions--governed by those decisions--and the need for responsible critical reflection is eliminated. Furthermore, the "... concentration of the material means of management in the hands of the master"(Weber, 1968:980) in the bureaucratic form of organization similarly reduces the individual official's sense of responsibility for the actions of the organization. Deprived of ownership and policy level decision-making, the bureaucrat is responsible only to the organization for the competent performance of his or her duties, and not to society for the consequences of the organization's activities. This attenuation of individual responsibility dissipates any concern for the potential harm of the intended or unintended consequences of the organization.

The bureaucratic apparatus, however, not only tends to impose ignorance and foster thoughtlessness within the organization but also without by adopting a policy of administrative secrecy in regard to the general public. According to Weber:

> This superiority of the professional insider every bureaucracy seeks further to increase through the means of keeping secret its knowledge and intentions. Bureaucratic administration always tends to exclude the public, to hide its knowledge and action from criticism as well as it can (Weber, 1968:992)

Administrative secrecy is used by bureaucracy to prevent the free dissemination of information about the organization to the general public in order to preclude the comprehensive understanding necessary for constructive criticism. The absence of an informed public protects the bureaucracy from criticism, and prevents it from being held accountable for its harmful effects, and thus the public remains its unwarned, defenseless victim. Thus protected from criticism from the outside, bureaucracy protects itself against criticism on the inside, as noted above, by means of the hierarchial distribution of information, the negative effects of which are reinforced by the norm of formal relations within the organization itself. As Merton observes:

> Formality is manifested by means of a more or less complicated social ritual which symbolizes and supports the pecking order of the various offices. Such formality is integrated with the distribution of authority within the system ...(Merton, 1968:249).

227

While this formality of relations has the positive function of minimizing interpersonal friction, it has also the negative function of inhibiting a free exchange of information about the organization among its many functionaires. The limitation of their official interaction to the minimal interchange of knowledge necessary to the coordination of tasks reduces the possibility for an accumulation of different perspectives on the organization, and the development of a comprehensive understanding of its potentially harmful consequences.

The restriction of information, and inhibition of reflection initiated originally by the hierarchial distribution of authority, responsibility, and areas of jurisdiction and competence, and reinforced by the formality of relationships within the organization is supported also by the requirement for specialized training. Each official is required to possess expertise in his or her area, and this specialization of knowledge within limited areas militates against his or her comprehension of the relation of his or her actions to those of other officials, the interaction of all roles and activities within the whole organization, and the relation of the organization's activities to the welfare of the public. Finally, as was noted in regard to dehumanization, the individual bureaucrat's willingness to submit to this confinement of his or her cognitive process, and to adopt a passive, uncritical perspective is insured by the concentration of resources for production in the bureaucracy. That is, in order to live the individual must earn a living, and to earn a living he or she must be employed by the bureaucracy that controls the resources of production. The bureaucracy provides the individual with the means of livelihood, and encourages competent performance and devotion to duty through the incentives of graded salaries, promotion by seniority, social esteem of office, esprit de corps among the workers, and pensions. Thus the individual is motivated to comply and conform to the organizations' requirements.

As in the case of dehumanization, the inherently pernicious nature of these bureaucratic features will be demonstrated through examples drawn from the Nazi regime. Bureaucracy has been shown to constitute a world in itself apart from the realm of private existence. It prescribes distinctive regulations for thought and conduct, which within the

228

structure of the organization, have the force of law.
As a citizen within the bureaucratic realm, the individual official is morally obligated to abide by its
governing laws. To transgress against these laws in-
vokes negative sanctions. Hence, whether the organization as a whole is manifestly oriented toward the
perpetration of good or evil, the individual participant is expected, required, and motivated to support
the organization. In the Third Reich, Hitler was
the highest official in the three interrelated bureaucracies of the civil service, the Party, and the army—
and his orders had the force of law. Through his
rise to power, Hitler gained the position of the ultimate arbiter of the legal order, and as such instigated
the legalization of genocide which transformed Germany
into a criminal state. For the law-abiding individual
official of the Third Reich, participation in the destruction process was morally obligatory, and opposition to the process constituted criminal behavior.
As Arendt remarks in regard to the Eichmann case:

> This was the ways things were, this was the
> new law of the land, based on the Fuhrer's
> order; whatever he did he did, as far as he
> could see, as a law-abiding citizen. He did
> his duty...he not only obeyed orders, he
> also obeyed the law (Arendt, 1973:135).

Thus, even when a bureaucracy turns toward
the blatant execution of evil, its status as a legitimate institution, and the legal authority inhering in
its regulations, impede individual recognition of institutional evil, and of personal complicity. Such a
recognition becomes virtually impossible within the
context of the bureaucracy's self-protecting hierarchial distribution of jurisdictional areas, authority, responsibility, and most importantly, information. As
Hilberg notes, this differential distribution of information insured that each Nazi bureaucrat could seldom
see beyond the restricted purview of his/her own jurisdiction (Hilberg, 1961:31). Similarly, Arendt comments
that in Eichmann's case "...he had never been told more
than he needed to know in order to do a specific, limited job" (Arendt, 1973:84), and hence he was completely
ignorant "...of everything that was not directly, technically, and bureaucratically, connected with his
job..." (Arendt, 1973:54). The typical Nazi bureaucrat
was not ordinarily sufficiently informed about all the
processes of the organization to perceive its ultimately evil end, and his or her own complicity in genocide. Moreover, even when an individual official began

to suspect the true goal and consequences of the organization, his or her suspicions and moral unease were
alleviated by the knowledge that the administration was
directed by people better informed than himself or herself, and his or her own responsibility was negligible
compared to that of the higher officials. In a related
vein, Himmler contended that the responsibility for
murderous actions did not belong to the lower eschelon
officers who performed them but to the higher eschelon
officers who ordered such actions:

> He pointed out that the Einsatzgruppen were
> called upon to fulfill a repulsive
> (wilderliche) duty. He would not like it if
> Germans did such a thing gladly. But their
> conscience was in no way impaired, for they
> were soldiers who had to carry out every or-
> der unconditionally. He alone had responsi-
> bility before God and Hitler for everything
> that was happening (Hilberg, 1961:218-219).

Finally, at the same time that the bureaucracy sought to undermine individual reflection and
criticism within its own ranks, it endeavored also to
prevent criticism and resistance from the general public by cloaking its operations in a veil of secrecy,
and by the dissemination of false information. Thus,
the Party attempted to quell rumors about extermination
by advising the public that the Jews were being deported to work camps in the east (Hilberg, 1961:300). Secondly, the success of the killing operations depended
upon the maintenance of secrecy. As Hilberg notes, the
administrators of the death camp devised elaborate
strategies to conceal their mission from everyone outside the system, and to deceive the victims until the
very end (Hilberg, 1961:621). Apparently such methods
are eminently successful for history bears witness to
the fact that many of the victims remained ignorant of
their fate until the last moment, and among the perpe-
trators of these atrocities criticism, protest, and
resistance failed to emerge.

The various causes of this second precondition of social destructiveness—i.e., thoughtlessness—
which have been identified within bureaucracy are listed below. (1) The tunnel vision focuses attention on
the client's immediate situation, excludes recognition
of the consequences of official decisions, and is generated by the requirements for precision, speed, unambiguity, continuity, discretion, knowledge of the

files, reduction of friction, and strict subordination. (2) A decrease in the sense of responsibility and concern for the effects of bureaucratic activity arises from the separation of ownership of the means of production from labor, and lack of participation in policy level decision-making. (3) Elimination of public criticism or rebellion is expedited through the use of administrative secrecy. (4) Restriction of the free flow of information and of the development of comprehensive understanding within the ranks of the organization is promoted by the hierarchial structure of authority, the norm of formal relations, and the specialization of training and function. (5) Voluntary adoption of the bureaucratic perspective is induced by the provision of the means of existence. The cumulative effect of these various factors is manifested as an erosion of the motivation and capacity for individual reflection, moral judgment, and of the sense of personal responsibility for one's own actions. Incapable of deducing the final goal of the organization's activities, and convinced, in any case, of personal exemption from the burden of responsibility, the individual bureaucrat, who quite genuinely has no intent to do wrong, may be so effectively shielded against and psychologically removed from reality, that he or she voluntarily but nonetheless unwittingly acquiesces or actively participates in the commission of criminal atrocities that threaten the existence of the human race. The logical end of the bureaucratic subversion of the critical faculties is the unknowing complicity in evil. Like Eichmann, the individual bureaucrat may be transformed into a criminal, because under the conditions of his or her official functions, he or she simple never realizes what he or she is doing.

The phenomena of the transcendence of societal evil—of the bureaucratic generation of conditions conducive to social destructiveness (i.e., dehumanization and thoughtlessness)—has been defined as consisting, on the one hand, of a fundamental awareness and respect for the humanity of others, and, on the other hand, of an attitude of skeptical distrust of the world. With regard to dehumanization, the sources of transcendence have been identified as the establishment of informal groups within formal organization, and the experience of role conflict. The particular cause of transcendence implicit in both these sources entails an arousal of the mechanism of identification. The ego mechanism of identification, according to Diamond:

231

> ...is a powerful psychological force of mor-
> ality and civilized human conduct.... To
> have a sense of compassion and ethicormoral
> feeling toward another, one must be able to
> identify with the other, to have a libidinal
> investment in the other person as a love ob-
> ject or at least as a narcissistic projection
> (Diamond, 1971:127-128).

Identification with the other as a human being like oneself—the imagination of oneself in the other's role or situation—evokes an empathy for the other that mo- tivates just and humane treatment, and militates against the infliction of harm. Although the several bureaucratic factors of dehumanization tend to under- mine the mechanism of identification, the countervail- ing influences of informal groups and role conflict tend to stimulate and strengthen identification. In the first place, the normative organizational require- ment for secondary relations characterized by a minimal involvement of self and other which conduces to object- ification and indifference is counterbalanced by the normative requirement of informal groups for primary relations characterized by a maximal involvement of self and other conducive to identification and empathy. Secondly, although interaction in the bureaucratic set- ting is required to be in the mode of secondary rela- tions to the exclusion of primary relations in contra- distinction to the vascillation between the two modes characteristic of private life, the existence of the primary relations of informal groups within the context of the formal organization, and hence in juxtaposition to the required secondary relations, constitutes a sit- uation which, at least superficially, resembles that of private life. Hence, this situation may be interpreted or understood as calling for the rational and pragmatic vascillation between primary and secondary relations as is the case in private life. The resemblance between private and professional life initiated by the estab- lishment of informal groups within the bureaucracy thus counteracts the erosion of the identification mechanism generated by the norm of impersonal secondary rela- tions. Similarly, the confusion of behavior arising from the conflict of roles—as when a friend of the bu- reaucrat enters the domain of his or her professional activities—induces a deviation from the norm of imper- sonality, and injects a personalization of the official attitude toward the other (client). The trauma of such conflict militates against the resumption of a rigor- ously impersonal attitude, by evoking in the individual bureaucrat an awareness of the other (client) as a human being, and hence fosters an empathetic identification antithetical to the forces of dehumanization.

Thus, the net effect of experiences within informal groups and of role conflict is to undermine the bureaucratic segmentation of private and public life and the concomitant compartmentalization of private morality and professional duty by the creation of a similarity of the bureaucratic to the private realm which in turn calls for the practical vascillation between primary and secondary relations characteristic of private life. As the bureaucratic situation comes to resemble that of private life, its normative requirements are invalidated and displaced by those of private life and personal morality. The bureaucratic subversion of identification is itself subverted by a strengthening of the identification mechanism.

With regard to the evil of thoughtlessness, the sources of transcendence have been identified as the influences exerted by informal groups, modern education, and role conflict. In brief, the transcendent function of informal groups is to provide a forum for the exchange of information, discussion, and use of the critical faculties. The function of modern education is to inculcate principles of logic and to exercise the critical faculties. The function of role conflict is to stimulate doubt concerning the bureaucratically defined givens, and to generate critical reflection on those problematic aspects of the world. The specific cause of transcendence inherent in each of these sources is critical reflection, or the immanently transcendent nature of human thought. As Louis Wirth states in the introduction to Ideology and Utopia:

> ...what is not so easily recognized is the fact that thought, even in the absence of official censorship, is disturbing, and, under certain conditions, dangerous and subversive. For thought is a catalytic agent that is capable of unsettling routines, disorganizing habits, breaking up customs, undermining faiths, and generating skepticism (Mannheim, 1936:xiv-xv).

For the individual bureaucrat, either the experience of the free-flowing discussions in informal groups or of the behavioral confusion stemming from role conflict, may render problematic aspects of the occupational world-view which he or she has previously

233

taken for granted and never thought to question--such as the predetermined irrelevance of the consequences of official actions for the clients, or the need for administrative secrecy, and so on. The arousal of even the smallest doubt gradually diminishes the validity and sanctity of these preordained domain assumptions peculiar to the official role. The meticulously skeptical reflection on the previously unexamined givens of the bureaucratic context--the implicitly ideological values, definitions, concepts, and expectations--makes possible perception of the false or distorted nature of these givens. The utilization of logic and imagination or intuition in the reflective process--initiated by the arousal of doubt and grounded in skepticism--allows the bureaucrat to recognize the falsity of the hierarchially distributed information, and to perceive the organization's hidden reality by means of, on the one hand, logical deduction of the probable consequences of organizational activities, and on the other hand, intuition of the possible but unpredictable alternative consequences of his or her own actions, and those of the organization as a whole. Through logic and intuition the individual bureaucrat can reason from the known to the unknown, and can discover the evil truth shrouded by the bureaucracy's deceptive practices. As Hilberg observes, even the all-powerful SS could not combat or eliminate the transcendent function of human thought:

> If the SS and Police could do little about the rumors, it could do nothing about the intellectual power of deduction and prediction: one may conceivably hide killing centers, but one cannot hide the disappearance of millions of people (Hilberg, 1961:624).

Hence, the end effect of exposure to informal groups, modern education, and role conflict is to reduce ignorance and the generation of thoughtlessness by stimulating doubt and distrust of the organization and critical reflection on the nature, goals, and consequences of individual official activities and those of the entire organization. The bureaucratic subversion of thought is in turn subverted by an invigoration and intensification of thought.

Processes of Evil and of Transcendence

To delineate the process of manifestations of societal evil and transcendence of evil, a brief recapitulation and ordering of the aforementioned structures and processes is required. Beginning with the process of manifestation of evil, it must be recognized, in the first place, that human thought is determined by the social conditions of existence, that the social conditions of existence are largely determined by the existing mode of production, and hence that human thought, to a great extent, is a function of the mode of production. Accordingly, since bureaucracy is a form of the organization of production, it generates a distinctive mode of thought and behavior. The foregoing analysis has shown that the mode of thought and behavior peculiar to bureaucracy is fashioned primarily by the normative requirement for impersonality in social relations and the hierarchial distribution of information. Specifically, in contradistinction to the general tendencies of social life--i.e., vascilation between primary and secondary relations--the bureaucratic norm of impersonality requires interaction in the mode of secondary relations to the exclusion of primary relations. This tendency undermines self-development, and further, through the objectification of self as well as other, leads to dehumanization. Secondly, the structural restraints on the availability and adequacy of information ensuing from the hierarchy of authority--in contrast to the societal generation of both critical reflection and mindless conformity--militate against critical reflection, and induce mental conformity or thoughtlessness instead. Thus, the mode of thought and behavior fostered by the bureaucratic organization of production entails inclinations toward dehumanization and thoughtlessness. That bureaucracy is, consequently, conducive to the evil of social destructiveness is evident in the fact that both dehumanization and thoughtlessness are necessary if not sufficient preconditions for social destructiveness. In this respect, the function of dehumanization is to exclude the victim from the sanctified realm of humanity and the protection of moral imperatives. The function of thoughtlessness is to impede realization of the ultimately harmful effects of the individual bureaucrat's specialized activities, and those of the organization as a whole. Thus, the pernicious combination of dehumanization and thoughtlessness eliminates the moral and psychological obstacles to social destructiveness, and further constitutes a positive sanction for participation in the perpetration of destructiveness.

Turning to the process of the manifestation of transcendence, it is necessary to recognize that human thought arises from human activity, that the mode of production is only one of a multitude of human activities, and that each type of activity generates distinctive ways of thinking and behaving. Accordingly, since informal groups, modern education, and role conflict are types of human activities, each generates a characteristic mode of consciousness and conduct. Within the context of the bureaucratic setting, the perspectives arising from these three forms of activity function to mitigate, and militate against the genesis of dehumanization and thoughtlessness.

Specifically, in the case of dehumanization, exposure to role conflict and the primary relations of informal groups sustains and reinforces the awareness of the humanity of others. Moreover, the juxtaposition of these primary relations to the required secondary relations of the bureaucratic order creates a similarity of bureaucracy to private life which calls forth the mode of relation in private life--alternation between primary and secondary relations--and effectively invalidates the compartmentalization of private morality and professional duty. As the bureaucracy comes to resemble--or is interpreted as resembling--private life, dehumanization is replaced by a personalization of relationships. Secondly, with regard to thoughtlessness, exposure to the free-flowing discussions of informal groups, and the traumatic experiences of role conflict stimulates doubt and distrust of the organization and generates skeptical reflection on the accepted perspective. Such reflection--grounded in skepticism, enriched with the more adequate information obtained in informal groups, and utilizing the precepts of logic and insights of intuition inculcated through education, penetrates through the deliberate deception of bureaucracy to its hidden evil reality, and the attendant harmful consequences for the public. Thus, the inclinations to dehumanization and thoughtlessness are counteracted by the influences of informal groups, role conflict, and education which awaken awareness of the humanity of others and the consequent need for relation to others as human beings.

Furthermore, these influences generate doubt

236

and distrust of the organization, provide adequate data for reflection, and induce critical and skeptical reflection on the nature and consequences of the organization which eventually culminates in realization of the implicit potential for evil in bureaucracy. Hence, the individual bureaucrat, who, through exposure to these influences, has developed a comprehensive understanding of the organization and its detrimental effect on the thought processes, is enabled to resist the organization, and to mitigate its destructive consequences for others.

Consequences of Evil and of Transcendence

This investigation of the bureaucratic order has revealed it to be not only a powerful instrument of evil but, more importantly, a primary and potent source of societal evil. Granting this, what are the prospects for a triumph of evil--the implementation of social destructiveness or of the transcendence of evil-the prevention of social destructiveness? On the one hand are the factors conducive to social destructiveness: (1) the dehumanization originating from the norm of impersonality, and (2) the genesis of thoughtlessness by the restriction of information ensuing from the hierarchial structure of authority. On the other hand, these are counteracted by factors conducive to the prevention of social destructiveness: (1) the humanizing influence exerted by the primary relations of informal groups and role-conflict, and (2) the invigoration and intensification of thought evoked by exposure to the discussions in informal groups, the training in logic in education, and the problematic doubt aroused by role conflict. The forces of evil and of transcendence appear to be equally balanced-- both the implementation and the prevention of social destructiveness are immanent possibilities.

However, it is possible that there is another significant factor, perhaps the decisive one, which is not social, and is not predictable on the basis of analysis of purely social factors--that is, the element of individual choice. If it is assumed that all of the above antithetical forces of evil and of transcendence are present in the bureaucratic setting, that an individual may be subject to socialization into dehumanization and thoughtlessness, and yet also become aware of this pernicious process, then it would be a matter of

237

individual decision whether he or she chose to ignore
the implications of evil and voluntarily conformed to
and complied with the organization's requirements, or
whether he or she chose to heed the implications of
evil, and freely rejected and refused to comply with
the organization's requirements.

If indeed, individual decision is the determinative factor in tipping the balance of forces for
evil and for transcendence, then it may further be
hypothesized that this decision will reflect the relative strength of an individual's inclination to protect his or her own self-interest or to protect the
welfare of others. That is, if an individual--having
been led to recognize the potential for evil in bur-
eaucracy--still chooses to support the bureaucracy, this
decision may well indicate that he or she prefers to
gratify self-interest with the seductive allurements of
the organization's incentives--i.e., salary, promotion,
pensions, and so on. On the other hand, if he or she
chooses to reject and rebel against the bureaucracy,
this decision reflects his or her greater selfless
and humane interest in the welfare of others. If this
is the case, then the prediction of the implementation
or prevention of social destructiveness would, ultimately depend on an analysis of individual differences of
inclinations toward self-interest or the welfare of
others--and such is beyond the scope of a purely
sociological analysis of social structural factors.

However, the possibility of individual decision being the crucial factor in determining the course
of social destructiveness calls attention to the implicit and difficult issue of individual responsibility
and culpability for societal evil. This investigation
has exposed the very subtle subversion of the sense of
humanity and of the critical faculties engendered by
bureaucracy--yet it has also revealed that very powerful forces of transcendence are also endemic to the bureaucratic setting. If both these conclusions are correct, then the person who participates in the bureaucratic perpetration of evil does so willingly, with
certain though perhaps limited knowledge of the criminal nature of his or her acts. Despite the fact that
an individual may, initially, conceive of the bureaucracy with a great deal of innocence and naivete, the

inevitable exposure to conflict within the organization dispels that naivete, and evokes doubt and suspicion of the organization. Secondly, although the individual may receive only very limited or even false information about the organization, the use of logic and intuition in reflection will lead to perception of the hidden evil reality. Therefore, in spite of the fact that bureaucracy creates conditions in which it is difficult to distinguish right from wrong, an individual cannot escape the burden of guilt for complicity in societal evil. Although this burden of guilt is not absolved by the extenuating circumstances created by bureaucracy, it may be somewhat reduced. That is, if a person is judged to be normal—not insane or mentally incompetent —and hence capable of reason, then the degree of his or her responsibility and culpability will depend on the adequacy of the information he or she had at their disposal. The more informaiton about the organization the individual possesses, the greater is the burden of guilt for complicity in evil. If the forces of trans- cendence endemic to bureaucracy do indeed invariably lead to the realization of the bureaucracy's potential for evil, then the individual official is morally res- ponsible and legally culpable for the failure to reason from the known and false to the unknown and true—with- in the limits of the information available—for the failure to acknowledge, and abide by the implications of that realization. Thus, for instance, Adolf Eich- mann—a "normal" man in an "insane" situation—was con- victed for his failure to acknowledge and oppose the evil consequences of the bureaucracy that employed him. Morally and legally, the insanity of a situation is no justification for evil behavior. Individuals within evil institutions are also culpable for its injurious consequences, but the degree of their guilt varies ac- cording to the extensity of their knowledge about the institution. While the individual bureaucrat may have no intent to do wrong, he or she is culpable on the grounds of the failure to recognize the evil intent of the institution.

In conclusion, the consequences of the bu- reaucratic cultivation of dehumanization and thought- lessness may be summarized as the eradication of the moral and psychological obstacles to destructive ag- gression. Furthermore, these inimical bureaucratic conditions establish a positive sanction for social de- structiveness, and in fact invite and induce destruc- tive aggression against those identified as victims.

The subversion of the sense of humanity and of the critical faculties signifies that the ultimate end of bureaucracy is genocide—as Hilberg observed:

> It is the bureaucratic destruction process which, in its step-by-step manner, finally led to the annihilation of five million victims (Hilberg, 1961:29).

Conversely, the consequences of the countervailing factors of transcendence—of exposure to the primary relations and the free exchange of information in informal groups, to the discipline of logic in education, and the traumatic confusion of role conflict—may be summarized as a heightened consciousness and appreciation of the common bond of humanity uniting all people, the arousal of doubt and distrust of all perspectives or world-views, the strengthening of the tendency to critically and skeptically examine the domain assumptions and consequences of all perspectives, and a very considerable and depressing decline in a person's naive belief in the innate goodness of his or her own society. But, surely, the loss of innocence is a small price to pay for the prevention of social destructiveness.

With regard to the central issue of human judgment, there are, most certainly, processes within the bureaucratic order hostile to and destructive of human judgment, but, in the last analysis—as this study has revealed—it cannot be eliminated. The existence of human judgment may be taken for granted though its exercise cannot, for individuals may freely and knowledgeably choose to ignore or neglect to use this faculty. They are, however, morally and legally culpable for such negligence.

CHAPTER 16:   Toward a Sociology of
            Evil and Transcendence

                Introduction

Few anthropologists would today defend without important qualification Ruth Benedict's
famous statement (1934:278):   "...the coex-
isting and equally valid patterns of life
which mankind has carved for itself from the
raw materials of existence."   ...the abandon-
ment of the doctrine of untrammeled cultural
relativity is a reaction to the observation
of social consequences.   If one follows out
literally and logically the implications of
Benedict's words, one is compelled to accept
any cultural pattern as vindicated by its
cultural status: slavery, cannibalism, Nazism, or Communism may not be congenial to
Christians or to contemporary Western societies, but moral criticism of the cultural patterns of other people is precluded (Kluck-   ⌐
hohn, 1962:266).

You believe (and I share your belief) in cos-
mopolitanism, i.e., that the natural barriers
and prejudices which until now have impeded
the free intercourse of nations by the egoism
of their national aspiration, some day will
fall before the light of reason and consciousness, and that the peoples will then
start living in one congenial accord, like
brethren, sensibly and lovingly striving for
universal harmony (Dostoevsky, 1949:577).

Mankind's salvation lies exclusively in everyone's making everything his business, in the
people of the East being anything but indif-
ferent to what is thought in the West, and in
the people of the West being anything but in-
different to what happens in the East (Solzhenitsyn, 1973a:30-31).

                    241

> If the One World is not to destroy itself, it
> needs a new kind of man—a man who transcends
> the narrow limits of his nation and who ex-
> periences every human being as a neighbor
> rather than as a barbarian; a man who feels
> at home in the world (Fromm, 1971:171).

The implicit and, hopefully, clearly explicated value judgment which motivated this study is analogous to Kluckhohn's critical assessment of ethical relativism in anthropology as indicated in the above quo-
tation. That is, in brief, the social consequences
which ensue from the scientist's adherence to the doctrine of ethical neutrality—as in the case of the an-
thropologist's observance of ethical relativism—vitiate the ostensible validity of that doctrine. According to this view, scientific neutrality with respect
to moral issues and problems has contributed considerably to the unstable and perilous state of the world
today. In this case, the scientific community is morally obligated to renounce and discard the obsolete
and inexpedient position of ethical neutrality, to incorporate an ethical ideal which postulates the pursuit
of knowledge for the sake of the betterment of humanity
rather than for the sake of knowledge alone, and, under
the aegis of such an ideal, to confront directly the
fundamental moral issues of evil and transcendence. To
this end, an ethical ideal, constructed on the basis of
the lessons of history, and which envisons the well-
being of humanity, was tentatively suggested as an appropriate standard for the reorientation of science toward moral issues. Essentially, the central postulate
of the ideal is that the quality of human life depends
upon the fate of human dignity and moral judgment—that
the quality of life deteriorates as a result of violations of human dignity and moral judgment, and conversely, the quality of life improves as a result of
preserving human dignity and moral judgment. In terms
of this ideal, then, the role of science with regard to
the phenomena of evil and transcendence of evil entails
empirical identification of the conditions of life on
the individual, interpersonal, and societal levels
which constitute or foster violations of human dignity
and moral judgment, and conversely, identification of
the conditions of life on the individual, interpersonal, and societal levels which are conducive to the preservation of human dignity and moral judgment. Furthermore, scientific activities should be directed toward the innovation of strategies designed to reduce
the incidence of the former, and increase the incidence

of the latter. Accordingly, this study was designed to
survey the theories of selected novelists and social
science scholars who have dealt with the problem of
evil and transcendence in an effort to obtain at least
a preliminary indication of the various types of phenomena which can be designated as manifestations of evil
or of transcendence, and thus, moreover, to demonstrate
the relevance and potential fecundity of scientific inquiry with respect to such intrinsically value-laden
issues.

Major Conclusions

As an exploratory and theory-oriented prelude
to empirical investigation of evil and transcendence,
this study has revealed several significant conclusions
with regard to the exoteric manifestations of evil and
transcendence. These conclusions are listed below.

(1) All of the diverse phenomena defined as
evil are characterized by a common conception of a deterioration in the distinctive human faculties—however these
are variously identified. Conversely,
all of the phenomena defined as transcendent share a common conception of
the continuing development of these faculties.

(2) Six (Chekhov, Solzhenitsyn, Freud,
Fromm, May, and Arendt) of the nine
scholars whose theories were examined
concur in assuming a dichotomous conception of the locus of causality.

(3) The sources of evil and transcendence
identified within the causal realms of
human nature, interpersonal interaction,
and social reality are comprised primarily of combinations of factors within
these realms, and secondarily of interactions of factors between the three
realms.

(4) The majority of the specific factors
conducive either to evil or to transcendence were identified as conditions of
social reality. Of the remaining factors, a greater number were identified
as predispositions of human nature, and

the least number were identified as processes of interpersonal interaction. Secondly, social reality was found to contain the greater number of factors conducive to evil while human nature contains the greater number of factors conducive to transcendence.

(5)   The processes from which the phenomena of evil and transcendence emerge were described as involving the transformation of latent potentialities into manifest effects.

(6a)   Wherever there are factors conducive to evil in any one of the causal realms of reality, these factors are counterbalanced by other factors conducive to transcendence, and originating either within that particular realm or within one of the two other realms of reality. For example: when evil arises from certain predispositions in human nature, it is opposed by other (transcendent) predispositions of human nature, or by processes of interpersonal interaction, or by conditions of social reality. Thus, a tenuous balance exists between the antinomic forces of evil and transcendence.

(6b)   The ultimate consequence of all the various phenomena identified as evil is the fatal subversion or annihilation of the unique human faculties which may occur (1) on the individual level, through the repression or restriction of innate and/or learned needs, (2) on the interpersonal level, through the inhibition or nullification of the self-and-other confirming process of symbolic communication, and (3) on the societal level, through the totalitarian subjugation and domination of the individual by the collective. Alternatively, the ultimate consequence of the phenomena identified as transcendent consists of the continued maturation of the unique human faculties which results (1) on the individual level, from the freedom to express

244

innate and/or learned needs, (2) on the interpersonal level, from the confirmation of self and other in the process of symbolic communication, and (3) on the societal level, from the freedom of the individual to react or rebel against as well as to conform to the particular patterns of thought and behavior prescribed by his or her society.

In terms of the implication for empirically-oriented research, these conclusions suggest, in the first place, that two of the three possible causal realms of reality—human nature and social reality—should be the principal targets of investigation. Secondly, the investigation of human nature and social reality should focus on determining the probable combinations and interactions of factors between these realms which comprise sources of evil and transcendence. And thirdly, the distribution of specific causal factors between the two realms indicates that research oriented toward eliminating evil should focus on reconstructing pernicious societal conditions, whereas research oriented toward expediting transcendence of evil should concentrate upon stimulating the transcendent faculties of human nature.

These observations, drawn from the philosophical speculations and theoretical formulations of scholars concerned with the problem of evil and transcendence, support the view that social science and, by extension natural science also, can in fact fruitfully contribute to the needed understanding of contemporary manifestations of evil and transcendence. By abandoning the perspective of ethical neutrality, and adopting an ethical ideal such as the one herein suggested which advocates empirical investigation of evil and transcendence, the scienfitic community will be in a position to contribute not only to the understanding such phenomena, but also to the practical resolution of the typical dilemmas that disrupt individual, interpersonal, and societal life. Furthermore, above and beyond the eminently desirable prospect of actually ameliorating the quality of life, the dual strategy of, on the one hand, inventing techniques to alleviate or eliminate the conditions identified as detrimental to the well-bing of humanity, and on the other hand, inventing techniques to stimulate and increase conditions identified as beneficial to the well-being of humanity, will also expedite the emergence of a cosmopolitan consciousness of common humanity among the peoples of all societies. This consciousness of common humanity would transcend the divisive conflicts of ethnocentric values and interests, and constitute the essential psychological foundation for the establishment of international interdependence and world peace. Finally, this study illustrates that the proposed ideal of preserving human dignity and moral judgment was supported by a consensus of opinion among the selected novelists and scholars who agree that destruction of the distinctive human faculties (which were previously identified as the ontological foundation of human dignity) produces a decline in the quality of life, whereas preservation of these faculties enhance the quality of life. The information which would become available as a result of Scientific inquiry into the nature of evil and transcendence could be meaningfully utilized in the validation of existing, or proposed, and perhaps universal ethical norms.

Furthermore, it was discovered in the course of this study, that the attribute of moral judgment was considered by a majority of the selected novelists and scholars to be by far the most powerful, and therefore the single most important evil-transcending component of the constellation of distinctive faculties comprising the special worth or dignity of human beings. Thus, a comprehensive understanding of the nature and function of human judgment is crucial to the ethical enterprise of resolving the problem of evil. According to each of the theories examined, the nature of human judgment was conceived as a consciousness of fundamental moral principles pertaining to both individual behavior and the activities of society—which concurs with Berdyaev's contention that society as well as individuals is in need of moral evaluation. The transcendent function of human jdgment was defined in terms of the ability to recognize the intrinsic evil of individual or collective egoism, to become aware of, reflect upon, and critically evaluate the implicit and unexplicated givens of society, and to expand narrow egoistic or ethnocentric interests to the wider system of interests involved. In terms of origin, this individual and societal-transcending faculty was variously perceived as deriving from an inherent moral consciousness (Lawrence, Solzhenitsyn, Arendt), from the emergent nature of reason (Chekhov, Freud, Fromm), from an innate ethical sensitivity (May), from the processes of role-taking and the prevision of gestures (Mead), and from negative thinking (Marcuse). Despite this

246

variation in origin, moral judgment was in all cases considered to be a latent faculty peculiar to human be-ings which is aroused and brought to fruition by either universal social processes or conflictual situations endemic to human life. The existence of this faculty, in other words, is inevitable and thus can be taken for granted.

More importantly, the fact that this faculty is necessarily aroused by unavoidable conditions of human life was interpreted by five of these nine the-orists (Lawrence, Solzhenitsyn, Fromm, May, and Mead) to mean that the exercise of human judgment—the aware-ness of good and evil, and the construction of behavior on the basis of this knowledge—is likewise unavoid-able. Both the existence and the exercise of human judgment are inevitable, and can be taken for granted. This interpretation—which concurs with the symbolic interactionist thesis that human beings freely con-struct and hence, control their actions, and are there-fore endowed with moral responsibility for the benefi-cial or harmful consequences of their intentions—sig-nifies that the perpetration of evil cannot be attri-buted to the victimization of unwitting individuals by circumstances, but rather, follows from the witting and irresponsible choice of individuals to relinquish their control of circumstances. That is, every prospective action confronts the individual with a necessary choice between enacting evil—initiating a course of conduct detrimental to others—or enacting transcendence—ini-tiating a course of conduct beneficial to others. Therefore the manifestation of evil derives from ei-ther: (1) a voluntary choice of the evil alternative, or (2) a witting and voluntary decision to ignore the potentially injurious consequences of an intended act, or (3) errors of judgment arising from an incomplete or inadequate understanding of all the values involved in a particular situation, and hence a miscalculation of the probabilities of evil and transcendence.

In each of these three cases individuals are morally culpable for the evil which they initiate al-though the degree of guilt varies with the nature of their intentions, and the extensity of their knowledge of the situation. That is, the maximum degree of cul-pability is illustrated in the extreme case where a person possesses adequate knowledge of the situation, is fully cognizant of the issues and values involved, re-cognizes the probability of injurious consequences, and yet, despite all this, chooses to enact the evil alternative. Conversely, the minimum degree of moral culpability is demonstrated in the other extreme case where a person does not intend evil but is hampered by inadequate or faulty knowledge of the situation which distorts his or her judgment, prevents recognition of the probability of evil consequences, and thus induces selection of an ultimately harmful course of action which vitiates the person's genuinely good intentions. The median degree of guilt issues from the case where a person possesses an adequate knowledge of the situation, and is thus capable of rationally determining the harmful or beneficial consequences of prospective alternative actions, but freely decides not to make this evaluation, and chooses a course of action unmindful of its consequences.

According to this examination of the nature and function of human judgment, the control which human beings exert over their behavior invests them also with moral responsibility for the consequences of their actions, and with moral culpability for the evil they initiate. There are no conditions which excuse or justify individual perpetration of evil, although there are conditions which mitigate the degree of culpability. The degree of individual culpability depends upon the nature of a person's intentions, and the extensity of his or her knowledge of a situation. The range of individual guilt is illustrated by the three indicated prototypical categories— (1) premeditated choice (maximum degree of guilt) (2) culpable negligence (median degree of guilt),[2] and (3) culpable ignorance (minimum degree of guilt).

The conclusion that the existence and exercise of human judgment can be taken for granted signifies that human beings are capable of morally evaluating their own actions, the actions of others, and the projects of their own society. According to the several theories here considered, such moral evaluation is a function of the reflective (prevision) and empathetic (identification) aspects of human consciousness. In the first place, the reflective aspect refers to the fact that human beings construct their actions by means of the imaginative completion of the act which enables them to anticipate before the fact the probable consequences of their intentions, and the range of possible

---

[2]My thanks to Professor Sjoberg and Professor Littrell for suggesting the concept of culpable ignorance.

alternative courses. In the second place, the empathetic aspect refers to the tendency to identify with or
take the role of the other which places the actor in
the position of the other whom he or she is affecting
and enables the actor to feel and realize—through his
or her own responses—the harmful or beneficial effects
of his or her actions on the other. Similarly, human
beings evaluate the actions of others and the projects
of their society by imagining themselves in the position of the recipient other toward whom individual or
societal action is directed, and then determining the
harmful or beneficial nature of these actions according to their own negative or positive reactions. Thus,
human beings morally evaluate the actions of individuals (themselves or others) and the projects of their
society in terms of their own spontaneous reactions to
an imaginatively anticipated effect. The impetus to
make such an evaluation—with respect to either individual or societal activities—is aroused by the universal process of social interaction and/or the experience
of conflictual situations. Both of these experiences
induce an awareness of the hidden underlying values
that structure human intentions, expose discrepancies
or inconsistencies in these values, and thus render such
values problematic or questionable.

     In the case of social interaction, the coor-
dination of self and other activities depends upon the
actor's ability to ascertain both the other's intentions and the meaning of his or her own intentions for
the other, both of which require imaginative identification with the other in order to experience and understand the other's reactions. If, in the process of
this imaginative identification, the actor discovers
that his or her intended action will produce a detrimental effect on the other, he or she is necessarily
compelled to question the ethical validity of that intention, and of the underlying value which motivates
that intention. The actor is compelled to reflect upon
and re-evaluate the morality of his or her individually
or socially-derived values which had heretofore been
taken for granted as unexamined givens. Similarly, in
the case of conflictual situations, the personal trauma
of such experiences—i.e., the spontaneous negative
reaction against an injury to the self evoked by the
repression of eroticism, the agony of isolation, the
demoralizing degradation of incarceration, the anxiety
of sexual frustration, the sense of being unfulfilled,
the uncertainty which follows from a loss of a center
of values, the isolation which ensues from anti-social

249

activities, and the loss of a sense of self as the individual is subordinated to the collective—also stimulates an awareness and suspicion of the societal values which must exist as the normative substructure that makes such conditions possible. The individual is again confronted by a transformation of the previously unexamined and unexplicated given into the ethically-suspect problematic which must be rationally reconsidered and re-evaluated in order to restore the necessary continuity of the world.

Thus, the exercise of human judgment is elicited by the universal process of social interaction, and by the inevitable experience of ubiquitous conflictual situations, both of which bring hidden societal values to the level of consciousness, expose their questionable ethical validity, and induce reflection and re-evaluation of these values. This evaluation proceeds through, and is determined by spontaneous individual reaction against real or imagined injury to the self. By virtue of these processes, then, human beings are capable of transcending the limitations of the given social construction of reality into which they are socialized, and of evaluating the morality or immorality of their own society. And, furthermore, having recognized the moral deficiencies of their society, human beings are also capable of transforming an evil society into a good one, through the imaginative construction of a society without those deficiencies, which vision provides the inspiration, motivation, and direction for needed social reform. By virtue of their special qualities—of judgment, reason, and imagination—human beings are far more than the passive products of omnipotent society, and are indeed the creative inventors of moral and social change.

In conclusion, the evidence of this study suggests that the resolution of the problem of evil which confronts the modern world can and should be facilitated by the contribution of science which will serve to complement and reinforce the transcendent function of human judgment, which moreover, in agreement with Hannah Arendt's position, is definitely not "...the last thing to be taken for granted in our time" (Arendt, 1973:295). When human beings "...behave according to the rules of society..." (Horton and Leslie, 1970:31) which at times requires individual participation in the perpetration of evil, they do so not "...partly because it never occurs to them to do otherwise..." (Horton and Leslie, 1970:31), but because they freely and wittingly choose to do so.

BIBLIOGRAPHY

Arendt, Hannah

    1971   The Origins of Totalitarianism. New York:
           Meridian Books, The World Publishing
           Company (second enlarged edition).

    1973   Eichmann in Jerusalem: A Report on the
           Banality of Evil. New York: The Viking
           Press (Revised and enlarged edition).

Berdyaev, Nicolas

    1945   The Destiny of Man. Translated from the
           Russian by Natalie Duddington, M.A.
           London: Geoffrey Bles, The Centenary
           Press.

Berger, Peter L. and Thomas Luckmann

    1967   The Social Construction of Reality: A
           Treatise in the Sociology of Knowledge.
           Garden City, New York: Anchor Books,
           Doubleday and Company, Inc.

Bernard, V. W., Perry Ottenberg and Fritz Redl

    1971   "Dehumanization." Pp. 102-104 in Nevitt
           Sanford, Craig Comstock and Associates
           (eds.), Sanctions for Evil: Sources of
           Social Destructiveness. Boston: Beacon
           Press.

Buber, Martin

    1970   I and Thou. Translated and with a
           Prologue by Walter Kaufmann. New York:
           Charles Scribner's Sons

Burg, David and George Feifer

    1974   Solzhenitsyn. New York: Stein and Day
           Publishers.

Chekhov, Anton P.

    1964   Chekhov: The Major Plays. Translated
           by Ann Dunnigan, and with a Foreward by
           Robert Brustein. New York: A Signet
           Classic, the New American Library.

1965   Anton Chekhov: Ward Six and other Stories.
        Translated by Ann Dunnigan, and with an
        Afterword by Rufus W. Mathewson. New York:
        a Signet Classic, the New American Library.

Cooley, Charles Horton

1970   "Primary Group and Human Nature." Pp.
        156-158 in Jerome G. Manis and Bernard N.
        Meltzer (eds.), Symbolic Interaction: A
        Reader in Social Psychology, Second Edi-
        tion. Boston: Allyn and Bacon.

Diamond, B. L.

1971   "Failure of Identification and Sociopathic
        Behavior." Pp. 125-135 in Nevitt Sanford,
        Craig Comstock and Associates (eds.)
        Sanctions for Evil: Sources of Social
        Destructiveness. Boston: Beacon Press.

Dostoyevsky, Fyodor M.

1949   The Diary of a Writer, F. M. Dostoiesky.
        Vol. II. Translated and annotated by
        Boris Brasol. New York: Charles
        Scribner's Sons.

1958   The Brothers Karamazov. Translated with
        an Introduction by David Magarshack.
        Baltimore, Maryland: Penguin Books, Inc.,
        (2 volumes).

N.D.   The Best Short Stories of Fyodor
        Dostoyevsky. Translated with an Introduc-
        tion by David Magarshack. New York: The
        Modern Library, Random House.

Duster, Troy

1971   "Conditions for Guilt-free Massacre."
        Pp. 25-36 in Nevitt Sanford, Craig
        Comstock and Associates (eds.), Sanctions
        for Evil: Sources of Social Destructive-
        ness. Boston: Beacon Press.

Freud, Sigmund

1962   Civilization and Its Discontents.
        Translated and edited by James Strachey.
        New York: W. W. Norton and Company, Inc.

1965 "Thoughts for the Times on War and Death."
Pp. 206-222 in Benjamin Nelson (ed.), On
Creativity and the Unconscious: Papers
on the Psychology of Art, Literature,
Love, Religion—Sigmund Freud. New York:
The Cloister Library, Harper and Row,
Publishers.

1972 "Civilized Sexual Morality and Modern
Nervousness." Pp. 20-40 in Philip Rieff
(ed.), Sexuality and the Psychology of
Love—Sigmund Freud. New York: Cullier
Books.

Fromm, Erich

1955 The Sane Society. Greenwich, Connecticut:
Fawcett Publications, Inc.

1965 "Character and the Social Process." Pp.
117-124 in Gardner Lindzey and Calvin
Hall (eds.), Theories of Personality:
Primary Sources and Research. New York:
John Wiley and Sons., Inc.

1971a The Heart of Man: Its Genius for Good
and Evil. San Francisco, California:
The Perennial Library, Harper and Row,
Publishers.

1971b Beyond the Chains of Illusion: My Encounter with Marx and Freud. New York:
A Touchstone Book, Simon and Schuster.

Goodheart, Eugene

1963 The Utopian Vision of D. H. Lawrence.
Chicago: The University of Chicago
Press.

Gould, J. and William L. Kolb (eds.)

1964 A Dictionary of the Social Sciences.
New York: The Free Press of Glencoe.

Hall, Calvin S.

1954 A Primer of Freudian Psychology. New
York: A Mentor Book, the New American
Library.

Hilberg, Raul

    1961   The Destruction of the European Jews.
            Chicago: Quadrangle Books.

Hingley, Ronald

    1966   Chekhov: A Biographical and Critical
            Study. London: Unwin Books.

Hochman, Baruch

    1970   Another Ego: The Changing View of Self
            and Society in the Work of D. H. Law-
            rence. Columbia. South Carolina:
            University of South Carolina Press.

Horton, Paul and Gerald Leslie

    1970   The Sociology of Social Problems. New
            York: Appleton-Century-Crofts.

Jay, Martin

    1973   The Dialectical Imagination: A History
            of the Frankfurt School and the Insti-
            tute of Social Research, 1923-1950.
            Boston: Little, Brown, and Company.

Kluckhohn, Richard (ed).

    1962   Culture and Behavior: Collected Essays
            of Clyde Kluckhohn. New York: The
            Free Press of Glencoe.

Kornhauser, William

    1959   The Politics of Mass Society. Glencoe,
            Illinois: The Free Press of Glencoe.

Lawrence, D. H.

    1962   Lady Chatterly's Lover. New York: The
            Grove Press, Random House, Inc.

    1969   Women in Love. New York: Bantam Books,
            the Viking Press, Inc.

Lukacs, Georg

    1970   Solzhenitsyn. London: Merlin Press.

MacIntyre, A.

    1970   Herbert Marcuse: An Exposition and a
             Polemic. New York: The Viking Press.

Mannheim, Karl

    1936   Ideology and Utopia: An Introduction
             to the Sociology of Knowledge. Trans-
             lated from the German by Louis Wirth
             and Edward Shils, with a Preface by
             Louis Wirth. New York: Harcourt,
             Brace and World, Inc.

Marcuse, Herbert

    1966   One-Dimensional Man: Studies in the
             Ideology of Advanced Industrial Society.
             Boston: Beacon Press.

Marks, R.

    1970   The Meaning of Marcuse. New York:
             Ballantine Books.

Martindale, Don A.

    1960   The Nature and Types of Sociological
             Theory. Boston: Houghton-Mifflin.

Marx, Karl

    1904   A Contribution to the Critique of
             Political Economy. Chicago: C. H.
             Kerr.

May, Rollo

    1967   Man's Search for Himself. New York:
             W. W. Norton and Company, Inc.

    1972   Power and Innocence: A Search for the
             Sources of Violence. New York: W. W.
             Norton and Company, Inc.

Mead, George Herbert

    1964   "Scientific Method and the Moral
             Sciences." Pp. 248-266 in Andrew J.
             Reck (ed.), Selected Writings--George
             Herbert Mead. Indianapolis: The Bobbs-
             Merrill Company, Inc.

    1967   Mind, Self and Society--From the Stand-
             point of a Social Behaviorist: George
             Herbert Mead. Edited and with an Intro-
             duction by Charles W. Morris. Chicago:
             Phoenix Books, the University of
             Chicago Press.

Means, Richard L.

    1969   The Ethical Imperative: The Crisis in
             American Values. Garden City, New York:
             Doubleday and Company, Inc.

Meltzer, Bernard N.

    1970   "Mead's Social Psychology." Pp. 5-24 in
             Jerome G. Manis and Bernard N. Meltzer
             (eds.), Symbolic Interaction: A Reader
             in Social Psychology, Second Edition.
             Boston: Allyn and Bacon.

Merton, Robert K.

    1968   Social Theory and Social Structure.
             New York: The Free Press.

Miller, David L.

    1973   George Herbert Mead: Self, Language and
             the World. Austin: The University of
             Texas Press.

Mirsky, Prince D. S.

    1958   A History of Russian Literature: From
             Its Beginnings to 1900. Edited by
             Francis J. Whitfield. New York:
             Vintage Books, Random House.

Neilson, W. A., Thomas A. Knott, Paul W. Carhart

    1956   Webster's New International Dictionary
            of the English Language. Second Edi-
            tion, unabridged. Springfield, Mass.:
            G. and C. Merriam Company. Publishers.

Pfuetze, Paul E.

    1954   The Social Self. New York: Bookman
            Associates.

Roazen, Paul

    1968   Freud: Political and Social Thought.
            New York: Alfred A. Knopf.

Sanford, N., Craig Comstock, and Associates (eds.)

    1971   Sanctions for Evil: Sources of Social
            Destructiveness. Boston: Beacon Press.

Sjoberg, Gideon and Paula J. Miller

    1973   "Social Research on Bureaucracy's Limi-
            tations and Opportunities." Social
            Problems 21 (summer): 129-143.

Solzhenitsyn, Alexsander I.

    1972   Cancer Ward. Translated from the
            Russian by Nicholas Bethell and David
            Burg. New York: A Bantam Book, Farrar,
            Straus and Giroux, Inc.

    1973a   Nobel Lecture. Translated from the
            Russian by F. D. Reeve. New York:
            Farrar, Straus, and Giroux.

    1973b   The First Circle. Translated from the
            Russian by Thomas P. Whitney. New York:
            A Bantam Book, Harper and Row, Inc.

    1974   August 1914. Translated by Michael
            Glenny. New York: A Bantam Book,
            Farrar, Straus, and Giroux, Inc.

Theodorson, George A. and Achilles G.

    1970   Modern Dictionary of Sociology. New
            York: Apollo Edition, Thomas Y.
            Crowell Company.

Tiryakian, Edward A.

    1968   "The Existential Self and the Person."
            Pp. 75-85 in Chad Gordon and Kenneth J.
            Gergen (eds.), The Self in Social Inter-
            action, Vol. I. Classic and Contemporary
            Perspectives. New York: John Wiley and
            Sons, Inc.

Toumanova, Princess Nina Andronikova

    1937   Anton Chekhov: The Voice of Twilight
            Russia. New York: Columbia University
            Press.

Uris, Leon

    1974a   Exodus. New York: Bantam Books,
            Doubleday and Company, Inc.

    1974b   QBVII. New York: Bantam Books, Double-
            day and Company, Inc.

Weber, Max

    1963   Max Weber, Selections from his work and
            an Introduction by S. M. Miller. New
            York: Thomas Y. Crowell Company.

    1968   Economy and Society: An Outline of
            Interpretive Sociology. Edited by
            Guenther Roth and Claus Wittich. New
            York: Bedminster Press.

9316